THE FUNCTION OF GEOGRAPHY IN THE GEOPOLITICAL PUZZLE

Vassilios Moutsoglou

Copyright ©2020 Vasilios Moutsoglou
ISBN: 9798688667776
First English – language Edition

All rights reserved

No part of this book may be reproduced, or stored in a retrieval system, or transmitted in any form or by any means, electronic, mechanical, photocopying, recording, or otherwise, without express written permission of the publisher.

Cover design by Vassilis
Library of Congress Control Number: 2018675309
Printed in the United States of America

First English – language Edition

Copyright of Greek Edition ISBN 9789607922960
©2018 Vasilios Moutsoglou-Tsoukatos Editions
All inquiries for the Greek edition may be addressed to info@tsoukatou.gr

TABLE OF CONTENTS

INTRODUCTION 9
THE GEOGRAPHIC PILLAR OF GEOPOLITICS 13
    The Essentials of Geography 13
    The Clash of Civilizations 29
    Globalization 34
    The persistence of borders 39
    Sanctions and geography 48
    The demographic boom 49
    Migration 52
    Climatic change 55
    The Entropy in Politics 59
    The Arctic 61
GEOGRAPHY IN SHAPING HISTORY 67
    Historical evolution 67
    Shaping Europe 83
    Migration in the Balkans 94
    Developments in Western Europe 100
    North America 107
    Africa 108
    The Silk Road 110
    The Jewish diaspora 111

    The Age of Adventure 112
THE ARABIAN PENINSULA AND ISLAM 117
    The advent of Islam 117
    Islamic conquests 119
    Saudi Arabia 120
    The Geopolitics of Islam 122
THE TURKMENS AND THE OTTOMAN EMPIRE 125
THE 19th CENTURY 139
    Baghdad Railway 149
    The Macedonian question 152
    America 155
GEOPOLITICS OF THE 20th CENTURY 162
    Western Power's interventions in the Balkans 166
    The First World War 170
    The post-war period in the Balkans 185
    The blockade of Berlin 187
    The Middle East and imperialist policies 188
    The bipolar system and the Cold War 189
    The end of the Cold War 195
THE BALKANS 200
    Political shaping of the Balkans 205
THE CURRENT TURBULENT FLOW OF HISTORY ... 209
    The international situation after 9/11 218
    The 4th Generation Wars 220
    The post-Cold War era 224

- Western incitements in Georgia and Ukraine .226
- The East-West confrontation..........................234
- China's growing influence.............................241
- The shift of focus to Asia 243
- The grid of international cooperation in Asia ..252

AFRICA AND AMERICA..257
- Sub-Saharan Africa..257
- Latin America...260

THE MIDDLE EAST...263
- The Palestinian issue..271
- Syria 273
- North-East Africa 279
- The MENA region...283
- Turkey 286

THE MAGHREB..303
- Western Sahara 304
- Sahara 307
- Western Sahel Geopolitics..............................308
- Terrorism in Algeria and beyond 311
- Libya...315

THE ARAB SPRING...317
- The events in Algeria.......................................319
- Tunisia: The beginning of the Arab Spring ..320
- Egypt 322
- Libya 323

7

- Syria 326
  - The spread of events 327
  - Roundup 330
- EUROPE 333
  - The European Union.................................... 337
    - The European External Action Service 345
  - The Mediterranean 346
    - The geopolitics of pipelines and energy...... 351
  - Greece 354
    - The Delimitation of the Maritime Zones..... 358
  - EPILOGUE 359
- ANNEX 367
  - The U.S.'s re-engage the world. 367
  - Biden administration's new Global policy........ 370

INTRODUCTION

Geography is the schematic depiction of the world and everything it contains. Consequently, it has been a critical factor in shaping political, social, and economic history.[1]

One of the main parameters of global political and economic processes is geography. As a science, geography studies the distribution of phenomena on Earth, the procedures, the characteristics, and the human interaction with the environment.[2] Sorts of the various phenomena compare, generalize, search their causes, trace the laws of nature, and record their effects on humans.[3] Geography is also related to many disciplines.[4]

History is the systematic study of human activity in the depth of time to conclude the present and the future. However, historical phenomena do not only evolve in time but also space; consequently, they are related to time and geography and, with the function of the political factor, become geopolitical.[5]

History has no regularity; events happen only once and are not repeated, at least precisely in the same way, even when the circumstances that create them are similar.

---

[1] Claudius Ptolemaeus, 2nd century A.D.
[2] *Hayes-Bohanan, James (29 September 2009): «What is Environmental Geography Anyway?».*
[3] *Hughes, William. (1863), The Study of Geography.*
[4] *Hornby, William F; Jones, Melvyn (29 June 1991), An introduction to Settlement Geography Cambridge University Press.*
[5] *Rediscovering Geography: New Relevance for Science and Society Washington DC: The National Academies Press. 1997.*

Moreover, history is written by individuals who have their perceptions. On the contrary, geography is a much more objective science. The influence of geography on history depends on economic means, objectives, and human potential. Thus, the economy is added as a formative factor in history along with geography. Historical and economic factors create conditions in favor of the status quo, which persists even when the reasons for its formation cease to exist.[6]

Geopolitics is the study of the effects of geography on international relations and politics.[7] Geopolitics also plans a country's security policy, considering the geographic factor.[8] Geopolitics, as a theory of local interdependencies and historical causality, analyzes and associates stable and variable geographic factors. It comes to conclusions regarding the sharing of power in the international arena[9]. Geopolitics is a method of studying foreign policy to understand, explain, and ultimately predict the behavior of international political actors through geographical variables. These variables include climate, environment, culture, topography, demography, natural resources, nations' character, history, and factors such as the economy.[10] However, geopolitics does not

---

[6] I.D. Pintos: Economics of the Area (in Greek).
[7] *Devetak et al. (eds), An Introduction to International Relations, 2012.*
[8] Nicholas John Spykman: The Geography of the Peace,1944.
[9] *Lambros Kafidas, Military Review, Nov – Dec 2009* (in Greek).
[10] Evans, G & Newnham, J., (1998), "The Penguin Dictionary of International relations".

10

explain everything[11]. Furthermore, the winds of geopolitics are changing frequently and quickly, in contrast to the more stable geography.

---

[11] Tim Marshal: «Prisoners of Geography».

THE GEOGRAPHIC PILLAR OF GEOPOLITICS

The Essentials of Geography

Natural geography, primarily, is not considered a variable factor. Instead, it is characterized by stability to the extent that something is stable only on a scale defined by time measured in millennia. However, it can provide variable results regarding its elements and their utilization in connection with human activities and politics. This variability is reflected in geopolitics.

The introduction of agriculture, the permanent establishment of human groups in a place, and the ensuing "ownership" of the land individually and collectively constituted the basis of civilization and the beginning of geopolitics.[12] However, the character of the term "property" and the subsequent term "property of land" have undergone many changes during human history, and the ownership, in itself, and particularly ownership of land, has a different meaning or is not recognized at all in specific historical circumstances but also by certain ideologies.

"Multiply and fill the earth and subdue it". When these words were written, humankind had already spread in the world. The reasons for the spread of the human species from very early on and the continuing migration were economic, political, social, and personal. Initially, the food-gathering economy imposed constant movements in search of food, with the scarcity of food and water resulting from population growth and climate change. It was followed by issues of politics and power-sharing that

---

[12] The historian Numa Denis Fustel De Coulanges respond to the theories about a primitive agricultural communism in his book "The Origin of Property in Lands"

forced selected groups to migrate. Finally, the migrating groups created colonies in the ancient world, though the connection with the place of their origin continued. More rarely initially and more commonly later, political, social, and personal reasons were the leading migratory causes.

According to economist Perroux, the modern age man has shaped geography just like he shaped historical evolution.[13] The man brought about changes in nature and geography, initially by creating rural exploitation areas with swamp drainage and river flow arrangements and later by opening canals and altering the marine environment. Due to the Lessepsian species migration, Suez transformed the eastern Mediterranean into a quasi-tropical sea. Bridges and tunnels changed geographic and geopolitical data. Islands were united with the mainland coast; continents were connected by bridges or separated by canals. The sea became land and the sea land. The man intervened in the landscape, perforated mountains, and built ports where none existed. With its industrial actions, man partly brought about climate change, perhaps even melting ice in the Arctic. The changes made are crucial up to a point to talk about a new, human-made geological period, the "Anthropocene."[14] In this sense, geography is now both anthropocentric and mutable.

Besides, a change in geography as a component of geopolitics is also taking place in terms of perceptions. Maps are not innocent. They create impressions; they take root in collective opinions and geopolitical ideas. In a sense, geography is mutable and evolves according to the perceptions that are sometimes artificially constructed. The process of "making" the judgments, according to Prof.

---

[13] I.D. Pintos: Economics of the Area (in Greek).
[14] As it was named by Paul Crutzen.

G. Prevelakis, has persistent effects over time, while after their creation, it is difficult to overturn them.[15] Although this was not intentional, the Mercatorian map projection imposed the picture of larger (in comparison) geographical sizes when distant from Ecuador, i.e., Europe and North America. British perceptions regarding continental Europe differ from those of the rest of Europe. The "invention" of an "Eastern Mediterranean" entity serves geopolitical purposes. The actual perception of Westerners regarding China is different than in the past. The same applies to the Soviet Union, the Russia of Yeltsin, and the Russia of Putin.

In the Aegean, the border between Greece and Turkey was conventionally drawn between the eastern Greek islands and the Turkish coast, shown in Turkish maps until 1970. Maps not showing it led to the perception of having the actual border in the middle of the Aegean. The reference of the FYROM as Macedonia[16] in the world maps established this name in the world's common perception.

The geographical configuration and the morphology of the space in which the economy takes place are essential factors and significantly impact it. Therefore, spatial planning, regional development, and, more generally, geographical conditions constitute a significant economic objective. The drafting of a geo-economic charter is a prerequisite for implementing financial programming. The geographical area's economic research includes studying the natural environment, the influence of man on it, the form of industrial organization, the climate, and the geographical morphology of the space,

---

[15] Article by George Prevelakis (in Greek).
[16] The name of the country changed to North Macedonia, by the Prespes agreement, 2018.

15

together with the possibility of transport and communication by sea or river.[17]

Geographical data affects international relations and politics and is essential in developing international relations. History is about structured groups' social, political, and economic development within a specific national framework. The activity of the individuals becomes political if there are enough general interests and solidarity to become the object of this activity and cause some form of integration. The focus of politics can be the nation, a geographic region, or even an international or a supranational organization such as the E.U.[18] The unit could extend to cover the entire world (United Nations). Without the territorial-geographical element, no nation could ever exist in the state's sense.

As Max Weber pointed out, the state results from the evolution of political institutions. It is a sovereignty relationship based on "legal violence." The State legitimacy is based on "custom," on the "charisma of the leader," or on "reasonable rules," and not on geography. A political organization where the administrative staff controls the respective means is regarded as a "class-structured" organization.

The vassal of the fiefdom paid the costs for the administration and justice of his fief. The legitimacy of a manor's occupation and the feudal lord's social prestige emanated from his superior in the hierarchy, the ruler. In class society, the "lord" governs with the help of an autonomous aristocracy, sharing power with him. It is based on his "house" members and the landless peasants attached to him. The evolution of the modern state begins

---

[17] I. D. Pintos: Ibid.
[18] G.K. Vlahos: Political Theory (in Greek).

with the action of the ruler. The ruler appropriates the power of the autonomous bodies of the administrative authority that existed alongside him. In the modern state, the administrative staff is wholly separated from the means of administration.[19]

Geopolitics studies the effects of geography on relations between states, international relations, and international politics. This effect proves to be reliable, perhaps decisive for historical developments. Geopolitics is, among other reasons, the use of geography for the political purposes concerned. It differs from the states that came and gone in every historical period. Active international decision-making centers sometimes create geopolitical dynamics to form balances, sometimes artificially. They produce national ideologies for non-existent nations. They "recall' human rights that have never been violated or even claim non-existent people's rights in self-determination. However, geopolitical dynamics are created by a culture, an ideology, a language, an economy, an army, or a robust demographic increase.[20]

According to a theory, it is immoral and cowardly to believe that impersonal forces such as geography, the environment, or national characteristics define people's lives and draw the direction of international politics.[21] Despite R. Kaplan's astute observation, Geography does not take revenge. Nevertheless, the deterministic approach is considered an inevitable reality to a certain extent. It was already observed that these elements do not

---

[19] D. Tsakonas: Anthology of texts on sociology, 1972 (in Greek)
[20] I. Th. Mazis: Geography of the Islamicist movement in Middle East 1992, p.109 (in Greek).
[21] Isaiah Berlin: Historical Inevitability, 1954.

define but affect it.[22] Historians sometimes approach developments in the prospect of "inevitable." However, many times, the results are due to randomness. Events occur based on probability, although sometimes they occur following the citizens' will or even based on the political line imposed by the leader. Geography is not an absolute determining factor in history. However, it is "probably decisive"[23] in the sense of the non-direct existence of a perfect cause-causal relationship to events and policies regarding the inclusion in this relationship of other factors that could drive a result.

Foreign policy is exercised in a geographical area, always considering its specificities. Geographic analysis precedes the geopolitical and affects its probability. Various factors and scientific parameters govern geographic clusters, sometimes regardless of the administrative regime they interact with. The cultural, political, and economic elements work drastically with the geographical area, shaping its geopolitical character. The complexes of geographic areas are in continuous interdependence, competition, or conflict, constituting the geopolitical background of the world.[24]

"Geography," in any case, interacts with the "human population." The two concepts are in a function. Culture grew faster in places where the possibility of communication between large groups of people existed, at least in the historical past, related to geographic proximity: north-eastern Africa, the Middle East, and Eurasia. The

---

[22] Robert D. Kaplan: The Revenge of Geography, p.61, 2012.

[23] Probabilistic determination theory.

[24] I.Th. Mazis: Geographic Time and Economic Area,1988 (in Greek).

remote or rugged communication and contact areas, sub-Saharan Africa, America, and Australia, were unknown in the then ecumene[25] and initially remained culturally backward. Civilization was born and developed in the vast single landmass, Eurasia. Its speed of development and dissemination depended on the ease of travel of colonists and, afterward, merchants. The role of geography in this regard is undisputed. However, with the widespread use of the Internet, satellite television, and mobile telephony, technology development takes communication out of any geographic terms, multiplying it to the utmost and creating new global cultural standards.

The very nature of man that directs him to civil cohabitation led to civilization's birth and development. The distribution of projects, the possibility of using products or intellectual achievements of others, and the increased potential emerging from stability and security have contributed to the development of culture. Culture could develop primarily in such an environment. The possibility of advancing technology, education, science, philosophy, and art depends on the degree and the way of the organization and operation of the societies.

The cultural development of humanity is not universally similar in terms of degree and style. The physical configuration of the space and the geographic proximity between the geographic entities play an essential role in formulating common or similar cultural characteristics such as language, religion, values, and traditions, which sometimes transcend the boundaries of nations. As a result, the civilizations that grow in each place do not always have an upward direction but are

---

[25] The ecumene is a Greek term for the known, the inhabited, or the habitable world dating from antiquity.

differentiated and transformed into other cultural shapes. The most significant differentiation occurred not only with the lapse of time but also by violent or peaceful "migration" of population groups with different cultural characteristics. In this way, an alteration of the cultural level of Europe and Anatolia was historically observed, most of the time, to a deteriorating direction.

Geo – Culture is the conscious use of culture in the international distribution of power and the states' competition based on geography. The use of geopolitical tools presupposes, in principle, the existence of a cultural element that could qualify for international recognition and acceptance. Any expression of cultural activity, including religion, could be exploited for geopolitical purposes.[26] In antiquity, but without any particular awareness of its geo-cultural ramifications, Alexander the Great and the Roman Empire acted in this way in large part of the then-known world. During imperialist expansionism, the Western powers imposed Christianity in South America and Africa. At the same time, French culture was adopted in West Africa and Europe, especially during the interwar period. Finally, the imposition of American culture worldwide after the Second World War contributed to the USSR's defeat in the Cold War.

Territorial continuity and easy access by the sea, the degree of convenience that nations could communicate and trade, have been the basis for cooperation and development. However, territorial continuity has caused disputes and conflicts between nations and states, especially with no natural geographical boundaries.

---

[26] G. Poukamisas: Foreign Affairs, Hellenic Edition, issue of Oct- Nov, 2017 (in Greek).

Powerful countries were always interested in the geopolitical arrangement of their broader environment. Geopolitical plans still include securing roads, ways, and means of transit for trade and strategic aims. The ability of a country to communicate freely to keep open the transit routes for its citizens and goods was an issue that led the states even to wars.[27] Besides, from the earliest times, the countries sought to influence the geopolitical design of areas they considered necessary for their general interests. On the other hand, the countries that have understood the specific interest of stronger Powers for their region have included this parameter in their plans and political decisions.

In the modern era, European countries ensured stable conditions at territories where oil pipelines pass and maintained open inland transit routes for commerce.

Geopolitical aspirations have been, politically and historically, an obvious criterion for shaping states' foreign policy. The neighbors of the countries are those they are, and this element should always be considered a constant. However, historically, even recently, efforts have been made by countries that have occasionally succeeded in changing the geopolitical status of their geographical neighborhood. For example, Great Britain demonstrated the highest possible interest in the political shaping of the continental coast across the Channel and Europe in general, even declaring twice war against Germany in the previous century on this issue. Beyond its ideological character, the Cold War also had geopolitical implications as the "warring" parties tried to create safe and friendly surroundings with satellites or states-bastions. Italy's

---

[27] The U.S. justified its war against Native American Indians by their prohibition on travelling.

stance was to avoid integrating North Epirus into Greece after the First World War. The purpose was that a weaker state, Albania, controlled the shores across the Italian peninsula. Albania would be susceptible to Italian sway, as indeed has been.

Among the factors mainly taken into account in this context, the specific geopolitical conditions of the region, including the correlation of forces, the strategic aspirations of neighboring states, and the wider area, as well as access to energy sources and commercial roads, could be included. The conflict between Western European nations and Russia in the 19th century, culminating in the Crimean War, resulted from Britain's interest in the Mediterranean and maritime routes and Western engagement in the Middle East. At the beginning of the 19th century, the Powers engaging in the Battle of Navarino aimed mainly at geopolitical interests rather than Greece's independence.

As it is formed not only by geographical but also by broader geopolitical criteria, a region's character is always considered in states' decisions concerning their foreign policy. The European Union has made a particular account of the neighborhood by establishing the so-called "Neighborhood Policy" to create in its periphery regions with prevailing principles of the rule of law, democracy, and liberal policies. They chose the term neighborhood deliberately instead of the vicinity to declare the specific bonds of "community" created by the long-term proximity and community of interests with the neighbors of the E.U.

States, particularly the powerful ones, are always looking for "strategic partners" and "stable foundations" in the regions of their interest, either close to hostile states or in areas of instability, especially when adjacent to wealth-producing sites. In the context of the "arrangement" of the space under their particular interests, powerful states are involved in various methods, including policies of threats and provision of "exchanges." The U.S. offensive in Iraq to overthrow Saddam does not seem to have targeted any non-existent arsenal of weapons of mass destruction but to create a pro-Western stronghold in this sensitive oil-producing region. After its venture in Afghanistan, the U.S. targeted to develop a strategic network that would broaden the stability zone under American sway to control the Middle East. Access to wealth-producing resources that provide energy, water, and raw materials, and the acquisition of power to regulate their trade, always has been a decision-making criterion in international relations, both economic and political.

Order and subordination to legitimacy are above any excessive limits of liberty since to paraphrase Plato, freedom without order is slavery. This aphorism applies both internally and externally at the international level. Domestically, the states have enacted penal laws and established police forces and courts. However, in Western Europe, long-term and strict observance of rules that enforce order has led to a culture of respecting laws without always requiring violent enforcement. The democratic regimes try to act in this direction. The mature peoples are also voluntarily trying to overcome the preliminary stages of civilization and achieve harmonious coexistence without the need for violent enforcement of order. However, it is wrong to believe that the criminal confrontation of antisocial and criminal delinquency is unnecessary. Humans are political beings, and there will always be exceptions.

In the context of international relations, there is no empowering force to ensure order; thereby, the efforts to achieve it focus on consultation, the conclusion of agreements, the development of transnational organizations, or even supranational organizations at the regional or continental level. Organizations or agreements aimed at avoiding wars, trade organizations, or preventing climate change have been established at a global scale that transcends geography in part but not entirely. Membership in specific international organizations implies legal or moral obligations for member-states, such as respect to certain principles, e.g., solidarity among members, or rules, such as abiding by the international law for the United Nations members. The obligation to apply a standard policy of some regional organizations creates misunderstandings, as the traditional global system generally recognizes only independent states and regional organizations. Thus, sometimes, within the framework of the OSCE or U.N., there are complaints about failing to formulate a policy "under democratic conditions" due to the observance of a line agreed upon outside the framework of these international organizations, e.g., by the member-states of the European Union.

These obligations sometimes create significant distortions in marginal organizations with outdated purposes, such as the Organization for Islamic Cooperation, where the requirement to apply a standard pro-Islamic policy is sometimes contrary to the U.N. principles.

Unlike Europe, the traditional idea of independent states as the international system's basis remains strong in Asia, and the Asian nations do not wish to cede powers to a global or supranational organization. However, at the same time, solidarity between them is so strong that, for example, Japan, a like-minded country with democratic values, did not join the European Union in its effort in 2003 to restore democracy in Burma/Myanmar.

During the Cold War, doctrines of avoiding interference in the differences between the North Atlantic Alliance allies and the non-involvement in the "internal affairs" of the opposing coalition in Europe constituted criteria for making decisions. In addition, the members of the two blocs shared, within their alliances, common positions on the issues relating to the East-West conflict.

On the other hand, E.U. member-states mostly align their foreign policy in agreed lines within the European Council, vis-a-vis countries outside their geographic area. Nevertheless, again, the sway of the most influential states and the E.U.'s bureaucracy, gradually becoming independent, distort the democratic process, even in the Council of the E.U., the more respectful institution of this procedure. Moreover, sometimes, decisions taken at the collective level may harm individual member-states. This situation does not seem promising for the continuation of the concession of powers to the Union's central bodies by the member-states.[28]

Political maps and reality

Geography defines and informs. However, political maps do not always tell the truth.[29] For example, a single color does not mean homogeneous control or separate nations. Still, it sometimes demonstrates the diversity of countries as the basis of international conflicts. At times, the borderlines on the map, particularly in the Middle East

---

[28] V. Moutsoglou: The criteria in international politics, Athens, 2015 (in Greek).

[29] Black: Maps and History.

and Africa, have little to do with national reality or the integration of peoples.

In the Sahel, a region of many races and languages and with newly formed nations, the borderlines separating states have often been decided in absentia of the peoples and based on the areas held by the previous colonial regimes. Regarding the Sahara, the desert is a vagueness factor in the borders' demarcation. The post-colonial distribution of land to nations violated the traditional boundaries and particularly the way of life of the people there. The region's people were used to the free movement of the caravans and nomadic life. For them, passports and border controls are devoid of any practical meaning. The lines drawn by the colonial powers on the maps are not visible to the Saharan people on the sands.

In the Middle East, the Sykes-Picot agreement concluded in May 1916 between Great Britain and France, with Russia's consent, allocated the Middle East territories of the Ottoman Empire to zones of influence and control among Great Britain, France, and formerly, Russia. The allocation was made arbitrarily, based on the victors' interests, neglecting the conditions on the ground. As a result, human geography remained sidelined, defeated by the political interests of the great powers. The result was a persistent local but also broader continuous friction.

Prof. G. Prevelakis and V. Pantazis showed that maps are not objective and guiltless.[30] Maps are institutions of ideology, and their effect on understanding history is significant. For example, the choice to put the North Pole at the top of the charts unconsciously creates the impression of a "superiority" of the northern countries, i.e., Europe and North America. At variance, the

---

[30] V. Pantazis: Maps and ideologies, 2018 (in Greek)

geographer Eratosthenes' maps (296 BC – 195 BC) had the South Pole up. At first sight, maps of Australia with the South Pole at the top seem incomprehensible to the observer used to the reverse image.

Nevertheless, for the peoples of the Northern Hemisphere, it is technically advisable to place the north up. The Mercator projection of the global surface on a level map shows that the northern hemisphere is much larger than the equatorial region. Therefore, Europe is shown as more significant than Africa. Whether ulterior motives or not, colonial Powers of the time appeared larger and, thus, more significant on the maps.

Colonialism constituted from the outset an "unnatural" situation with the whole of Africa painted in three or four colors, a condition that could not last for long in the 20th century. Eventually, the colonial powers were forced to leave. Sometimes, they did it peacefully. Elsewhere, they resisted fiercely, as it happened, for example, in Cyprus, Vietnam, and Algeria. Britain generally followed a vengeful policy, provoking situations of instability and war-induced almost everywhere where it was forced to withdraw. It cannot be by chance that many of the outbreaks of turmoil in the world occur in its former colonies, the Indian subcontinent, Cyprus, the Middle East, and Ireland. Together with other Western and Arab nations, France has responsibility for the situations created after the "Arab Spring" period in Libya and Syria.[31]

Wherever the colonial powers achieved to bring about changes in demography, they were successful in

---

[31] Washington Post, 29.11.2017: Kaddafi was ousted by the USA and France.

perpetuating their control.[32] Elsewhere, they left their language and culture, Spanish in Latin America, French in West Africa, Portuguese in Brazil and other African and Asian (Lusophone) countries, and English in East Africa and the Indian subcontinent.

Chokepoints

In military geography, a chokepoint is a geographic formation on land, such as a valley, a passageway, or a bridge. A chokepoint at sea could be a strait or a cluster of islands preventing free passage.

Chokepoints allow small military forces to repel superior troops in military operations. However, regarding trade, it can add costs or create difficulties. The oldest historical examples are the Thermopylae battle and the Salamis naval battle. Among choke points are the Straits of Marmara (Bosphorus and Dardanelles) between the Black Sea and the Aegean, the Strait of Hormuz in the Persian Gulf, the Bab – El Mandeb at the south end of the Red Sea, Gibraltar, the canals of Suez and Panama, the Strait of Malacca in Malaysia,[33] Cape of Good Hope and Cape Horn.

Any power controlling the choke points has additional leverage in commercial and military domains. Examples are many. The Ottoman Empire and its

---

[32] E.g., the Falkland Islands, Gibraltar, Northern Ireland, Martinique, and Ceuta and Melilla.

[33] This strait is the main naval crossing between the Indian and the Pacific, connecting the economies of China, South Korea and Japan with India and Pakistan as well as Europe (South Naval route via Suez). Up to 100 thousand ships sail annually through this strait, transferring about a quarter of the world's goods, including oil.

successor, Turkey, have historically fully used (up to abuse) the Straits' advantages for strategic and commercial matters. Tankers carry half of the worldwide oil pass from the Strait of Hormuz between two hostile forces, the Sunni Arab Emirates and the Shia Iran. Therefore, it has great strategic importance. The U.S. Navy and the navy of other powers have a continuous presence in the region. The significance of the Suez and Panama canals and the oil pipelines that pass parallel to them is also high for commercial reasons. When Nasser nationalized the Universal Company of the Maritime Canal of Suez, Britain, and France wedged a war against Egypt, not for the fiscal regime but for the control of the Canal. The U.S. has shown interest in controlling the Panamanian government because of the Canal and intervened whenever it lost control.

The Clash of Civilizations

Geography plays a crucial role in the theory of the conflict of civilizations, which imposes its own "geographic boundaries."[34] A few years after the end of the Cold War, Samuel Huntington expressed the opinion that the competition of the superpowers ceded its place to the "clash of civilizations."[35] In the new world order after the Cold War, the most critical conflicts would no longer

---

[34] It is queer that American theories such as Francis Fukuyama's "End of history" or Samuel Huntington's "Clash of Civilizations", which proved to be either inaccurate or flimsy, had such a broad resonance. This could probably be attributed to the timing of the publication, that is, precisely after the USA victory in the Cold War.

[35] Samuel Huntington: The Clash of Civilizations and Remaking of World Order (1996).

concern social classes or groups of economic interests but different cultural entities. Huntington rushed to define the two camps of the "clash of civilizations" that foreboded: on the one hand, the (enlightened) Western civilization, and on the other, the (dark) Orthodox East and Islam. However, although this is a non-scientific and non-historical theory, Huntington has found a broad audience to take him seriously.

Huntington drew a vertical line from north to south, starting from the Russian-Finnish border that crosses and separates Europe between East and West. The boundary between the Habsburg Empire and the Ottoman Empire identifies the track. The regions west of this line are dominated by Christian Protestantism and Catholicism, the Western "good" religions. Christian Orthodoxy and Islam prevail in the east, two religions that "seemingly," according to Huntington, do not differ much! On the western side of the line, it is easier to develop democratic systems as they have experienced regeneration, reform, and the industrial revolution. Despite this idea, fascism and Nazism were born there.

On the contrary, Huntington considered the east of the line economically (and culturally) underdeveloped. It argues that the West has been battling Islam on this border for 1300 years. Especially after the Second World War, the Arab World developed nationalism and became more potent because of the oil. As a result, conflicts occurred between the West and the Arab countries. Huntington neglects that wars are not carried out on lines but surfaces, while the fiercest battles occurred on the Huntington line's west side.

A cause of the theory of the conflict of civilizations is the mentality that it was already formed centuries ago in Western Europe. It systematically underestimated the

"East," separating it from its overpriced self. It constructed supposedly sympathetic images of the "mystical East" of irrational societies, distinguishing them from the superior, rational Western nations. Old expressions like "Bon pour l'Orient" resulted from this approach.[36] Edward Said's "Orientalism" examines the extent to which its thirst for power formed the European-Western knowledge of the rest of the world. Orientalism is a way of thinking based on an ontological and scientific distinction between East and West. "Human reality" is divided into concepts "we – them," where the meaning "we" in the West is perceived only as discrimination in the sense of "them." These concepts, however, are merely historical and cultural constructions.

A variant of orientalism is the perception of the "Balkans," resulting from the region's problems created during the fights for the Ottomans' expulsion. The first phase of the Macedonian issue, the Balkan Wars, the competition of the Great Powers, the place of the pretext for the explosion of World War I, the permanent claims, the ethnic conflicts, and instability are the components of this term, which is both ironic and contemptuous.[37] The Balkans, enslaved for centuries to the Ottomans, were alienated from the rest of Europe. They ended up being considered dismissively as the "East" with the ancient synergy of the Catholic Church. The latter succeeded in extending only in areas controlled by the Habsburgs, hence the dividing line of the Huntington. The term "Balkans" cultivated the image of a region of uncivilized barbarians

---

[36] Eduard Said: Orientalism,1978.
[37] Maria Todorova: Balkans, the Western fancy, 2000.

prone to self-destruction and, therefore, needed the guardianship of the West.[38]

Westerners perceive geography as influenced by their ideological origins and rivalry with Russia (and later China), which they express at every opportunity. Promoting their interests was always tainted with pretexts of democracy or support of Human Rights. The liberal internationalists of the U.S. and Western Europe agreed and outbid the West's offensive against Yugoslavia primarily because the latter did not adhere to the West as all other Eastern European countries did. They considered the attempt to maintain the unity of the federal state as an offensive war, disregarding their stances on similar situations in the West and the atrocities committed by opponents of the central government.

When a part of the Bosnian population sought to secede violently from the Federative state without complying with the constitutional procedures, Yugoslavia attempted to preserve unity by force. The West considered unjustified the Yugoslavian acts of war in Bosnia. In contrast, the American bombing of Belgrade to detach territory (Kosovo) from Serbia, a blatant violation of international law, was justified.

Europeans (half-hearted) disagreed with the U.S. offensive in Iraq. Still, they agreed on the attack on Assad in Syria (a country with almost a secular regime) in alliance with the Jihadists.[39]

In general, Westerners think and act as if the Huntington line exists. According to Robert D. Kaplan, "Remember that communism, while an extension of the totalitarian tendencies within Eastern Orthodox

---

[38] Natasa Stasinou.

[39] V. Moutsoglou: The Arabic Spring, 2014 (in Greek).

Christianity, and, therefore, an affront to liberalism, was, still, an ideology of the industrialized West." [40] In a sentence with so many inaccuracies, it would hardly fit more contempt for the Huntington line's east side.

Huntington's theory is wrong. Orthodox East and Islamic civilizations have nothing in common; they are adversaries. Eastern European cultures, including the Russian, are the same Western civilizations as in the rest of Europe, heirs of ancient Greek and Roman civilizations. Even between Western and Oriental cultures, i.e., the Chinese and Japan, there is no clash, although different. If there were a clash, this would be between the Islamic world[41] and others, not only between the civilizations but at all the coordinates of life, world views, and ideologies. History witnessed the constant clash between Islam as it was represented by Arab and Ottoman expansionism against Christian Europe. Although it cannot be considered a "clash" but a peaceful one, this expansionism is currently expressed by the extensive Muslim immigrant flows to Europe. Short-sighted politics should not determine political science.

Essentially, there is no clash of civilizations; world civilizations have found a modus vivendi among them. Differences are political and not cultural. Muslim democratic Algeria is not the same as Muslim monarchical Saudi Arabia. In some cases, geography has played a more significant role than culture.

---

[40] Kaplan: The Revenge of Geography, p. 74.
[41] As represented e.g., by Saudi Arabia or Erdogan's Turkey.

Globalization

Globalization, reflecting the reality of the increased contact between countries and cultures, could be perceived as opposing the theory of conflict of civilizations. Globalization aims to create conditions for integrating the economy and culture globally. The advanced means of transport and communication in the 20th century contributed to the accelerated interdependence of the economic and cultural activities of the nations. According to the IMF, four issues falling within the scope of globalization are commerce and trade, capital and investment, migration and movement of persons, and the dispersion of knowledge and culture.[42] Concerns of broader geographic interest, such as climate change, environmental pollution in the sea and air, and overfishing, are added to these issues.[43] Although some experts believe that globalization is a phenomenon of modern times, others consider that its beginnings could be traced even before European exploration. In fact, although the term was not used then, globalization started in the 19th century.

Globalization has resulted from the evolution of both air travel and global trade, as well as the easiness of communications in the electronic age, through decisions initially taken by developed countries. Thus, customs duties were reduced to ensure that each state offers the highest quality products at the most reasonable prices for

---

[42] International Monetary Fund. (2000). "Globalization: Threats or Opportunity." 12 April 2000.
[43] Bridges, G. (2002). "Grounding Globalization: The Prospects and Perils of Linking Economic Processes of Globalization to Environmental Outcomes". *Economic Geography*.

the benefit of producers and consumers in terms of free competition. The result was the reduction of global poverty. Consequently, the developed countries lost resources in favor of the less developed. Nevertheless, geography is again present since the cost generated due to this parameter (travel, transport, packaging, maintenance,.) is added to the final price of the products.

Globalization is indeed about many more than economic relations. It aims and achieves, to a certain extent, conditions for the development of common elements worldwide, such as moral and social values, as well as ecological conscience. Using English, French, or Spanish helps disseminate the same information and commentary on people of different national and cultural backgrounds. At the same time, the image through the screens conveys broadly the thrill of events as well as seasonal trends such as fashion. The aim of creating a common human culture is in the statute of the United Nations. The creation of a global community with the full meaning of a "world village" can contribute to the very survival of human civilization, if not the very survival of humanity. The latter eventually realized that individual actions may damage the entire planet. In this direction, efforts should be deployed in a coordinated way. The particular "geographical" civilizations would be preserved, and geography will always be there to generate differentiations.

Globalization turned out to be, in a way, a significant hazard. The rapid economic rise of the so-called Third World countries has impacted the developed countries. The transfer of funds and resources has drained the economic potential of relatively poor Western countries and prevented their economies' growth. This led broad vulgar strata of the population to unemployment and poverty. The national markets have suffered a critical blow. The shifting of wealth and, by extension, of power from West to East had geopolitical consequences. It degraded the state's role in the West and its regulatory capabilities.[44] Large companies of developed countries exploited the cheap workforce of developing nations. They gained huge profits at the working class's expense, not only for the host countries but also for their own countries. Developed countries, as well as less developed but organized countries, were the winners. China and India were among them, with billions of inhabitants' income to rise tenfold in a decade. Losers were the middle and working class of developed and relatively developed countries that lost entire production sectors.

The ideological lumpenproletariat opposes these positions. They consider that the opposition to globalization and migration is right-wing populism. However, the advocates of the liberal right believe both globalization and migration are profitable. Globalization contributes to capital efficiency, and migration increases the workforce, reducing labor costs.

According to the founder and executive chairman of the World Economic Forum, Klaus Schwab, globalization is a phenomenon driven by technology and the circulation of ideas, people, and goods. At the same time, global warming is an ideology that rewards the neo-liberal world order against national interests. Globalization is a reality. However, whether policies should be "global" is debatable.

In any case, globalization will not disappear; global economic crises sometimes slow down its results, but they do not stop it. It will cease neither through peaceful procedures nor protest demonstrations. Globalization

---

[44] Ignasio Ramone: The Geopolitical of Chaos, 1997.

means, before all, change, permanent change, and accelerated change. Change means needing to adapt each time to new realities but creates insecurity at the same time. It offers unique opportunities to those who can manage them, but there are also losers, individuals, groups, peoples, and nations. If globalization is not managed correctly, even today's winners will become losers in the long term.[45]

The reasons for transforming global geography towards modern globalization are mainly technological since technology does not recognize national boundaries. The states can no longer control the flow of information, incoming or outgoing. The Internet, telecommunications, and satellites have neutralized restrictive state systems regarding the movement of ideas and information. The fall of the empire of the Soviet Union inaugurated the general current for border degradation. Thirty years after the exponential increase in the movement of goods, capital, people, information, and ideas, along with positive results, negative consequences have emerged, particularly in some parts of Western societies. Social inequalities have been enlarged; substantial financial resources have been transferred from the impoverished layers of Western nations to countries in Asia. Many Muslims migrated to Europe, causing the remodeling of European values.[46] Thus, in the Western world, the reaction to migratory flows increased, despite an activist movement's actions, which mixed up immigrants and refugees and succeeded in depicting as politically incorrect, at least in Western Europe, any voices against illegal immigration.

---

[45] Michael Reiterer: Asia – Europe, do they meet? p.97.
[46] Tzeni Lialouti.

Globalization eliminates the possibility of applying Keynesian economics in some less productive countries. Any additional financial resources available through income redistribution, rather than contributing to internal economic development, leak abroad through cheaper imports, neutralizing the economic multiplier. The result is the generation of a necessity for economic austerity policies and a tendency towards protectionism. In the context of the European Union, the north-European countries, enjoying competitive advantages, try to impose models of financial rigor on the Mediterranean countries, as the latter, having waived the customs barriers, but also because of the common currency without fiscal integration, are not capable of defending their economies.

The Trump administration's dissenting approach to trade agreements, i.e., the North American Free Trade Agreement (NAFTA), the Trans-Pacific Partnership Agreement (TPP), and the Comprehensive Economic Agreement between Canada and the E.U. (CETA), had provoked reactions. However, it was argued that these agreements' objective was protecting investors and safeguarding intellectual property rights instead of promoting international trade.

Direct foreign investments are not always advantageous for host countries. They could have an overall negative impact depending on the economic sector of investment. Usually, an investment that does not aim to raise employment, augment exports, or reduce imports may not be advantageous for the host country's economy. It could be considered as a kind of external loan. Investments to exploit natural resources (tourism or subsoil) or property purchases are not beneficial for the host country.

Excessive globalization could lead to the restoration of the nation-state and "hard" borders and consequently to the weakening of supranational institutions with implications for the European Union.

The persistence of borders

The world is divided among sovereign states; a sovereign state is an organization on a territory; without the latter, it cannot exist.[47] The definition of a state provides for the existence of land. The border defines this territory, and historically, the countries clashed many times to expand the territory they controlled, both for economic reasons and for reasons of power.[48] Moreover, the demographic boom led to a further lack of space, which had become "valuable" even from ancient times.

Within borders, the territory has value, on the one hand, as an area for living and developing the people's political, economic, cultural, and social activities. On the other, as financial wealth. The state control exercised on its territory provides for the exploitation of arable land, mineral resources, and maritime space, as ensured by the U.N. Convention on the Law of the Sea. At the same time, state territory is the area of the people's sovereignty. People function within the borders of a territory, and the borders enclose their existence. Without borders, they do not exist as people, a state constituent, even if they existed as a nation.

Political borders are sometimes based on geographical – topographical data, mountains, sea, lakes,

---

[47] View of Ambassador Robert Strausz- Hupe, a partisan of the world federalism.

[48] As it is cited by Steven Pinker, an American- Canadian psychologist.

and rivers; occasionally, they are undefined on the ground. They could be a theoretical line at sea, on a lake, on the sands of the desert, or a plain. A theoretical line without a topographical datum can divide two different worlds, two distinct ideologies, i.e., a NATO country from a country of the Warsaw Pact, a Muslim country from a Christian or Buddhist one. Nevertheless, even when ideologies change, geographical or not, boundaries remain etched in people's memories.[49]

Although the land in Europe was initially widely available for economic exploitation, politically, it has always been the subject of bloody controversy. The relation between the search for fertile land and the political-military expansion is not direct. The struggle between Germans and Slavs during the Middle Ages, Germany's geopolitical plans in the 19th century to create a zone of influence in Anatolia and the Middle East, and Austria's efforts to occupy Balkan regions at the expense of the Ottoman Empire are due to the principle of political expansion based on the control of territories. On the contrary, wide-ranging colonization took place in America, Australia, New Zealand, and South Africa, where Aboriginals did not realize their value. Especially in North America, the expansion to the West, the "Manifest

---

[49] Tim Marshal in his book "Prisoners of Geography" takes as an example the border between Syria and Turkey, where there are no topographically defined borders (sic), pointing out that on the one hand there is a NATO country and on the other hand, at the time that it was written, ISIS and the jihadists, who were considered as a danger not only by Ankara but the entire Western World. Many Westerners consider Turkey as belonging to the Western world disregarding that is a country pursuing its own interests, as its leaders declared.

Destiny," is due to the search for agricultural land and the exploitation of forests and mines. In Argentina, the mapping out of the borders was based on farmland and pasture, resulting in indefinite natural boundaries, arid areas in the West and south, and forest areas in the north. In Australia, the boundaries are defined throughout the land by oceans, and in this case, economic activity and colonization depended on agriculture, pastures, and mines.[50]

    The borders separate two political units but also form a line of contact. The social and economic life of societies is influenced by the political, social, and economic system of the country and the geographical characteristics of the region. It is also influenced by the proximity to a political construction, the borders. The geographic proximity to an area adjacent to another country, sometimes with a completely different system or to an area of uncertainty, creates unique conditions, unlike other regions.

    Internationalism is a political dogma that transcends national boundaries and seeks greater political and economic cooperation among nations and peoples. It aims to integrate on a higher than the national level. However, in a particular form, it takes a hostile stance towards the nation and the homeland, despises the national symbols, aims at abolishing the national borders, and assumes an activist position to achieve these goals. Internationalism sometimes is confused with "proletarian internationalism", a Marxist perception based on the view that capitalism is a universal system. Therefore, the working class must act in global terms to confront it. This

---

[50] N.K Deniozos: Foreign Affairs, the Hellenic Edition, Aug. - Sept. 2018 (in Greek).

confusion leads some left-wing forces to identify with views in favor of abolishing borders for crossings, a peculiar laissez-passer, although this is a liberal perception.

On the other hand, cosmopolitanism is an ideology that considers all of humanity as a single community of the same moral values without expressing views on borders, except the belief that they should not impede passage. However, British Prime Minister Theresa May said, "If you believe you are a citizen of the world, you are a citizen of no state." However, this approach constitutes a violation of human rights.

Globalism is a term describing a national policy that considers the whole of the world as a scene for political sway (on the part, e.g., of the U.S., Russia, or China) and a policy that considers global interests to be above the interests of each nation (e.g., agreements on tackling climate change). According to a theory of the German officer of the Nazi army and geographer Karl Ernst Haushofer in a pre-war (before WW1) wording, borders are not fixed. Only weak states in decline seek stable borders; for solid nations, they are nothing but a transient obstacle. From this point of view, the borders are not rigid political or natural boundaries of races and nationalities, but they are changeable, succumbing to the will and needs of influential ethnic and racial groups. Internationalism has nothing to do with this expansionist approach.

According to U.S. President Trump, and in the context of his anti-immigrant rhetoric in that capacity, the borders make the state: if there are no (guarded) borders, there is no state. However, the American journalist Joshua Keating considers that ambitious ethnicities and de facto countries exist without regulated borders.[51] He refers to entities missing one or two elements necessary for their statehood, i.e., territory, people, organization (government), and international recognition. The reference is to autonomous Somaliland, Catalonia, Kurdistan, Palestine, entities not having international recognition, states with no single government, and failed states (such as Libya after the Arab Spring). Keating observes that organized life and international relations are based on the state. For a long time, borders separating countries remained stable and, in their majority, undenied. However, in Europe, e.g., Ukraine, Greece, and Cyprus have neighbors that question them, this remains an exception. Keating, forgetting Turkey, argues that Russia is the main nationalist force that disputes the borders. Turkey disputes the borders of almost all its neighbors.

Another issue is the case of island states such as Kiribati, which may disappear in a cataclysmic climate change event if the sea level goes up. The peoples of such countries shall be transferred elsewhere. Still, for the continuity of the state, the element of the territory will no longer exist. Kiribati bought (in 2014) an area of about 26 square kilometers on the island of Vanua Levu of Fiji with the prospect of resettling its citizens (a little over 110 thousand then) in case of its land flooding. However, the question is if, following the possible disappearance of the island, its "people" could continue its statehood in the new territory under the old name, I-Kiribati, while retaining the relevant rights deriving from it. Until recently, in the sense of the state, the element of international recognition was not included; it has been added later. It is, therefore, a question of how the international community would react

---

[51] Joshua Keating: Invisible Countries.

juristically to a lack of territory, particularly concerning the state rights of those peoples. Issues could be raised regarding the Exclusive Economic Zone of the state at sea, the international agreements they have concluded, or even the seats they hold at the UNO. However, in cases of military occupation of territory in the modern era, the international community did not accept the change, respected the relevant international law, and continued to recognize the rights of the state that possessed the area legally.

The geography of hunger and violence arises due to natural conditions and the mismatch of the demographic factor with the territorial one. Countries suffer from the population's degradation by force and warfare or by a peaceful-legal or aggressive-irregular migration. In searching for another socio-economic system, the problem is transferred through migration to other states, neighboring or not. Irregular, unorganized immigration in Europe has led to the misery of aspiring immigrants, occasionally leading to their death in their attempt to enter Europe illegally. The inordinate grant of rights to national communities of different cultures resulted in the adoption of a multicultural model. In this model, immigrants do not adopt domestic rules and sometimes try to impose their own -religious or social- laws. Also, the misunderstanding about the host countries' possibilities, the vision of European prosperity that no longer exists, causes such a migratory momentum that makes borders permeable, almost open. These create a sense of ending the territorial area of shared ownership by the host country's nationals. The result is the loss of the neighborhood, the community, the village, and ultimately, the common property held by those "lacking any property," i.e., the territory within borders. [52]

The change of borders in modern times has always been problematic; it was sometimes consensual, such as the split of Czechoslovakia. In this case, the Czech Republic and Slovakia remained in the Visegrad initiative. Westerners remained neutral.

Occasionally, secession was violent, such as in the Yugoslav states' case, which brought about a war. Westerners were allied militarily with the secessionists against Serbia.

In the West, the states opposed vigorously, although not by arms – except in Ireland and the Basque countries – to the secession actions. In the case of Catalonia, the central government used legal deterrence with the dismissal of the local government and imprisonment of its members. In the case of Quebec, with threats of financial sanctions. In the 19th century, the United States fought fiercely against the secessionist Confederate States in the South to preserve the Union.

For the unification of Germany, Westerners acquiesced "half-hearted." While they reacted strongly in the case of Crimea (a formerly Russian region inhabited by Russians) with sanctions, their reaction regarding the military occupation of part of Cyprus (an independent country with a Turkish minority of 18%) remains entirely theoretical level. In the case of Western Sahara, although they do not theoretically recognize the borders of Morocco, they hesitate to recognize the Saharawi state legally. However, according to the U.N. authorities, the latter has the right to be legally recognized. In the case of Sudan, an agreed split, the two states inherited the original

---

[52] Panagis Panagiotopoulos.

state's instability. In the case of Kosovo, a union with Albania was indirectly attempted with the decision to abolish the border controls. Eventually, the international reaction is always political and beyond current justifications and pretexts emanating from the interests of the powerful states.

The question of the concepts of state, nation, and people, as well as their relations and interactions, has a primary role in differentiating countries. This differentiation of ideas, at least in terms of general level and common perception, is mainly due to historical reasons and seems poorly influenced by globalization. Within their geographical boundaries, nation-states always remain the cell in which social, political, economic, and cultural life evolves. The -most often- common language, shared economic interests, and whatever elements constitute the nation are strong bonds that will not be easy to wipe off.

Like anarchy - the lack of any system- although an alluring utopia for many people, it is not capable of responding to the needs of people; in the same way, internationalism is not able, at the present stage of the evolution of the political civilization, to contribute to prosperity and progress. Even in an area such as Western Europe, where states have almost similar cultures and comparable economic growth, border disputes are generally missing, and nationality, based on historical parameters, remains decisive. The Schengen Treaty, which is criticized by the security authorities, including the U.S., even though it makes the borders porous, does not abolish them.

Therefore, the actual regional problems should be examined and resolved in the context of nation-states, such as collective security, economic cooperation, development, and the organization of the area. Notably, the imposition of communist regimes within the Eastern Coalition framework had created conditions. It brought about political and economic cooperation among the states of the region, which cannot be considered to have been imposed exclusively by force. However, such collaboration within a liberal regime is more challenging with the released social effects. The termination of the international bipolar system freed powers, the restriction of which would be onerous without the catalytic intervention of the West, the assimilation of which has been the ideal of the post-war era. In the new reality, more significant efforts should be spent to organize the area, which can only follow the most massive formations of the West, integrating the region's nation-states.

Although there has been a tendency by activist interest groups to break down nation-states, most populations believe that this would not improve people's living conditions. On the contrary, systems replacing the nation-states would either adopt federal institutions that do not respond to the people's particular interests by transferring all power to centers with different objectives or establish institutions for the exploitation of the people by an oligarchy, hereditary or aristocratic. In any case, the European peoples do not seem to be prepared to abandon the nation-states to adopt more federalist institutions.

The nation-states under democratic control will endure for a long time, with the introduction of institutions inclined to a higher capacity to integrate their populations, indigenous and immigrant, and increase cooperation with other states and other peoples. The deficit in democratic control could be gradually reduced if societies push in this direction, but this is not the case at present. However, the continuity of nation-states, even as unbreakable cells that could form the basis for federal solutions to practical problems, remains. Moreover, in multinational states, the federated states behave as nation-states, even if different nationalities constitute them.

In Western societies, but not only, and in modern times, nationalism – patriotism is the primary ideological reference. This trend emerged as the result of cultural developments but also when it was proved that the nation-state is the sole foundation that ensures the existence and freedom of people in democratic conditions.

Sanctions and geography

Sanctions taken by the U.N., the USA, or the E.U. do not hurt only the target state but have repercussions on third states, whether they are members of the collegiality that imposes the sanctions. Costs are different in each case. Among the factors determining these costs, depending on the sanctions' nature or content, the geographical aspect, particularly the vicinity, should be included.

Sanctions imposed, e.g., by the U.S. against Iran, were also affecting Iraq because of the interdependence of the two countries since Iraq cut off Iran from Syria and the overland route to the Arabian Peninsula. Still, Iraq's food, gas, and electricity supply depends on Iran. At the same time, Iran could divert rivers outside Iraq, leading the country to drought. Iraq would undoubtedly not want to displease the U.S. Still, on the other hand, the consequences of respecting the sanctions could be vital. Ironically, this interdependence of the two countries is primarily due to the U.S. invasion in 2003.

The demographic boom

In general, people consider that geography is as it is. Since 1942, when this aphorism was expressed, geographic characteristics have reshaped; technical and economic possibilities of human intervention in the environment have increased. Still, above all, the human population has increased exponentially. Being 2.5 billion at that time, it reached 7.6 billion in 2017. According to the United Nations, the human population will rise to 8.5 billion in 2030 and 11.2 billion in 2100. This figure was estimated to be approximately 370 million in the 14th century and has since increased continuously, reaching a top increase rate of 2.06% between 1965 and 1970. At the same time, the average age is growing, and the proportion of the active population is decreasing, though not to the same degree everywhere. The growth of Earth's population results in different age distributions. Another change is urbanization. In 1800, shortly after the Industrial Revolution, only 3% of the population lived in cities. This figure, in 2010, exceeded 50%. In terms of geography, the population's density is significant, which is, of course, higher in the temperate zone, as it is covered by land. Therefore, the enormous human population is concentrated in the northern hemisphere.

Unlike Europe and partly North America, the population on all other continents has a strong growth trend, with East Asia and sub-Saharan Africa recording high rates in this direction. Especially the latter, which in 1950 had a population of 180 million; if it continues at these rates, in the year 2050, it will have 2.2 billion. Food may not be missing, but economic growth will be prevented, and the environment will deteriorate. The U.N. predicts a decrease in the population growth rate in Africa, but smaller than in other regions. This image can change

family planning, women's education, and the Sahel's stability. According to the U.N. forecasts, the Earth's population will grow by one billion in Europe and America, two billion in Africa, and five in Asia. At the same time, the population of Africa will rise to 4 billion and the Earth's population to 11 billion. Other studies, however, showed that the world population would begin to decline after a population increase at around mid-century.

In Asia, the economy is growing. Some Asian countries that Europeans consider Third World are more economically developed than some European countries. The economy's center of gravity and markets will move to the Pacific-Indian Ocean region. It is estimated that China, India, and Indonesia will be among the four strongest economies in the world.

If the threshold of $2 per day is considered a sign of absolute poverty. In that case, the number of people living below this threshold is 745 million (2017), improved since 1990, when the Earth's population was 5.3 billion. Then, the number of absolute poor was around 1.9 billion. 3.4 billion, half of humanity, are just fleeing the absolute poverty threshold by living on about 5.5 a day. On the other hand, a few dozens of rich people control half of the world's income.

In any case, the improvement made is credited to Asia and globalization. However, India is one of the countries with the most deprived population, where 13% of its people live in absolute poverty. The more acute problem is in sub-Saharan Africa, where the absolute poor is around 41.1% of the total population and is rising. Moreover, due to the high birth rate in more impoverished social strata, the proportion of people living in conditions of extreme poverty is expected to increase, leading to increased migration.

People regularly consume energy in everything they do to move, warm up, cool down, keep their food in the fridge, and produce food or other products. The total energy consumption by humans has doubled since 1973. Although energy produced by renewable sources, Sun, wind, and hydro, has been increasing in recent years, much of the energy produced still comes from the combustion of hydrocarbons and nuclear fission. There is a reservation for their use after the significant accidents in nuclear reactors. On the other hand, it seems that fusion energy systems, clean and safe, are challenging to construct.

Advances in technology contribute to increasing the resources allocated to produce environmentally friendly energy. However, even the solutions invented to protect the environment by using, e.g., electric cars, will increase the total energy consumed. In contrast, limited resources such as rare-earth elements are used to manufacture batteries. People are already consuming far more resources than the planet can produce. As a result, they pollute the environment and cause damage to the ecosystem.

Scientists warn of drinking water availability, reducing marine life forms, deforestation, reduction of biodiversity, and climate change. All these problems are the result of the continuing growth of the population. Planet Earth cannot withstand such a large population of people. As it did in the past, it will rectify the situation if the man does not take the indispensable steps. Homo sapiens has changed to "Homo Pernicious", the destroyer of the environment in which he lives.[53]

If Earth's corrective action starts, it will be difficult to stop it, and the time required will be measured

---

[53] According to Professor Th. Lianos.

in tens of millennia. Scientists like Stephen Hawking, excluding risks such as a pandemic, predicted a continuation of human life on Earth only for a few centuries if preventive measures are not taken, noting that the damage already done is irreparable. The answer given by some scientists is that more calories could be produced, more heat and light, more kilometers traveled with less pollution, and a smaller ecological footprint through progress in anti-pollution technologies and intensification of cultivation. However, suppose there is a continuous increase in the global population. In that case, there will be a point at which the problem can no longer be tackled. One of the main issues is the disproportionate increase in the population of regions. It is noted that migration contributes to the rise of the planet's population by removing people from countries with a high birth rate, thereby allowing new population growth.

The global demographic problem also focuses on the aging of the population resulting from the development of societies. Demography issues should not be confused with problems in the organization. The latter gives solutions to both the large population density and the small one.

Migration

Recent history shows that the migration of people worldwide is inevitable and would be relatively advantageous for immigrants if this took place according to the rules. Otherwise, it would have adverse effects in the countries of origin, host countries, or both. The uncontrolled and illegal entry of migrants, as is mainly the case in Europe, has adverse effects on everyone. The proportion of criminal elements among irregular migrants is higher than in the countries they originate from, which is among the reasons for irregular migration. Illegal immigrants' ability and desire to integrate with host countries is unknown and often non-existent since their movement goals are irrelevant.

The leading cause of migration to Europe is the high birth rate of countries in Asia and Africa. In Africa, it is around 5; in Asia, it is around 3; in Europe, it is around 1.5. In addition, about a billion people, mainly Sunni Muslims, live on a few Euros and aspire to migrate to Europe that welcomes them. However, there, they live on granted allowances. Greece and Italy are among the primary hosts of illegal immigrants, receiving them on the grounds of being politically correct.

The wars in Syria, Afghanistan, and Africa have not been the cause of immigration to Europe. Illegal-irregular migration has been exerting intense pressure on potential host countries in recent decades, regardless of war, with significant portals of entrance to Greece and Italy and, to a lesser extent, Spain and France.

The migratory pressure to Europe indicates the difference in tackling global political and economic realities. The inability of the welfare state in Europe to respond to the needs of the weakest Europeans is a reality that does not seem to concern those who come to the continent with high expectations for subsidies and social services. Several Europeans, mainly attached to the left but not only with the strong advocacy of journalists and NGO activists, favor the advent and settlement of migrants from other continents in Europe. Others believe that they are punishing themselves for the old colonial oppression. Others want to be politically correct, supporting immigration enthusiastically. Migrants sometimes fall victim to the impression of the ongoing prosperity of

Europe prevailing outside the continent. Some migrants believe that Europe owes them; others want to exploit subsidies, and some – few – choose the European way of life. They all understand whatever is expressed in Europe in favor of immigrants as an invitation.

Religion creates another problem, as many immigrants in Europe are Muslims. Islam appears as a unified nation based on shared faith, i.e., Umma, outside the political sphere. Extremist elements of this "nation" have carried out terrorist acts, and the condemnation of their peers, if any, has not been proportional. The Islamic religion substantially differs from other religions since its rules exercise overall control of all aspects of a Muslim's life. According to an interpretation, a Muslim cannot exist under the Christian administration. Conciliation formulas exist, but this principle remains at the heart of fundamentalism. In this light, the difficulties of integrating Muslims into the European way of life are apparent; there are unsurmountable difficulties in reconciling the imperatives of Islam and the duties of the citizens of European states. However, for their part, the European nations prefer secularism and respect Islam over Christianity. Nevertheless, in a recent survey, 70% of Europeans declared themselves Christians in the broadest sense, 25% irreligious, and 5% Muslims.

The migrants are unaware of the journey's dangers to Europe, as traffickers hide them, resulting in many deaths. On the other hand, the hasty attribution of refugee status to, in fact, illegal immigrants harms the institution of protection of the refugees. At the same time, it damages their countries of origin, which would need the population that had fled elsewhere after their normalization.

Uncontrolled migration absorbed resources that would have been headed in weak resident European grassroots layers and deteriorated local culture and image. This is particularly evident in some Western European cities. Moreover, several European cities and regions have been unable to integrate migrants because of their large numbers and technical and administrative weaknesses.

Europe has, however, made efforts to ensure that the countries of its vicinity had the relevant economic potential to avoid the need for migration of their population. This has produced counter-effects. The rise of the cultural level has led to a better knowledge of living conditions in non-Muslim Europe due to its secular system and respect for human rights, prompting migration. The additional economic possibilities acquired by the aspiring migrants, through the help of Europe, provided them the means to attempt illegal entry. In any case, irregular immigration in the way it is in Europe cannot positively impact the host countries and only sparsely becomes favorable for the immigrants themselves. Europe cannot accommodate the millions of desperate people heading towards it, nor can it overlook the security issues arising from the uncontrolled entry of third-country nationals.

Climatic change

The Earth's climate is not stable but changing. Before the industrial age, climate change was caused by natural causes, either by the Sun's activity because of alterations in radiation reaching Earth or astronomical issues, such as mutations in the Earth's orbit and its axis inclination, regularly occurring in extended periods. Endogenous events, such as significant volcanic eruptions and activity of tectonic plates or disturbances due to oceanic processes (currents, water circulation), as well as processes due to the interaction of the geosphere, the hydrosphere, the biosphere, the atmosphere, and possibly others that we may not know, also contribute to climate change.

According to several studies, in the last two millennia, temperature increased between 950 and 1100 A.D., the so-called medieval warm period. Later, in the 17th century, lower temperatures were registered, and the period was named "the short glacial period."[54] After 1970, the temperature, according to many studies, increased continuously. This fact was attributed to significant carbon dioxide emissions due to industry and traffic. Other studies show that after the 17th century, there was constant temperature reduction up to the industrial age and a sudden increase popularized as the "hockey stick controversy." In contrast, others profess that the medieval warm period was warmer than today. In assessing the reliability of the studies, the interests of companies and oil-producing countries should also be considered, but in no absolute terms.

Present climate change is considered to be due to human activity, and changes brought about in the environment, such as deforestation and dam construction. According to some studies, human activity produces high concentrations of greenhouse gas emissions, contributing as much as 20%, but maybe more.[55] Washington Post detailed how some places on Earth are growing warmer faster than the rest of the planet, causing environmental

---

[54] It was linked to the depopulation of the Latin America by European colonists and the forestation of the previously cultivated land.

[55] Kimon Hatzibiros: http://users.itia.ntua.gr/kimon/LCA_dam9.doc. (in Greek).

devastation. It demonstrated "that extreme climate change is already a life-altering reality across 10 percent of the Earth's surface."[56] In other places, a temperature decrease is observed.

The earth system behaves as a single, self-regulating system consisting of the natural chemical, biological, and human elements. Global warming might cause significant damage to the economy, human health, and the environment, with possible annual losses in specific sectors amounting to hundreds of billions of dollars by the end of the century. If it continues, it will lead to drought in large areas and the destruction of farmland. At the same time, the probable rise of sea levels due to the melting of the ice and the expansion of marine waters due to their heating will remove ground and wipe out even whole islands. The lives of thousands of people could be endangered, and the survival of millions may be compromised. Substantial financial resources will be required to treat the problems created. Some effects, such as the rising sea levels from melting ice, even if not as significant as mentioned, will be irreversible for millennia. Others, as the extinction of species, will be permanent. In the Mediterranean, overfishing has dramatically reduced the volume of catches. Besides, the sea's overheating already led to the extinction of some fish species and the migration of others.

Scientists claim that it is not the wild animals that cause a pandemic. The causes of the pandemic of COVID-19 are deforestation, the loss of natural habitats of wild animals, the reduction of biodiversity, and the over-exploitation of wildlife resources that bring wildlife species into contact with humans in densely populated areas. The

---

[56] Washington Post won a 2020 Pulitzer Prize for this study

2020 crisis is the indisputable affirmation of the overload of the planet's ecosystems.[57] The message sent by the coronavirus pandemic was a reminder that the Earth does not belong to humans. Humankind must respect nature as nature could always take countermeasures.

Although greenhouse gas emissions, particularly carbon dioxide, may not be the sole cause of climate change, it is the only cause over which humanity could have some control. The effort to reduce emissions should be undertaken worldwide and, specifically, by the most industrialized countries. Attempts have been made to conclude international agreements in this direction, but the interests affected are big. The U.S., under President Trump, withdrew from the Paris Agreement of 2015, which provided commitments to restrict greenhouse gas emissions. This agreement limits the increase of the Earth's temperature to 2 degrees Celsius (but even this increase is considered catastrophic).

The possible rise of the sea level due to temperature-related factors would endanger island states such as the Maldives, Vanuatu, or Kiribati. Although an agreement was finally reached on limiting carbon dioxide emissions (Paris, 2018) to the 1.5% limit (instead of 2%) above the pre-industrial level, this may not be achieved because of possible infringements (e.g., the U.S. and China, but not only) as well as the action of other factors. Some island states are already taking measures to prevent the erosion of their coasts and protect the quality of their drinking water. Papua New Guinea moved the population of the coral islands Carteret to the land part of the country, but moving the entire population of an island country to another country's territory would create legal issues.

---

[57] Josep Borrell: The world after coronavirus, 2020.

The Entropy in Politics

The world is in flux; nothing stays as it is. The only constant is the mutation. According to Heraclitus, continual movement and change are the fundamental characteristics of reality, expressed by the philosopher with the image of a river that remains the same, although the water flowing through it changes continually. The philosopher did not believe in a universal flow and change but insisted on linking this change to fixed parameters. In thermodynamics, entropy is the concept by which disorder is measured; its maximum value reflects complete disorganization. The latter is equivalent to the homogenization of everything and, therefore, the cessation of evolution. "Life" is the opposite process that leads to the reduction of entropy through energy consumption and the restoration of order. In nature, entropy, "homogenization"', tends to increase with the release of energy. Therefore, energy must be consumed for a system to return to a degree of "less homogenization" to increase its potential.

The same is true for human societies, which, if not organized by "energy consumption," i.e., effort, are heading towards homogenization, i.e., the disappearance of production potential. Political entropy is a trend that is observed but cannot be measured; politics, in a sense, is precisely the collective effort to restore entropy to previous levels, reduce entropy with social energy consumption, and restore order.

Political society is organized with institutions, thus potentially producing a result. On the other hand, various social forces aim to disorganize the community. The natural tendency to increase political entropy leads to "homogenization" disorder, the dissolution of institutions, and any organized entity capable of producing a work. Where no specific political effort is made to this end, the tendency of societies is towards increasing entropy, i.e., in social terms, increasing disorder. Reverting to a previous entropy level entails energy consumption, i.e., in the case of societies, spending effort and resources. However, this effort will contribute to an increase in overall entropy. In contrast, the restraint from the outset contributes to a more minor increase in entropy. Therefore, prevention is preferable.

The attempt to contain entropy differs within the international community's organized groups, i.e., the countries. It evolves differently and more freely in international relations. Concerning the "opposite concepts," where the phenomenon of entropy occurs through its increase, Heraclitus considers that the tendency is toward balance to increase homogenization. Seemingly opposite situations, trends, and forces are linked to a coherent relationship that results in homogenization and disorder, i.e., necrosis.

According to Heraclitus, cold is heated and hot is cooled, but to return to the previous state requires energy consumption. The relationship of opposites is expressed as "war" - another aspect of harmony. This cosmic constant governs opposites and continuously produces, through conflicts, new balances, although it does it in a lower degree of order, therefore higher at entropy. War was seen as a natural phenomenon, the preponderance of the powerful over the weak, thus increasing entropy. As an increase in entropy, migration also works toward homogenization, as the war does.

On the contrary, the modern organization of international relations through international organizations and international law aims to maintain entropy, the "potential to produce work." When international organizations do not act in this direction, usually succumbing to power, entropy increases; thus, in international relations, entropy, in general, is increasing. Consequently, the potential for finding solutions that would reduce entropy, always based on energy consumption on efforts spent, is decreasing.

The model of Heraclitus with the image of a river that remains the same, while the water flowing through it is continually changing, does not apply in human societies and politics. The historical developments could be likened to the river water or the smoke of a cigarette flowing first smoothly and then with turbulent flow. Each time is a field of change from a relatively laminar flow to a rather turbulent one. As time passes, it is more difficult to restore order. The same conditions in turbulent flow cannot be achieved; the opportunity does not come twice. Turbulence will always go under greater entropy and irregular conditions.

The Arctic

According to scientific studies, the average Arctic ice level has fallen by 40% since 1980.[58] The melting of ice releases marine areas rich in resources. It has geopolitical implications, primarily because it would allow ships to cross the Arctic Ocean without the accompaniment of icebreakers, thus reducing the cost. Furthermore, it facilitates the exploration and extraction of the abundant reserves of hydrocarbons and other regional ores, e.g., manganese, uranium, copper, and iron. However, the relatively higher costs of exploiting these deposits should be considered with other regions with a more appropriate

---

[58] This phenomenon is not observed in the Antarctic.

environment. However, it is estimated that 30% of the non-recovered natural gas deposits and 13% of the corresponding oil fields are in the Arctic subsoil. Despite reducing the resources in fishing and hunting related to ice, the catches of the region are still notable. On the other hand, indigenous peoples of the Arctic comprehend their rights and the anticipated increase in their economic potential, giving them political strength. In the case of Greenland, this political strength boosts their request for independence from Denmark.

The melting of the ice and the release of transit routes create issues of national security, which relate to claims on maritime zones. Russia has already amassed strong forces in the region, and its demands reached the point of "posting" a Russian flag on the seabed near the North Pole. Russia also fears that the drilling rigs of Western states could include military monitoring systems.

The opening of the Arctic Road for navigation significantly reduced the maritime distances between Europe and Asia. Routes from Japan and China depend on the passage from the Strait of Malacca in Southeast Asia or Suez, avoiding choking points, the dangers of piracy, and increased traffic. The Arctic route also has disadvantages, such as the need for ships that can cross through the ice, which are more expensive to build and consume more fuel. Moreover, the crossing is not always ensured due to the yearly ice fluctuations and not only per season. On the other hand, Canada considers its northern archipelago as inland waters where harmless transit is not permitted. Therefore, additional difficulties are created in the Northwest Passage. Starting from the Atlantic Ocean, this passage passes south of Greenland from Baffin Bay and from the strait between the Banks and Victoria Islands, north of Alaska, to reach the Pacific through the Bering

Strait. On the contrary, Russia facilitates the passage through the route north of Siberia (Northern Sea Route), viewing side benefits. With the use of the Arctic Road, the route of the sea road between north-east Asia and northern Europe is reduced by 40% compared to the use of the Panama or Suez Canals, with the respective impacts.

The U.N. Convention on the Law of the Sea (UNCLOS), signed in 1982 and entered into force in 1994, provides in article 234, on the areas covered by ice, the competence of coastal states to enforce laws for the control of marine pollution by ships within their Exclusive Economic Zone (EEZ), without discrimination and without impeding harmless transit. These two points, the imposition of strict legislation and the innocent passage are contradictory as they have been formulated. Based on this stipulation, Canada has already issued a law to prevent contamination of Arctic waters. It is noted that a large part of the hydrocarbon fields is located outside the original EEZ of the adjacent states; therefore, controversies arise between the nations of the region.

According to Article 56 of the UNCLOS, coastal states have sovereign rights concerning exploiting, preserving, and settling financial resources within their Exclusive Economic Zone. The EEZ extends to 200 miles, including the continental shelf and its water resources above it. However, the states may assert their rights beyond this limit if it is scientifically proven that this zone is the natural extension of their land. Article 76 lays down the rules for such a claim; the request should have been submitted up to ten years after the Convention's ratification. The Committee on the Boundaries of the Continental Shelf consists of 21 scientific members elected after submitting their candidacy by the UNCLOS state parties. The Commission meets every six months.

Several Arctic countries have submitted claims under Article 56. Russia introduced a request for the North Pole region in 2002, which the Commission rejected for technical reasons. Russia resubmitted in 2015 its petition for a continental shelf above 200 miles, including, once again, the North Pole. Canada, Denmark, and Norway also submitted requests. Canada requested an extension of its continental shelf to the North Pole. Norway has argued for extending its continental shelf and EEZ beyond 200 miles to three Atlantic and Arctic ocean areas. Although Norway's natural gas deposits contribute to Europe's energy security, Norway exploits them for its benefit. Denmark submitted a request in 2014 for an area of 900 thousand square kilometers extending from Greenland and beyond the North Pole to the limits of the Russian EEZ. The fact is that among the coastal states, there are considerable differences over the extent and ownership of their EEZ. The dispute between Russia, Denmark, and Canada for the ridge Lomonosov and Mendeleev on the seabed is considered among the most serious. Moreover, the claims of Denmark north of Greenland, Russia, and Canada overlap, creating new potential outbreaks of tension.

Five states, the USA, Canada, Russia, Norway, and Denmark (through Greenland), have shores in the Arctic Ocean. Iceland, Sweden, and Finland also have territories or coasts within or near the Arctic Circle. These countries constitute the Arctic Council. The Arctic Council is an international forum for cooperation and coordination among Arctic states and indigenous communities regarding the Arctic, particularly sustainable development and environmental protection.

Greenland, having only 56,000 inhabitants (86% are indigenous Inuit), belongs to Denmark. Still, it withdrew from the European Community after a referendum in 1982 due to a dispute with Brussels on catches. It is a vast, sparsely populated polar island, the second largest in the world after Australia, with an area of four times France's extent. In the long run, The Inuit sought secession from Denmark and independence. Although Greenland belongs to the Kingdom of Denmark, it has had broad autonomy and self-government since 2009. All parties in the local House of 31 seats, except a small one, favor complete independence, but as all admit, this is a long-term affair.

The small population of Greenland and economic inadequacy would render the viability of an independent state uncertain. However, its eventual independence would attract the interest of many economic forces, neighboring or not, including China, attempting to open an "Ice Silk Road." Chinese companies are interested in expanding three airports and investing in the mineral sector. Greenland responded by providing more than 50 licenses for exploration, many of which were for Chinese businesses (for rare earth minerals like uranium).

The geopolitical importance of the country is also high. Since the Cold War era, Greenland has been a strategic stronghold between the Western Hemisphere, Russia, and Europe. In addition, the U.S. Airbase in the northwest, 2,000 km from Canada's shores, is strategically important. On the other hand, China's interest is not only economic. Asia's "red capitalists" want influence on Arctic affairs, and Greenland increasingly appears as an "entry point" in the region. However, Denmark, still managing Greenland's Foreign Affairs, reacted when a Chinese company attempted to buy an abandoned U.S. naval base in late 2016.

GEOGRAPHY IN SHAPING HISTORY

Historical evolution

The perception of geography varies over time; different elements shape its data in every historical period. The world civilization started with the introduction of agriculture and the permanent settlements of human communities around the ninth millennium B.C. It evolved with the interaction of different cultures created by every community in their geographic region. Communication has been the core of the evolution of civilization, and it was achieved initially by the movement of populations. History could be defined as the study of the fluidity of human continuity. A culture erodes when the complex circumstances that created it wear out or when immigrants in great numbers enter, or neighboring geographic countries swallow it.[59]

Agriculture has shaped the landscape of many regions. The primary concern was the search for fertile soils to establish the initial food-collecting nomadic populations near rivers, hills, or foothills of mountains. Subsequently, safety had the most considerable role in developing cultures, and security was directly related to geography. For example, ancient Athens was founded around the natural stronghold of Acropolis, Algiers on The Island (Al Djazair), Paris on the Île de la Cité, New York on the southern part of Manhattan surrounded by river water and a wall.

The first settlements in the plains of Europe, as they were created with the superimposed residential mattresses, date back to 6000 B.C., maybe older. The most ancient cities are located in the Near East and central and

---

[59] William Hardy McNeill: The Rise of the West, 1963.

south-eastern Greece regions. Initially, the preference turned to the mountain outskirts where wild wheat and barley were endemic, with adequate rainfall for agriculture. The agricultural cultivation was transported to the fertile soils of central and western Europe, near rivers that provided water and transportation facilities. Attention was focused on security provided by the geographic characteristics of each selected area. Settlements near the seashore are related to fishing, transport, and commerce.

Migratory flows between Greece and the Middle East created a cultural balance in Eurasia. Far in the east and geographically isolated, China developed a mostly independent civilization. Greece was saved by the mountain ranges in the north and the sea around. The desert protected Egypt, while the fertile valley of the navigable Nile ended at a Delta, which was not susceptible to attacks from the sea. Geography was primordial in the Greek islands, where an early civilization thrived. Crete is close to Egypt. The Cyclades are also relatively close to the coast of Anatolia, close enough to have cultural communication and far enough to be safe from raids due to their insular position.[60] On the contrary, the fertile region of Mesopotamia, the origin of the groups that colonized the east arc of the Mediterranean, was an exposed and completely insecure area for the moving people.

The protocell of civilization is the settlement. History is the advancement of cultures and relations between them. Political integration is caused when an actual society conducive to collective activity could become political, depending on the cultural

---

[60] East: The geography behind history.

interconnections and the created interests. Communication among people has always been the generating power of history. Both the creation of towns and the interaction between them depended on geography. Communication in antiquity meant access to the sea or navigable rivers since movement and transportation on land were difficult and dangerous. The distance of the hinterland settlements from their seaport and the ease of access were paramount. The number of settlements each harbor served and the number of ports at the disposal of each settlement were substantial for each region's development. Prehistoric populations were not static geographically; they moved around all the time.

    The first cities in the Eurasian area were founded in five regions: Egypt, the Aegean, Mesopotamia, the Indus Valley, and China. Politically, the monarchy was imposed in Egypt and China, while in Mesopotamia and India, the situation was vaguer. The system was generally monarchic, with varying degrees of authority. In the Aegean, the system was sui generis.

    Prehistoric Greece was inhabited by Proto-Greeks Pelasgians, who had spread their settlements throughout Greece, Anatolia, and Italy. Arcadia is considered the birthplace of Pelasgians; therefore, Peloponnese was originally named Pelasgia. The first Helladic city is considered to be Lykosoura in Mount Lykeion of Arcadia. From 2200 until 1900 B.C., most Indo-European Proto-Greeks had settled in Epirus, north-western Macedonia, and north-western Thessaly. They were divided into three dialectical disciplines. From 1900 until 1150 B.C., large groups of Greek races migrated further south and settled in various Greek peninsula areas. In these areas, they encountered pre-Greek peoples, whom they assimilated. The Achaeans, according to Homer, and Mycenaeans, according to archaeologists, dominated Greece at the latest from 1600 B.C. but certainly had arrived there quite earlier. Ancient Greek tribes were Aeolians, Ions (Athenians, Boeotians), Achaeans, Myrmidons, Magnates, Dorians (Lacedaemonians), and others. The gender of the Dorians, initially moved to Pindos and later to Macedonia, was referred to as Macedonians, of the Greek word Makednos - tall. In the first Greek colonization (11th-8th c. B.C.), the Greek tribes settled in Greece. They colonized the Ionian, the Aegean, Crete, and Anatolia in waves, creating the basis of Western civilization.

The Aeolian, Ionic, Doric, Achaean, and Arcadian colonization created significant centers for consolidating and disseminating Greek culture. The western coasts of Anatolia were populated by Ionians, who are considered descendants of Achaeans (Cyprus, South Anatolia, central Peloponnese) and Dorians (Macedonia, Peloponnese, Crete, Rhodes). In the second Greek colonization (8th-6th c. B.C.), Greek colonies were established throughout the Mediterranean and the Black Sea. Together with Byzantium, they contributed to the economy and arts development. They always maintained relations with the metropolis.

The region covering Greece, Anatolia, Egypt, the Middle East, and Persia, with sea routes in the eastern Mediterranean and the Southern Black Sea region, dominated the world culture during the first millennium B.C. The hub where the history of the era evolves, the history of the then inhabited land, the "ecumene," is the region where Eurasia meets Africa, with outlets to the Mediterranean and the Red Sea, the Persian Gulf, and the Indian Ocean. The sovereignty of the Greeks in the Mediterranean brought them into contact with the People of the Sea (of unidentified origin). The latter produced and sold raw materials - although there was no considerable shortage in Greece - and bought sophisticated Greek products.[61]

The geopolitical perception of the era evolves around Greece's territory, mainly toward the east, toward the Phrygians - an ancient Indo-European people who occupied the West-Central Anatolia after the fall of Hittites - and of Arameans in Mesopotamia, as well as of Chaldeans. The Kingdom of Phrygia was founded around the middle of the second millennium to the 1st Millennium B.C. It was conquered later by Lydia. Egypt was ruled at the time by the 21st dynasty.

Two centuries later, the region expanded toward the west to include Illyrians and Etruscans on the Italian peninsula. The Assyrian empire, including much of the Middle East, was founded in the southeast of Phrygia. Greece managed to maintain its culture, defeating the Persians. At the same time, Lydia, east of Ionia, in the interior of western Anatolia, achieved to remain politically independent until 546 B.C. The Assyria, Babylon, and Persia empires alternated successively in the Middle East.

According to Toynbee, the European continent has had favorable conditions of economic development and unfavorable conditions of life; coping with them has facilitated its development.[62] According to McNeill, Europe has vast fertile plains, timber and minerals, navigable rivers that cross them towards the north, and the Mediterranean coasts with ports that provide mooring facilities. The geographical terrain influenced the political and socio-economic life on the continent. Wherever the

---

[61] L.Th. Houmanidis cites J. Toutain.
[62] Arnold Joseph Toynbee: A Study of History (1934 – 1961).

plains prevailed, political life evolved differently from the fragmented areas by high mountain ranges or islands separated by relatively large sea distances. In Western Europe, the lack of physical barriers led to larger groups of people who spoke the same language, cooperated, or clashed. They engaged in commercial exchanges and interrelations, creating conditions of ethnogenesis and national rivalries.

The absence of geographic barriers facilitated the creation of large political entities, making a more effective administration possible. The flat terrain in a temperate zone, rich in agricultural production, provided the means for economic growth. This would lead to development in other areas of social and economic life, conditioning even political events. It is no coincidence that Napoleon considered Switzerland an inhabitable place, suitable only as a gateway. Geographical protection on the extensive European plains did not exist; the population was obliged to recourse to collectivities that could initially be formed only under the guidance of a lord. This person had the most significant power due to inheritance, property, or leadership qualities.

In the middle of the 4th Millennium B.C., Western Europe reached the Neolithic stage of civilization, quite later than the eastern one. The Indo-European cultures spread to the detriment of the Western Mediterranean groups. The Celts prevailed in Western Europe, succeeded by Gauls of Celtic origin. Iberians inhabited Iberia, Teutons North Europe, Illyrians the eastern Adriatic, and Etruscans the Italian peninsula. Thracians inhabited Thrace while further north, Cimmerians the region of today's Ukraine, Slavs the Dnieper, The Baltic peoples, and Fins inhabited the northernmost areas of Europe. Greece remained the center of the ecumene, expanding to the north.

Unlike Europe, the land is closed among mountains and sea in the Balkans, and the evolution has been different. Unity and dominance were hardly achievable. Geography led to the establishment of small political units of city-states.[63] Dialogue and compromise were necessary to ensure cooperation; thus, politics and diplomacy were born.

By providing the appropriate conditions, maritime contacts, and security in ancient Greece, geography was among the elements contributing to the enormous leaps in civilization and culture of the ancient Greeks. McNeil, contradicting the theories of the clash of civilizations, argued that contact and exchange among civilizations drive human history forward. He referred to societies formed to some extent through geography, standing on specific land, shaping their identity, and developing new cultural hybrids through interaction.

The organized colonies of the Greek world were the solution to address the population's growth in very narrow regions that could not sustain it and the problems of sharing power. Greek settlements have been established on all the Mediterranean shores, the coasts of Anatolia, North Africa, and southern Western Europe. The colonization in all these areas was generally peaceful; cooperation and the Hellenization of the indigenous people, especially in Anatolia, has been a natural result.

It is true that the Greeks, who fought the Persians, were far less than their opponents. Undoubtedly, they were brave, better prepared, and excelled their Persian opponents in many domains. However, geography had an

---

[63] 'However, McNeill points out that there were plains that were not separated by physical barriers; nevertheless, they were divided between different city-states.

essential role in the victories of the Greeks. The total equation should include the long course through rough areas and straits until the Persians and their allies reach the Greek land where the fight occurred. In Salamis and Thermopylae, geography played a crucial role; the wise choice of location of the battles favored the Greeks, both being choking points. Indeed, if the sites' geography were different, the numerous Persians would have won, and the world's civilization and political image would probably have developed differently. However, the geographical peculiarities in ancient Greece also led to civil wars and massacres. Instead of contributing to unity, the alliances and the federations caused bloodier and more generalized civil wars, which weakened the Greek nation, understood as a whole with a similar culture, language, and religion. Still, the notion of the unity of interests of the nation was missing in ancient Greece; consolidation existed only in cases of external risk, namely the Persian attacks. Finally, the Greeks fell into the "Trap of Thucydides." Spartans wanted to impede the rise of Athens and caused the bloody civil Peloponnesian War.

Herodotus, born in the early 5th century B.C. in Halicarnassus, under Persian occupation, narrates the Persian wars, maintaining a balance between geography and politics. His birthplace was an international port that facilitated the exchanges of Greeks with Egypt and the Persian Empire. Herodotus is considered the father of history and a grand geographer. Its analysis promoted an approach defined as partial determinism regarding the evolution of history by distancing it from the people's will.

Herodotus is considered the first historian to interrupt the Homeric tradition and manage history through research, systematically collecting his material and forming it into a historical narrative. His contemporaries and historians criticized Herodotus for mixing historical events with myths, not always without malice, according to the "ethics" of Plutarch's "On the Herodotus Malignancy." His "history," however, although sometimes inaccurate, contains many cultural, ethnographic, geographic, and other information, which was verified later. Herodotus revised excessive schematism based on his empirical observations. It highlighted the asymmetry of continents by replacing the oldest theory of the perfect cyclic world with Europe and Asia/Africa considered equal in size. However, it maintained the symmetry between the Nile and the Danube.

In the middle of the 5th century, Herodotus visited and described "for the sake of theory" areas outside the Greek peninsula, Colchis (exonym) up to Scythia, the interior of Anatolia and Pontus, Crimea, Cyprus, and the regions of Syria, Babylonia, Mesopotamia, Cyrenaic as well as Egypt, which he calls the "gift of the Nile." He admired Egyptians, to whom he attributed the discovery of the periodicity of year and the naming of the Twelve Gods. He noted that the Nile was vital to ancient Egypt's development. Its culture benefited particularly from this river. Herodotus had as the basis of his narratives the effort to give explanations. He dealt with the enigma of the River Nile flood during summer. Strabo also dealt with the same issue, resulting in different conclusions.

Herodotus examined the climatic conditions and administration forms of the people he encountered. He studied the Egyptians' climate and culture, which he considered superior to the Greek culture. On the contrary, Herodotus considered the Persian and Babylonian civilizations second-class. However, he showed interest in them, too, since he used the lists of the Kings of Babylon as a chronological system in its history. Herodotus separates Europe from Asia but understands Pontus and Scythia as part of Europe and criticizes the Persians' campaigns against the people of those regions.[64] Herodotus also wrote that Phoenician sailors who sailed Africa saw the sun rising on their right side, which perhaps alludes to the possibility that the ancient sailors sailed around Africa. Herodotus also referred to India and its culture. Despite criticism, many of Herodotus's geographical remarks have a scientific basis. Strabo has confirmed the ideas of Herodotus regarding the Black Egyptians, the Ethiopians, and the people of Colchis.[65]

Unlike many European regions, where the vast plains allowed large populations to create large groups, the Greeks "were always few." They became less through civil wars and by massacring each other. However, before they would succumb to the forces attacking from the west, they had one last chance. In the 5th century B.C., a contraction of the Greek world in the east for the Persian Empire's benefit. Alexander the Great counterattacked late in 4th B.C., expanding the Greek world to the depths of Asia, but his conquest was politically frivolous. The dominance of the Macedonian Kingdom, if established as a steady power throughout Greece for a more extended period, would create the conditions for creating a powerful, unified Greek state. However, Alexander the Great, instead of consolidating the state's authority and seeking expansion only in the neighboring regions, preferred to do "war tourism." After crashing Persia – something unnecessary at that historical moment – he did not return to Macedonia. It spread Greek culture more

---

[64] Kaktos, (1992) (in Greek)
[65] Diop (1981).

widely in Asia; still, culture cannot be maintained long without political power. In any case, it could not be ensured to such a large extent with a negligible and flimsy political-administrative system. The conquered are inclined to mimic the culture of their conquerors to the extent that this condition applies.[66] Moreover, the prolonged absence of Alexander from his headquarters would cause him to lose his authority.

The death of the Macedonian ruler led to the creation of several kingdoms under Lysimachus in eastern Macedonia and Thrace, Antigonus in Anatolia, and Seleucids in easternmost. The Kingdom of Ptolemaian dominated Egypt. In the west, Carthage emerged as a potent force fighting Syracuse. In the 2nd century B.C., the rise of Rome, showing primary interest in southwestern Europe, ended the Macedonian kingdoms. Over two centuries, it managed to control Western Europe, Greece, Anatolia, a large part of the Middle East, and Egypt.

The political continuity of Hellenism was interrupted by the Roman conquest. Latins excelled both in numbers and in terms of administration, organization, laws, and the military. The Mediterranean, a sea of communication and commerce, sailed by mainly Greek and Phoenician ships up to then, became a Roman lake. The Pax-Romana of the Mediterranean region was followed by Byzantine domination, which the Ottoman Empire later replaced. By the Middle Ages, the worldwide dominant force possessed the Mediterranean, or whoever dominated the Mediterranean was the dominant force worldwide. Together with their preoccupation to extend the territory they conquered, all the regimes in Eurasia had

---

[66] Ibn Khaldun.

as a primary concern the safeguard of trade routes, hence the importance of the Mediterranean Sea.

After Herodotus, the next great historian was Strabo (64 B.C.-24 A.D.). He was born in a Greek country in Amasia of Pontus, in the Roman Empire's time. As for philosophy, he was a follower of stoicism. The stoics were authentic cosmopolitans. They accepted the culture of their time, dealt with society's problems, and were interested in political life.[67] Although he was Greek, Strabo was politically a champion of Roman imperialism. His two most notable works are the "Historical Memos" and the "Geographic" (i.e., memos). Historical Memos consist of 47 books written on papyrus, mostly lost. His work "Geographic," composed of 17 books, is preserved intact and in excellent condition. In the prologue, Strabo stresses, among other things, the importance of geography for philosophers and politicians and criticizes his precursors (Eratosthenes, Posidonios, Polybius). In this work, Strabo describes the world, i.e., the inhabited and civilized part of the Earth, which identifies with the northern hemisphere. It is a brief but systematic textbook that informs about the data of his era. It presents a narrative history of people and cities from different regions of the then-known world.

Strabo traveled a lot, including to Egypt and Libya, to which his latest book refers. Regarding his visits to Hellas - Greece, he cites that Macedonia is Greece,[68] both terms used in the modern sense. In the geographical area of Macedonia, Strabo also includes upper Macedonia, according to the Roman administrative breakdown. He mentions Lyhnida (current Ohrid), the Heraclea Lygist

---

[67] Jostein Gaarder, 1994.
[68] Geographics, Book 7, chapter.1.

(current Bitola), and Styverra (Prilepa) as cities of this region. The ancient name of Prespa Lakes is Vrygiides Lakes, from the ancient town of Vrygion, located on the north shore.

Strabo described the Mediterranean starting from the strait at Heraklean columns (Djebel-i Tarik, Gibraltar) and cited that both its coasts, the European and that of Libya and Egypt, unite at the east, in Asia. For the European continent, he mentioned that it had "a variety of shapes and formed outstanding citizens and states. Regarding goods, Europe produces the most. That is because the whole continent is habitable except for a small uninhabited part that is cold. The mountainous and icy part of Europe is hardly inhabited due to the adversity of the conditions. However, even the hardly inhabited and predatory parts are civilized with worthy commanders. Thus, the Greeks, inhabiting mountains and rocks, lived very well because they provided for their polity, the arts, and the proper management of their life. On the other hand, the Romans adopted many savage peoples because they lived in a rugged land, without harbors, cold or otherwise difficult to inhabit places, achieved to connect the isolated, and taught the barbarians to live in a civilized way".

"The fertility and the temperate climate contributed to the population's civilization, peace, and happiness. On the contrary, pro-war tendencies and false heroics flourished on the barren land. However, in Europe, people are usually acting in solidarity. Many contribute by arms, others by producing goods and creating art, and others by formatting morals. Tangible is the damage caused when people are not in accord; the violence of those with the arms dominates, except in the case that the majority controls them." There is something unique –

Strabo points out – about this continent. "It is shaped with mountains and plains so that agriculture, an organized state, and arts coexist everywhere. In most of Europe, peace prevails thanks to the rulers. Europe is self-sufficient both in war and in peace. It has many warriors and farmers that maintain the cohesion of cities. The best products that are useful in life and many metals are produced there. Europe has plenty of livestock as well as a few wild beasts. It imports spices and gemstones, but those are things that, if someone does not have them, his life is not worse than the life of the one who possesses them. Therefore, this is the general description of the nature of the continent." Strabo, describing Europe two millennia ago, demonstrated the inherent superiority of this continent.

Claudius Ptolemy, a Greek of the Roman era of Alexandria, drew up in the early 2nd century A.D. the first relatively reliable maps. In his work, "Geography", he collects all the geographic knowledge of his time. He enriches it with seafarers' reports, resulting in a somewhat accurate description of Europe (with emphasis on the Mediterranean), North Africa, the Middle East, and the Arab Peninsula. He attempted to display the spherical Earth to a projection respecting the proportionality between points and cities. In the "Geographic Lecture," he gives instructions for drafting 27 maps about Europe, Africa, Asia (not without errors), Greece, and ecumene - the known inhabited world- with a grid of coordinates in a proportion of latitudes and longitudes. These maps had high geopolitical significance at the time. They were used to travel to trade, but mainly by the armies.

China's culture evolved earlier than that of Europe. China was geographically blocked and unknown in Europe until the last century of the 1st Millennium B.C.

Although Europe was the first to replace brass with iron, China quickly progressed in general technical developments. The communication and knowledge carried by Southeast Asian traders up to Bengal contributed to the region's growth. The silkworm was generally known in Asia, but China was the first to extract a continuous thread from the cocoons.

China imported wheat, precious jade from the West, animals, and rice from Southeast Asia. Europe imported silk, spices, and artifacts from East Asia as early as the second century A.D., exchanging them with raw materials, gold, and silver. The intermediate countries of the Silk Road contributed to trade by offering protection to caravans and collecting tolls. Palmyra and Petra were transit stations for caravans. At the same time, Alexandria had a central role with a large population and a safe harbor. Greek ships were sailing between the Red Sea and Indian ports. The Arabs were engaged in trade between India, the Persian Gulf, Abyssinia, and Somalia.

During the second century A.D., trade ties were strengthened. Darius's royal route, which served trade and geopolitical purposes, was more than 2,500 kilometers long. Babylon, Ecbatana, and Bactra in Afghanistan connect an even longer route. Seleucids continued the policy of facilitating trade from Seleucia to Persia.

North Africa remained detached from southernmost sub-Saharan Africa because of the obstacles set in by the Sahara Desert and the Atlas Mountains range, formed in a later geological period and, therefore, unworn, abrupt, and impassable. The populations there did not originate from sub-Saharan Africa; they had Mediterranean origins in historical times. Sahara in ancient times had a savannah climate; colonizers came from the

Mediterranean region. The earliest finds from millennia ago are those of the Neanderthals, who arrived from the Iberian Peninsula. The Berber tribe, considered a native of North Africa, was created by mixing Neolithic populations with Sahara people. Berberines used Phoenician symbols for writing and lived in regions of Algeria, Tunisia, and Libya. The ancient Greeks, however, called almost all of North Africa Libya.

Carthage has been the most potent political center in the region. The growing power of Carthage provoked the so-called Carthaginian wars with Rome; the constant defeats of Carthage eventually led to its destruction. The Romans created a bridgehead and dominated North Africa, which functioned as its breadbasket, founding colonies and brilliant cities, such as Cuicul (now Djémila) in today's Algeria.

Phoenician colonies founded in North Africa later evolved into Roman cities. The Hippo Regius (today's Annaba) east was then the Diocese of St. Augustine. The first road of the Old City of Algiers[69] to the sea is called Icosium Street in honor of the first inhabitants of Algiers. According to myth, those were the twenty comrades of Hercules who founded the city of Eikosion in that location. Icosium may not refer to twenty (Eikosi means twenty in Greek) but to home (Oikos in Greek) or something else. However, historically, the city was founded by the ancient Carthaginians of Tunisia, which had Phoenician origins. The Roman presence is also visible today, among others, at the rubble of Tipasa, an originally Phoenician -and afterward Roman- city west of Algiers.

---

[69] Algiers, Al Djezair, means "island". It is a small island united now to the land.

Further west of Tipaza is the city of Cherchell, whose name is a corruption of the Latin Caesarea, i.e., Caesarea of Cappadocia, from where a queen of Numidia came. In addition to Carthage, the other areas of North Africa were part of the Kingdom of Numidia, with Masinissa as their first king. Later, in the 5th century A.D., the Vandals who arrived in North Africa conquered Numidia, but the Byzantines ousted them.

The era of Romans, both West and the East, was succeeded by Islamic raids of Arabs crossing all of North Africa, Islamizing and Arabizing its inhabitants to a large extent. However, some local populations, such as Berberines or Amazigh in Algeria, retained elements of their culture. The Caliphate of the Fatimides founded there included North Africa and regions of the Middle East and the Arabian Peninsula.

Shaping Europe

The period of the transition of Europe from classical antiquity to the medieval world has shaped its current structural elements. At the time, the multinational Eastern Roman Empire was the central axis at the turn of the first millennium. It was restructured in terms of extent, administrative organization, and the social characteristics of its people. This transitional period covers the period that historical research calls Late Antiquity. This transition was made through a historical model of long-term and profound changes in all areas of human activity, including the European peoples' racial composition. The identity of modern Europeans is formed through the emergence of Christianity, the invasions from Asia, the peaceful or violent movements of populations for colonization or looting, and new states' creation within the Roman order. Although the people that migrated, usually violently from

Asia to Western Europe, brought their own culture, they gradually adopted and assimilated elements of the Greco-Roman tradition, forming an early medieval European civilization with several standard features.

The transition from the world of Greco-Roman antiquity to the Middle Ages is reflected in the gradual disappearance of pagan worship by Romans. The pagan cult was preserved in a few nuclei of the Roman Empire, the aristocracy of Rome, and the Neoplatonic philosophers of Athens. However, the pagan worship was limited by the legislative acts of Theodosius I (379-395) and Justinian I (527-565).

The Roman Empire, the "The Kingdom of Romans," had an excellent republican state composition under the emperor and possessed a vast territory around the Mediterranean, the latter becoming an inland Sea of the Empire, but also in Europe, Africa, and Asia. The domination of the Romans had imposed the "Pax Romana" throughout the ecumene. The Roman Empire reached its most considerable extent during Emperor Trajan around the 4th century, when nomads from the steppes of Asia, Ostrogoths, Huns, Avars, Bulgarians, Hungarians, and Alans began to invade all cultural centers of Europe.

Vandals were an East Germanic tribe that inhabited today's southern Poland. They staged numerous invasions in various countries, looted Rome, and founded kingdoms on the Iberian Peninsula. Crossing Gibraltar, they ended up in North Africa, occupying Numidia and Carthage in the 5th century A.D. However, the most crucial barbaric invasion was that of German-Teutonic tribes assisted by the Nordic ones. The Germans occupied the Roman countries of northwest Europe and were engaged in looting, leading to the region's devastation. Britain, a

Roman Province, had almost lost its original inhabitants and was repopulated by a Germanic race.[70]

The Alans, a nomadic people, had already been settled since the first two centuries A.D. in Brandenburg, Elba, and Main. The Franks, who attacked either coming through the sea from the Netherlands or the Rhine, proved to be the most dangerous invaders. This invasion restricted the contact between China and Europe, the transport and communication obstruction in the Mediterranean. Moreover, it impeded the connections between the Eastern Roman Empire and Western Europe.

In the 4th century, the Huns, a Mongolian-origin of a semi-nomadic tribe of mounted warriors, invaded Europe from Central Asia. The arrival of the Huns is linked to the migration of the Alans. The Huns subjugated the Ostrogoths in Eastern Europe and pushed the Visigoths to the northwest of the Roman Empire. A surge of mass fleeing followed the invasion. The leader of the Huns since 444 was Attila, whom Turks consider to be of the same nation. The sovereignty of this brutal leader extended from the Caucasus to the Carpathian basin, Hungary. The Huns made predatory raids inside Europe and threatened the Roman Empire. Eventually, Romans, Franks, and Visigoths came together and managed to defeat the Huns in 451. Attila died two years later, and the state of the Huns dissolved after a short period of political unrest.

Roman movements, military and economic, focused on the sea through which they ensured relatively easy and inexpensive transport. The attacks of German tribes on the west and northwest borders of the Roman Empire between the 3rd and 5th centuries and the establishment of various kingdoms as of the Huns (Central

---

[70] Peter Morris Green

Asia with an extension in Europe), the Franks (today's western Europe) and the Ostrogoths (today's northern Italy), resulted in the abolition of the West part of the Roman Empire in 476. However, the latter remained stable in the East, with the so-called Byzantine Empire (Eastern Roman Empire). Economic exchanges became local after the break-up of the Western Roman state due to these barbaric raids between the 3rd and 5th centuries. At the same time, piracy evolved into a scourge impeding not only transport and communication but also the development of coastal settlements and facilities.

The clashes continued in the 6th and 7th centuries with the emergence of the Avars and Lombards. The Lombards or Longbeards were Germanic people. In the first century A.D., they had already settled in the south of the river Elbe. From the 5th century, they spread in the region of today's Austria and Hungary. The Avars, nomadic warriors from the steppes, had moved to Europe after the Huns in around 555. The Lombards were threatened by their neighboring Kingdom of the Gepids as well as by the Byzantines. To address these dangers, they initially allied with the Avars. However, when the warmonger Avars turned against them in an attempt to subdue them, the Lombards were forced to leave Hungary's lowlands and invade Italy (568 A.D.), living in the region for 200 years. Avars dominated the land left by Lombards for the next 250 years. They practiced an aggressive policy and often threatened the Byzantine Empire's borders, imposing on the Byzantines' ever-increasing "contributions." In 626, the Avars, along with the Sassanides of Persia, besieged Constantinople without success. After this failure, their geopolitical scope was reduced, and they were forced to constrain their action at a local level. Finally, Frankish ruler

Charles (Charlemagne) conquered Italy in 774 and was crowned King of Franks and Lombards in Pavia.

All these raids from Asia to Eastern Europe and beyond used the north route through the plains of Siberia and Ukraine, where there were no physical obstacles apart from the Ural Mountains. The lack of natural geographic barriers that could identify state borders in large parts of Europe contributed to the high mobility of populations for a long time. It later shaped the security policy and political developments. On the contrary, the route followed by the Turkmens, south of the Caspian and through Persia and Anatolia, was challenging because of the mountainous territory and the relatively stable states along the way, including the Eastern Roman Empire.

Some historians consider European history "subservient" to Asia and the European culture as a result of the fight against the raids from Asia. The first state formations in Russia and Poland were created to address the Asian invasion; even Western European states were key formations for tackling Central Asia's nomads. However, the invaders from Asia are a constituent element of modern Europe, both racially and, in part, culturally.[71] Contemporary Western Europeans prefer this Euro-Asian ancestry to the Greek-Roman cultural heritage.[72]

The founding of the papal state on the Italian peninsula in 754, the Carolingian Empire (800–888) in western-Central Europe, the Viking Kingdom in northern France in the 9th century, and the Kingdom of Hungarians in Central Europe in the 10th century created new data in

---

[71] Mackinder, H.J., "The Geographical Pivot of History", The Geographical Journal, Vol. 23, No.4, (April 1904).

[72] See debates on "the Museum of Europe" and European Constitution.

an already volatile situation in Europe and the relations of the states of the region with Byzantium, the other pole of power in Eastern Europe. In particular, the Kingdom of Charlemagne (771-814), the largest and most organized state in Western Europe after the fall of the Roman Empire, is considered the beginning of "Europe" by modern Western historians, wanting to get rid of ideologies regarding the Greco-Roman Cultural heritage of Europe.

The second wave of invasions in Europe took place in the 9th and 10th centuries. The Vikings were invading Europe from the north, the Saracens from the south, and the Magyars from the east. The invasion of Vikings in Europe constituted a particular case. Their agenda was broad, depending on the opponent they had to deal with. The intrusions were either for looting, trade, or settlement. The first contact was in the form of exploration and colonization. Wherever no settled populations existed, they founded colonies, such as in Iceland, Greenland, or Newfoundland, in the New World. They settled in Russia, where they established their first state. Vladimir, baptized Christian and crowned King by the Byzantines, was Nordic. Scandinavians were the founders of Dublin in Ireland. In the British Isles and the Frankish Empire, they raided mainly easy targets, e.g., monasteries. As far as Vikings are concerned, the objectives of looting and trade were not far off the one from the other. They started with raids but changed tactics if the targets were challenging. Vikings, from Sweden in particular, when they arrived in Byzantium and the Khalifate of Baghdad, realized that their opponents were more vigorous in the military field; therefore, they proceeded to trade instead of raiding, as the large number of eastern currencies found in Sweden show.

Vikings had good knowledge of geography. Their ships were small and had low draught. Thus, they managed to interweave the ocean and continue their expeditions through the rivers. They used the sea the same way the Arabs used the desert. They moved with ease, knowing the whereabouts, and until the clumsy troops of Charles moved, they could plunder two monasteries a day. However, they avoided the problematic sieges, wherever they saw fortifications, left for elsewhere.[73]

The Eastern Roman Empire, from 330 A.D. onwards, limited itself mainly to the east. The historians named it the Byzantine Empire afterward, initially with a derogatory connotation for the Western world. The capital city of Constantinople, New Rome, Queen of Cities, and the Reigning of the Empire[74] was the center of civilization for the entire medieval world. With main characteristics, the Christian religion, and later the Greek language, the Greco-Roman tradition, and Roman law, this multinational Empire has been a pole of stability for one thousand years, the most significant and most organized state of the medieval period world, the forerunner of European civilization. An unchanged constant has been the imperial institution that incorporated the Hellenistic and Roman ideas of administration, the spirit of Christianity, and the Latin and Greek languages. Endorsed by a strictly structured state and ecclesiastical hierarchy, the emperor acted as an ecumenical leader. The Byzantine Empire reached its greatest extent during the Justinian period.

---

[73] Paul Freedman: Vikings / The European Prospect,1000 A.D.

[74] The meaning is that Constantinople remained capital of the state even when the Emperor was not there, contrary to Rome, which was capital only when Cesar was there.

Despite the persistent changes in its borders, Byzantium created an original civilization that shone for centuries. At the same time, politically, it decisively influenced the fortunes of the medieval world. In contrast to the decentralized medieval countries of Western Europe, the Byzantine state effectively controlled the crucial sectors of the economy. It cut coins, contrary to Western European practice, where the individual feudal lords cut them. It legislated regarding interest rates, certified measures and standards, and controlled trade in certain products. Alongside the use of Latin, the Greek language, being the language of the Church, gradually prevailed.

The spiritual influence of Byzantium on the Slavs who populated lands of its territory drove them to their Christianization. The Slavs appeared on the northern border of Byzantium around the 6th century. Initially, the Moravians, a group of them, asked Emperor Michael III, in 862 A.D., to learn the Christian faith. Missionaries from Thessaloniki, Cyril, and Methodius visited Moravia (today's Czech and Slovak regions). They invented an alphabet adapted to the needs of the Slavic language, by which the Holy Christian texts were propagated. The Christianity of the Bulgarians took place with the baptism of their ruler, Boris I, by the Patriarch Photios in 864. Regarding Russia and Ukraine, Christianity was established as the state's official religion by the Ros, under Vladimir I of Kyiv, in 988, at the time of the Byzantine Emperor Basil II.

For a long time, the Eastern Roman Empire had been the financial center of the Eastern Mediterranean. In the middle of the 7th century, however, the Arabs occupied the southern shores of the Mediterranean and advanced unrestrained. As a result, the economic network of Byzantium collapsed, trade declined, and the system shrank at a regional level. On the contrary, in the 9th and 10th centuries, the increase of Byzantium's population and production of goods, along with some recovery of Byzantine territories that inspired greater security, led to a period of economic growth that lasted until the end of the 12th century.

In the northwest of Byzantium, the founding of the Khanate of Bulgarians caused attacks that lasted until the 11th century. On the eastern side of Byzantium, the attacks of Muslim Arabs (starting in the mid-7th century) succeeded in the constant clashes with the Persians. Finally, in the Helladic part of the Empire, the raids and installations of Slavic tribes caused problems in communication, travel, and trade.

In the East, the Roman Empire had to deal with the Sassanids. The Empire of the Persian dynasty of Sassanids extended to the area currently known as Iran, Iraq, Pakistan, the eastern Arabian Peninsula, the east part of Anatolia, Syria, Armenia, the Caucasus, and Central Asia. The ultimate leader was the King, who carried the title of "King of Kings." Sasanians survived for 400 years, from 224 to 651, and significantly influenced the history of Iran – Persia. The Sassanid society was organized based on Avesta, the collection of Zoroaster's texts – one of the first monotheistic religions. Internal strife and wars with neighboring forces led to the weakening of the Sassanid Empire. The Conqueror and successor of the Empire, the Arab – Muslim Caliphate of Umayyad, was built and developed based on the foundations created by the Sasanians.

As adjacent to the Holy Land, the region of Egypt experienced the dynamic propagation of Christianity quite early. The Christianity of Egypt was associated with the evolution of monachism, and an essential part of the local

Coptic Church remained faithful to the Monophysitic doctrine. The pagan tradition ended after being confronted violently by Christians. Among its victims was the female Hellenistic philosopher and scientist Hypatia. After its conquest by Muslim Arabs in 641, Egypt joined the Islamic world.

The Kingdom of Charlemagne and his successors had Latin as their official language (as did Byzantium). Therefore, they accepted Greco-Roman cultural influences from the latter. But as the people of Byzantium spoke Greek, they were somewhat alienated politically. The Byzantine Empire also had relations with the Holy Roman Empire, especially after the marriage of Otto II to Byzantine Princess Theano in 972. The Arabs deprived Byzantium of many lands in the Middle East and North Africa in the 7th century. Still, their contact with the Greco-Roman tradition made Byzantium a source of civilization for the Umayyads of Damascus and the Abbasids of Baghdad (A.D.750).

Although Byzantium had been adapted to the Hellenistic period's experiences over the years, it also brought elements of ancient Greek rationality and Western economic and administrative model since it was the continuation of Rome. However, it did not have the same feudal structure as Western Europe since the central power had never been wholly shattered, nor was the economy of Byzantium entirely agricultural, as in Western Europe. For geographical and historical reasons, the economy of Byzantium has been a combination of urban and rural.

The invasion of the Turkmens and the mistreatment of Christian pilgrims in the Holy Land was the pretext leading to the Crusades.[75] The siege and sack of Constantinople in 1204 A.D., during the Fourth Crusade, marked the beginning of the fall of the Byzantine Empire. After the city's capture, a Latin Empire was established there. Baldwin of Flanders has been crowned Emperor Baldwin I of Constantinople in Hagia Sophia. The sack of Constantinople is a significant turning point in medieval history. Finally, the Greek Empire of Nicaea succeeded in expelling the Latins in 1261. Still, the Arab expansion and this Crusade caused the weakening of the Byzantine Empire with the final blow struck by the Ottoman state in 1453.[76]

The Byzantine Empire finally succumbed to the invasion of the Turkish-Asian tribes of Central Asia. The reasons for the decline and the inevitable fall of the Byzantine Empire are the continual wars, the devaluation of the state's influence, the religious conflicts, the political intrigues, the uprisings, the privileges of the monasteries, and the increased number of monks. The mismanagement of public finances, the increased taxes, and the enormous bureaucracy with the entailing misconduct and indifference led to social disintegration and moral decay.

The transition from Late Antiquity to the Early Middle Ages marks the general decline of the population in Europe, the exodus to the countryside, the invasions, and the movement of people. However, after the first millennium, the population of Europe increased, and advances in the technological and agricultural sectors along with climate change – the warm medieval period – have led to an increase in production. Large-scale

---

[75] Kaplan: Ibid., p. 93.

[76] L. Th. Houmanidis: Lessons on History of Economical life, 1969, Vol. B p.253 (in Greek).

invasions from Asia came to a halt, and trade flourished. The communities were organized under the feudal system.

Migration in the Balkans

The groups of Slavic races entered the Balkans in waves between the 6th – 8th centuries. They settled on the peninsula's northern arc, from the Adriatic to the Black Sea. The Slovenes arrived first and settled in the area northwest of the Adriatic. The rest of the South Slavic people came later; many went south to the Peloponnese and were quickly assimilated by the local Greek population. This was also the case with the Slavs settled in Hungary, who similarly were absorbed by the local community. On the contrary, the Slavs who settled in today's Bulgaria, although they were conquered politically by the Turkmens, who were kin to "Bulgarians", eventually assimilated them culturally.

As early as the era of the Eastern Roman Empire, the northern Balkan regions inhabited by groups of Slavic races could not compete with the southernmost part controlled by Constantinople, either economically or culturally. The reasons are related to geography, as a massive mountain range impedes the creation of sections of sufficient size to achieve satisfactory growth rates and hinder transport and communication, the relatively unfavorable climatic conditions, and the deficient soils, rather than political or social reasons. However, the mercurial border situation led to conflicts and wars, in which whatever financial surpluses were consumed to.

In 886 A.D., Czar Boris of Bulgaria was Christianized by missionaries Kirill and Methodius. In the 10th century, the First Bulgarian Empire defeated the Byzantines and the Serbs. Later, around 1200 A.D., the Second Bulgarian Empire, the medieval Bulgarian state of

94

Czar Samuel, confronted Emperor Vassilios II and was defeated. The Bulgarians, however, adopted the culture, legal system, and political organization of Byzantium.

The Serbs arrived in the Balkans in the 6th century simultaneously with the Croats, sharing culture and language. The Serbs were generally closer to Byzantium, adopting its religious and cultural characteristics and political and legal organization elements. The primary reason for establishing a state was to ensure protection from the Bulgarians. Under Stefan Dushan, the Serbian state achieved its medieval culmination in the 14th century. The Ottoman Empire subdued Serbia in the 15th century.

The Croats subdued as early as the 9th century to the formal sovereignty of Charlemagne and his successors. The Western Frankish missionaries followed, beginning a process that led to their Christianization; Croatia became Catholic. In 879, the Pope recognized the Croatian state. Unlike the Orthodox Serbs, who adopted the Cyrillic alphabet, Catholic Croatia, with a similar language, adopted the Latin alphabet.

The specific characteristic of the original Slavic groups was that they lacked a king. They were organized in small units under a local ruler. However, in the event of external risk, the need for rallying under a central administrative body arose. However, when the danger retreated, the local rulers ceased to acknowledge and obey the King they had chosen to deal with the threat. On the other hand, the Christianity of the King brought about the Pope's recognition of his ecclesiastical authority, reinforced his position, and led to the consolidation of his power.

The medieval Croat state reached its peak in the 10th century under Tomislav. Still, generally, the kings remained weaker than the local rulers. In 1102, the rulers formed a coalition. They agreed to be placed under the Hungarian King's authority, as his distant headquarters was more advantageous than the power of a geographically closer king. Since then, Croatia has remained a feudal state under the Hungarian King for some time.

Bosnia constituted the transition zone between the Croats in the north and the Serbs in the south. The difference between the Slavic groups of the time was not the nation but the religious dogma. After the schism between the Orthodox and Catholic Church of 1054, the Christian Slavs of Bosnia followed the Western Church's religious ritual rather than the Eastern Orthodox's. When the Hungarian kings became kings of Croatia in 1102, Bosnia managed to flee the direct control of Hungary, appointing its rulers. To advance their claims on Bosnia, the Hungarians convinced the Pope that the Slavs of the region were heretics. The medieval Church of Bosnians was connected, as the enemies of Bosnia falsely presented to the heretical cult of the manicheist Bogomils. This political incitement resulted in a Catholic Crusade in the mid-13th century, which was unsuccessful. The Church of the Slavs of Bosnia broke its relations with Rome but continued to observe the Catholic Church's rituals. This separate Church survived until the Ottoman occupation for two centuries.

After the Ottoman occupation occurred between 1450 and 1480, Bosnia gradually became a region with a substantial Muslim population due to Ottoman Islamization. According to Ottoman data regarding the collection of taxes, the conversion process to Islam has been long and gradual. In the late 16th century, Muslims were still a minority. Bosnia was described in 1648 as an area with half of its population being Muslim. Of the remaining half, two-thirds were Catholics, and one-third Orthodox Christians. A possible explanation for the Islamization was the superficial Christianity of the Slavs (overturned by the first difficulty), the lack of inspiring priests, and the memory of the Crusade of Catholics in the 13th century. Islam, the sovereign Ottomans' religion, brought financial, administrative, and social benefits to the conversed ones.

Several inhabitants of the Balkans were thus Islamized to pursue individual or collective benefits in the Muslim Ottoman Empire. The presence of the religious institutions and mosques of Islam in the area outranked the presence of the Christian ones. On an individual level, violent Islamization dictated by situations created by the Ottoman rulers also took place, as the success of the Islamic religion is morally rewarded, according to Islam. The same reasons apply to the Islamized Albanians, the Slavs of the Macedonian region, and the Pomaks of Thrace.

The ancestors of the Albanians, the Illyrians, supposedly arrived in the Western Balkans in 1200 B.C. The time gap in finds dating back then was interpreted as a break in the evolution of the civilization due to the descent of barbarians, the change of customs, and the introduction of new cultural elements. However, modern historians argue the correctness of this theory. Classical Greek writers considered Illyrians to be a non-Greek gender. Illyrians have left no historical or other written evidence of their civilization. Written proofs for their language also did not exist until at least 1555 A.D. Albanians joined the Islamic religion in a large proportion.

According to the Romanians, their ethnic origin dates to the era of Roman settlers intermingling with the local population of Dacia. Romanians appeared for the first time in historical records, located in Transylvania and Moldovlachia, in 1247. According to a Hungarian theory, the Romanians of 1247 are the ancient Dacians. During the Barbarians' raids, they fled to the southern Balkans and survived for a thousand years before returning to the area. As a result, Hungary argued that Transylvania did not belong to them. Western historians tend to accept the Romanian argument between these two theories since the Romanian language is based on Latin, lacking loans from the Greek language, which would inevitably be there if Romanians had lived a millennium in northern Greece. Although they spoke a Latin dialect as a second language, Greek Vlachs have no affinity with Romanians.

Hungary is not a Balkan nation; nevertheless, certain aspects of its history are interwoven with the Balkan nations' history. The Magyar nomads occupied the Hungarian plain in the 9th century and established a Catholic state during the second millennium. After their defeat at Mohacs by the Ottomans in 1526, the Habsburgs inherited the Kingdom's remnants, a depopulated land under Ottoman occupation. The Hapsburgs possessed only a strip of land, where they established their usual institutions, Diet, the King-Administrator, and bureaucracy. In the 17th century, the Turks were forced to gradually yield Hungary to Austria, culminating with the Treaty of Karlowitz in 1699.

Under the Ottoman administration, Hungary had a regime of tolerance for Protestants. However, the noble Magyar Protestants rebelled several times against the Catholic Habsburgs, claiming religious rights. In their dispute with the Magyar nobles, the Habsburgs followed the method of attributing various powers during the wars, removing them afterward. During the French-Austrian War of 1703, the nobles rebelled and asked Emperor

Charles VI to reinstate the old regime of privileges. The peace treaty concluded at Szatmar (present-day Satu Mare, Romania) on April 29, 1711, between the House of Habsburg emperor Charles VI, the Hungarian estates, and the Kuruc rebels. After that, no major war was held on the country's territory.

Since then, many new waves of immigrants, Ruthenians, Slovaks, and Germans, arrived. In 1780, the Magyars became a minority in Hungary. However, only 5% of the population exercised the civil rights possessed by Hungarian noblemen. For the Hungarian nobles, aristocratic class and national identity were synonymous terms. A citizen could only be someone belonging to an aristocratic class. This class claimed medieval rights, although its rise to the advanced level was relatively recent since most members of the older aristocracy were killed in the battle of Mohacs. The Habsburgs subsequently created a new order of nobles from the surviving landowners and officers of the Austrian army.

The efforts of Austria at the time of Joseph II to impose reforms threatened the interests of the Magyar nobles. The principles of their class were not compatible with the reforms in Hungary. Austria's war preparations against the Ottoman Empire caused the Magyars' uprising in 1788-1790, resulting in an impasse over reform efforts. Thus, the underdevelopment of the economy and the resulting social slowdown are the outcome of the political prerogatives attributed to a particular class in Hungary. In this regard, although Hungary moved on an advantageous orbit, different from the Balkan countries under the Ottoman Empire, the aristocratic class's attitude resulted, not differing much in terms of the country's development.

Developments in Western Europe

In Europe, the conditions – geographical, among others – favored the introduction of feudal systems. Feudalism was a social, political, and economic system formed as an integrated system around the 11th century. It prevailed mainly in the Western European states derived from the dissolution of the Empire of Charlemagne. The feuds were rooted in the last period of the Roman Empire and the so-called barbarian raids. The demise of the Roman state led to widespread insecurity due to barbaric invasions from the east and the north.

The raids of Arabs from the south and other tribes from the north, as well as the civil wars and independence tendencies of local rulers, caused turmoil in the territories of the former Roman Empire. This situation led to the destruction of roads and the decline of trade; economic activity focused on agriculture. An economic regime of soil fragmentation among various rulers was established. Feudalism was tenure by military service. Vassals paid their rent in spears and arrows against the King's enemies, who was considered their landlord. The King also often felt inferior to the Pope or the Emperor in feudal terms.[77]

The first step towards feudalism was the concession of land by the monarch to his noble subjects (vassals), with the obligation of an oath of faith to the King and supply of agricultural products. The impoverished peasants depended on vassals for protection from various dangers, such as grabs and looting. Feudalism drove the downturn of the economy (9th – 10th centuries). Shipping weakened, while the Church emerged as a fundamental social and economic life factor, condemning economic profit and trade. The era of monarchs' power ended, and

---

[77] G.K. Chesterton: A Short History of England, 1993.

all that remained were the formal vows of faith to the King. At the same time, the various nobles emerged as independent rulers within their fiefs. Feudalism evolved in three stages: the stage of tax as bid in work, bid in products, and finally, in money. Although this order was always the same, based on the history of economic life, the timing of these three different types of feudalism was different at each place, as the circumstances in each region had also played a role.

The population growth in Europe after the 11th century led to the expansion of trade, the flourishing of new ideas, and the creation of urban centers. Cities became trade hubs and safe shelters for liberated serfs and free growers. The new conditions boosted the crafts and contributed to creating capital. The trade gave rise to money transactions. Agriculture retreated, resulting in the fragmentation of feudal property and having as a political result the wane of the power of the feudal lords and re-strengthening of the monarchy. Merchants bought estates, and a land-owning bourgeois class was created.[78] Ultimately, the bourgeoisie was destined to prevail as a European and global model. Later, various kinds of democracy with a liberal economy became Europe's "natural" political system. It always prevailed under normal circumstances, except in cases where it was grasped by armed minorities or suspended because of extraordinary internal or international situations.

Economists and historians have tried to distinguish various stages of economic development regarding geographical − -intrinsic characteristics.[79] The economy evolved based on travel and transport possibilities.

---

[78] L. Th. Houmanidis: Ibid., p.298 (in Greek).

[79] L. Th. Houmanidis: Ibid. Introduction, p.16.

Depending on the industry, they identify the period of hunter-gatherer societies, the period of nomadic communities, the period of agriculture, and the period of trade.[80] Regarding trading instruments, they identify the stages of the barter economy, monetary economics, and credit economy. On the relations regarding production, they distinguish the phases of primitive common property, serfdom – feudalism, capitalism, communism, and the free economy. In terms of the scope of transactions, they identify the domestic economy, the urban economy, the national economy, and globalization. Concerning the political context, they identify the stage of the closed economy up to the 11th century, the urban economy (11th – 14th century), the Large Area economy (14th – 16th century), the national economy (16th – 19th century), and the international economy (twentieth century and after that).[81] From the point of view of regulations to a free or restrictive economy, individual and social, democratic or not, closed or open, livelihood or transactional. Many other scientists and philosophers have distinguished the economy in terms of the spirit that governs it, i.e., the economic order.

The Crusades that began in 1095 on the pretext of the liberation of the Holy Land from the Muslims were a connecting factor of state formations, allied on this purpose, and constituted the first expression of Western Europe's unity. However, the Kings, who in this context became leaders of the unified nation-states, contributed to restoring order but fended off the possibility of a kind of unification that would include all the European states. Plagues, hunger, epidemics, and wars, significantly

---

[80] Friedrich von List.
[81] Gustav Schmoller.

reducing the population of Europe, characterized the late Middle Ages. The epidemic of the "Black Death" killed between 1347 and 1350 about one-third of Europeans. Sects, the Inquisition, the schism between Catholics and Protestants, inter-state wars, internal conflicts, and rebellions were the causes of the disasters of that period.

At the same time, trade promotion associations such as the Hanseatic League were created, associating in this predominantly trade union, Germanic cities, mainly in the Baltic and the North Sea. The Hanseatic League developed primarily in the 13th century when the formation of German cities on the east of the Elbe and new markets led to the need for a kind of organization in commercial associations. The German towns collaborated to control the Baltic trade and, in 1275, achieved a ban on the entry of the ships of Flemish cities into the Baltic Sea. Gradually, the network expanded, and in 1370, Hansa, which numbered 77 cities at the time, coerced Denmark's King Valdemar IV to recognize it and guarantee free shipping and exemption from customs duties.

The Centennial War has been a conflict, intermittently interrupted by truces, between the dynasties Plantagenet and Valois and, through them, between England and France. The war lasted over 100 years, from 1337 to 1453 (116 years). Among the root causes of the conflict were the "medieval recession," which resulted from the increasing financial burden of feudal claims and the controversies over the feuds of Guyenne. The war pretense was the competition of the contenders for the throne of France after the death, in 1328, of the childless King of France, Charles IV. Philippe VI de Valois, the closest cousin of the deceased, was immediately proclaimed King (1328-1350), and by Edouard

III, already King of England (1327-1377), nephew of Charles, claimed the throne.

Together with the decision of Edward III to claim the Crown of France, The leading cause of the war was the control of the prosperous Flanders and other areas in the greater France. France wanted to expel the English and the English to abolish the vassalage of Guyenne to France, and ensure the return of Normandy, Anjou, and other areas. The Earl of Flanders, Louis de Never, was supported by his overlord, the King of France, while the Flemish bourgeois were Anglophiles. Despite the revolutionary spirit of various expatriate French who had fled to England and their aspirations in France, the war had geographic and commercial objectives. Although more extensive in area and wealthier, France proved initially weak in military power. The Kings waged war with the political framework of the feudal system of the time, that is, by the mere assistance of the feudal lords and nobles.

On the contrary, England converted the succession controversy to a "national" struggle, achieving the consensus of the bourgeois, who were interested in the wool trade, the main product of Flanders. After many battles in which the English army defeated the French troops, later, with the animation of Jeanne d'Arc, the French side had a few victories and concluded an agreement. With the Treaty of Picquigny (1475), France agreed to pay an annual allowance to King Eduard VI of England, and the latter renounced his claim to the throne of France.

Cultural and technological developments, as well as the Greco-Roman culture that emigrated to the West by refugees from its last guardian, the dissolved Byzantium, contributed to European society's transformation, marking the Renaissance's beginning. In the first half of the

17th century, the Holy Roman Empire (region of Germany) was politically fragmented and religiously divided. The Habsburgs, who were separated in the Austrian and Spanish septs from the time of the resignation of Charles V, cooperated closely with their common denominator, Catholicism, in their struggle against religious reform, resulting in the pursuit of common foreign policy objectives. The rivalry between France and the Habsburgs regarding the politically fragmented area of the Italian peninsula continued. Spain wanted to keep its old possessions there. At the same time, France, pretending to be the protector of the independent Italian states, sought the annexation of their territories to the House of Savoy.

The territory of the Holy Roman Empire experienced continual changes throughout its history (962-1806). In the era of its most significant expansion, it included areas of today's Germany, Austria, Switzerland, Liechtenstein, Luxembourg, Czech Republic (Bohemia), Slovenia, Belgium, and Holland, as well as large parts of today's Poland, France, and Italy. In contrast, it did not include Rome within its boundaries for a long time. Throughout its history, the Empire was not organized into a unified state. Instead, it consisted of many smaller kingdoms, principalities, ducats, counties, free imperial cities, and other Lander, continuously changing, dividing, merging, joining, and splitting. The lack of physical–geographical borders and the shared culture has always led Europe to consolidation efforts – usually through violent conquest. On the contrary, doctrinal differences prevailed over the universal Christian faith and caused bloody wars. Although Catholics and Protestants finally reached a compromise, Orthodoxy was always considered a foreign body in Europe.

The Thirty Years War (1618-1648) is considered a landmark of the political transformation of medieval Europe into modern Europe. With this war, the Catholic Church of Rome and the House of Habsburgs attempted to unify Europe by eradicating Protestantism and establishing a pan-European Catholic monarchy. This idea was dissolved in the fields of bloody battles and disappeared during the Westphalia Peace negotiations. This Treaty has been the historical starting point of creating a secular and independent state system in Europe.[82]

Fighting took place mainly in Central Europe, and most of the victims were residents of the Holy Roman Empire. The war started initially between the Protestant and Catholic Lander of the Holy Roman Empire, after the attempt of Emperor Ferdinand II to enforce Catholicism all over the Empire, to be generalized as a war of all Great European Powers expressing the competition between Austria and Habsburg for the political supremacy in the continent. Catholic France took the part of the Protestants against the Habsburgs. One of the results of the disaster that suffered the German region was the idea of pan-Germanism, presenting later the dangers of a divided Germany as the primary justification for creating the German Empire in 1871.

After the Peace of Westphalia, the political class of Europe was altered. The rise of Bourbon France, the retreat of the aspirations of Habsburgs, and the ranking of Sweden among the Great Powers have created a new balance of power. As a result, reinforced France emerged as the dominant force at the end of the 17th century.

---

[82] Th. A. Hristodoulidis: Diplomatic History Issue A (in Greek).

In the middle of the 18th century, a new European war broke out with ramifications in America, Africa, and South Asia. The causes of the Seven-Year War (1756-1763) were the efforts of France, Prussia, and Britain to dominate and expand their territory. France to constrain the increasing power of the British Empire, and Prussia allied with Spain (Pacte de Famille, 1761). Austria and, initially, the Russian Empire (until 1762), both rivals of Prussia, joined the alliance. When Britain attacked lands claimed by France in North America, conflicts broke out between Great Britain and France. At the same time, the rising Prussia competed with Austria in the struggle for the legacy of the Holy Roman Empire in Central Europe. Prussia annexed Saxony, and France, together with Spain, invaded Portugal. After the seven-year war, the hostilities ended with the Treaty of Paris (1763), which included various exchanges of territories. However, conflicts in Europe do not end there.

North America
Early British policy for North America was one of salutary neglect. It mostly left the settlers there alone to govern themselves. The thirteen original colonies initiated the American War of Independence (1775–1783) against the Kingdom of Great Britain over their objection to Parliament's direct taxation and lack of colonial representation. The American colonials, having no representatives in the British Parliament, rejected Parliament's authority to tax them. They proclaimed, "No taxation without representation," starting with the Stamp Act Congress in 1765. Protests steadily escalated to the Boston Massacre in 1770 and the Gaspee schooner's burning in Rhode Island in 1772, followed by the Boston Tea Party in December 1773. The British responded by

closing Boston Harbour and enacting a series of punitive laws that effectively rescinded Massachusetts Bay Colony's self-government rights. The other colonies rallied behind Massachusetts. A group of American patriot leaders set up their government in late 1774 at the Continental Congress to coordinate their resistance to Britain. Nevertheless, not all the colonists followed; several retained their allegiance to the Crown and were known as Loyalists.

The war started, but when the Revolutionaries realized they could not win without alliances, the Second Continental Congress decided on an agreement with France that was eventually reached in 1778, contributing to the American victory. The overthrow of British rule established the United States of America as the first republic in modern history.

Africa

Africa is the second-largest continent after Asia. However, it is the most sparsely populated continent; its population in 2020 was 1.34 billion, i.e., one-sixth of the world's population. Geopolitically, but also in terms of natural geography, environment, and resources, it consists of two separate sections: North-Mediterranean Africa and sub-Saharan Africa.

North Africa is geopolitically linked to Europe and the Middle East; Sub-Saharan Africa is considered a separate continent. Deserts cover most of North Africa, the Maghreb, and Egypt except a relatively narrow zone bordering the Mediterranean, which – in some regions – is fertile. In Northwest Africa, south of this productive zone, the mountain ranges of Atlas protect it from the heat and windstorms of the Sahara, creating in parts of the region of today's Algeria, Morocco, and Tunisia a perfect

108

Mediterranean climate. The Atlas Mountain range and the Sahara Desert prevented population movements from sub-Saharan Africa, resulting, before the arrival of Arabs, in the prevalence of the Mediterranean culture in most of North Africa. Modern nations of the region benefited greatly from the wealth of oil, natural gas, and Saharan minerals. The Nile, through the unique geographical conditions generated, facilitated the creation of Egypt, the first sophisticated civilization of the Mediterranean region.

Sub-Saharan Africa is comprised of eight unequal-sized geographic areas: the Sahara Desert, the Sahel at its rim, the Savannah in its south, the Swahili coast in the Indian Ocean from Somalia to Mozambique, the tropical rainforest area, the Great Lakes region, the Ethiopian Highlands, and South Africa.

Sub-Saharan Africa suffered from difficulty in communication; the two sides of the inverted triangle were cut off between two oceans, the Atlantic and the Indian. The triangle's base is the almost impassable Sahara. Although much larger as a continent, Africa's coastline is smaller than Europe's, and it has virtually no natural ports. It has a few floating rivers, impenetrable rainforests, and deserts. As a result, sub-Saharan Africa, until the 15th century, was mostly unknown in the "Ecumene."

Africa is weak regarding the two resources necessary for primary production and capital accumulation: the fertile soils and the irrigation potential. Moreover, it does not extend parallel to the equator in a temperate zone like Eurasia. Like South America, its axis has a north-south direction with climatically benign areas occupying relatively limited spaces.[83] Therefore, its rich subsoil in ores and oil could not contribute to growth since,

---

[83] Jared Diamond.

for this, a substantial industrial economy is indispensable. The fact is that sub-Saharan Africa has not been able to develop any remarkable civilization and had remained rather primitive until its "discovery" and the arrival of the colonialist Europeans, slave catcher Americans, and various adventurers. This development can only be attributed to the natural conditions prevailing in geography. In contrast, South America, which was in a similar or worse state regarding lack of communication, succeeded in developing several cultures (albeit savages in some respects) until its "discovery," which led to their destruction and their population's annihilation.

The invasion of colonialists and exploiters in sub-Saharan Africa was done in two phases: first, with the slave trade, and afterward, with colonialism.[84] The subsequent development of sub-Saharan Africa and its human geography has resulted from the actions of Europeans and Americans. On the contrary, the fate of North Africa after the Mediterranean civilizations and its conquest by the Romans was determined by the Arab invasion. The colonial powers followed Arab domination until its final delivery to the Arabized populations of the region.

The Silk Road

The great fortune amassed by Marco Polo from trade with Mongolia and China confirms the story in his famous book. Since the 14th century, European merchants have traveled to Mongolia and China following various routes. Traders and travelers could go to China via Trapezus to Tauris, subsequently to Hormuz, and through

---

[84] Asteris Houliaras, Sotiris Petropoulos: Africa and the others, 2016 (in Greek).

the naval way, the Bay of Bengal, Indochina, and from there, to China. After Tauris, an alternative to this road was to Samarkand and from there to China. A third road was through Crimea, Astrakhan, and Turkestan.

China, geographically, is far from the economic centers of the other pole of development, Europe. Therefore, both Europe and China sought trade routes for their interconnection. The network of these roads through land and sea was named by the German geographer Ferdinand von Ribera in the 19th century Silk Road, silk being one of the essential monopolistic products of China at the time. Other products were spices, glass, porcelain, and precious stones. China's know-how of producing paper and gunpowder was transferred to Europe. The land network crossed Asia and reached India, Persia, and Europe. The products of China were transported to Indochina, India, Persia, the Arabian Peninsula, and East Africa through the sea routes.

Silk Road contributed to the communication and development of cultures not only between the starting and ending points but also the ones that were along with it. The spread of Buddhism and Islam, and to a lesser extent of Christianity, is partly due to this path. Later, in the 15th century, the expansion of the Ottoman Empire interrupted the passage to Europe, leading to the search for new access routes from the West.

The Jewish diaspora

For two thousand years, the history of the Jews has been characterized by their geographical spread and increased internal coherence, demonstrating, in this exceptional case, the secondary but not absent role of geography in creating a nation. The Jewish people's essential diaspora began in the Roman conquest age.

Later, in the 13th and 14th centuries, with the Catholic Church's incitement, the Jews were expelled from England and France and forced to move to Eastern Europe. In the 14th century, expelled from Spain, most found refuge in the Ottoman Empire.

Jews are a national-religious group and a nation. They originate from the Middle East, the land of Israel, and appear in history in the second millennium B.C. They reside, apart from Israel, worldwide, without a specified territorial range. The spread of Jews throughout the Western world and in Africa, according to R. Kaplan, is not related to geography or racial homogeneity. However, the Semitic tribe prevails, especially in the Mediterranean. However, geography contributes to the creation of different customs and cultures, such as Ashkenazi (Northern and Eastern Europe) and Sephardic (Spain), as well as variations in language, such as in addition to Classical Hebrew, Ladino (Spanish-Hebrew language), and Yiddish (German-Hebrew language). The Jews suffered persecution and genocides, especially by Germans, to the degree of the Holocaust.

Jews, regardless of their country, but especially those in central Europe and later in the USA, thanks to their hard work and intelligence, offered significant achievements in science, fine Arts, literature, philosophy, and economics, contributing substantially to the advancement of the world's culture. Israel politically is closely linked to the U.S., mainly through the Jewish community; most of them are Ashkenazi born in the United States.

The Age of Adventure

The state policy of colonization, i.e., imperialism, is a phenomenon that began in the 15th century following the Age of Exploration. The discovery by the Portuguese and Spanish of the American continent, the coasts of Africa, India, and East Asia created the first empires that multiplied the number of continents and spanned the covered land across the globe. Along with North Africa, Eurasia was regarded as "the ecumene" until the beginning of the 15th century; later, the exploration era transformed geography into world science. Beyond man's natural tendency towards expansion, the search for gold and silver, but mainly the search for knowledge and new commercial roads, was the reason for the beginning of the era of exploration. The obstruction of journeys to Asia due to Ottoman conquests led to the search for other routes for trade in silk and spices. Portuguese, Spanish, Italian, and English navigators pioneered the change of the world's geographic map and discovered two new continents.

Seeking alternative routes to India to transport its rare products and traveling west, Columbus discovered in 1492 the islands of San Salvador (Bahamas) and Hispaniola (Haiti and the Dominican Republic). The Portuguese later, seeking precious metals, arrived in Brazil. The Spaniards conquered the entire region from the south of the United States to the southernmost tip of South America, decimating the Aztecs in Mexico and the Incas in Peru. England, France, and Holland also created overseas empires competing with each other. English and French ships reached the shores of North America, Newfoundland, the estuaries of the Hudson River, and Manhattan (1609). The first English colony in North America was Jamestown, Virginia (1607). The French founded the city of Quebec in 1608, and the Netherlands installed a commercial station in today's New York in 1624. Magellan attempted to make a complete tour of the globe, searching for alternative pathways for Asia. Captain James

Cook mapped many places that had not been explored until then. Britain raised claims to eastern Australia as late as 1770, while the Arctic and Antarctica were studied in the 19th century.

While the Western European countries had spread with their fleets to the oceans, extending their sovereignty to various new places, Russia expanded, according to Mackinder, its territory on land from Siberia to the border with Islamic Iran. Russia is a land force, a victim of invasions in the past, which defines its policy.

The era of exploration ended in the early 17th century when sea travel became more manageable because of sophisticated ships and mapping, and the number of unexplored places was reduced. The era of explorations contributed considerably to the advancement of geography by mapping the entire Earth and increasing scientific knowledge with information gathered from the vast tracts discovered. Interest in geography rose. New navigation methods were devised and developed. Additional details on ocean routes and marine currents were added to the maps, and new species of flora and fauna were discovered.

The reversal began in the 18th and 19th centuries when the European colonies in America gained their independence. Spain was weakened because of the Napoleonic Wars and, afterward, losing its possessions in the New World. Britain, France, Portugal, and the Netherlands turned their interest to Africa, India, and Southeast Asia. In the 19th century, the period of new imperialism, the struggle for the conquest and distribution of Africa intensified. The exploration of Africa by the Europeans concluded only in the early 20th century. While Europeans controlled only 10% of Africa in 1870, this figure reached 90% in 1914, with Ethiopia, Somalia, and Liberia alone remaining independent. According to Morgenthau, the imperialist spread in geographic lengths and widths in the vast, relatively empty areas has removed the conflicts among the Powers out of Europe, at least for some time.

The colonies of the defeated nations in the First World War were delivered as "mandates" to the victors. The end of the Second World War meant the beginning of the second phase of decolonization, not without bloody struggles or problems created deliberately by the withdrawing colonial power. Britain had become a vast empire thanks to its egoistic self-esteem as a tremendous geopolitical power. At the same time, it succeeded in retaining its colonies for some time, obscuring its violent policies with its cultural prestige. Thanks to this prestige, the image of the British colonialists as brave, intelligent, and benefactors of the colonies prevailed and persisted until historical figures highlighted the facts and the implications of these "masons of destruction" committed from Cyprus to Malaysia and from India to Palestine and South Africa.[85] France also was accused of brutality in Algeria and Vietnam.

The colonial period, which lasted for six centuries, ended in 1999 when Macau, the last colonial enclave of Portugal, was handed over to China. However, Western Sahara continues to be regarded by the U.N. as a region "non-self-governing". Culturally, France's sway continued mainly in West Africa, England's in East Africa, India, and Pakistan, Portugal's in its former African possessions, and Brazil and Spain's in Central and South America, mainly with preserving the language.

Hunger has been the greatest scourge of humanity for centuries, sometimes leading to mass exterminations

---

[85] Article by Pankaj Mishra.

that reached the percentages of ten and twenty percent of the total. It has contributed significantly to population movements since the origins of history. The next greatest plague has been the epidemic. The epidemics have exposed the population of ancient Greece more than once. In the Middle Ages, the plague spread to Asia, Europe, and North Africa, resulting in the elimination of one-third of the population of Eurasia, with people not being able to understand the causes of the "Black Death." European explorers carried germs to their discoveries, to the Mayas and Aztecs, to populations that had not developed immunity against them by eliminating, in some cases, even 90% of the people, as happened in Hawaii. Hunger, epidemics, and war were the three main scourges of humankind. Man has succeeded in dealing with them scientifically without eliminating them definitively.[86]

---

[86] Yuval Noah Harari: Homo Deus.

THE ARABIAN PENINSULA AND ISLAM

The advent of Islam

The desert dominates the Arabian Peninsula. The climate is tropical, and the humidity on the coasts is unbearable. Geography influences economic life in a highly negative way. The camels and the sea surrounding the peninsula are the main ways of communication and transportation. However, high on the plateaus, the landscape and climate of Saudi Arabia changed. There is no heat, no humidity, no desert, no sand. The scene resembles the Mediterranean coasts. Sometimes, there is a slight chill, stones, mountains, Mediterranean vegetation, and a clear blue sky. Taif, Mecca, and Medina in Saudi Arabia are typical cities of the Middle East. The oil is located east, in the Persian Gulf.

The advent of Islam has marked and catalytically shaped life in the Arabian Peninsula. Islam, geographically and culturally, is set in the context of significant currents of world history. According to Professor Hodgson, the region where Islamic culture was formed is negatively determined, i.e., by the absence of Greek and Sanskrit traditions, which are at the roots of European and Indian culture.[87] Hodgson attempts to explain Islam geographically. It argues that the Arabs, not having sufficient fertile land to cultivate, turned to trade utilizing the geographic position of the Arabian Peninsula in the middle of trade routes.

---

[87] Marshall Hodgson: The venture of Islam, Conscience and History in a World Civilization, 1974.

Honesty is an indispensable qualification for successful trading; therefore, Arabs had to be honest and appear as such. In addition, they had to develop qualities such as "commercial capacities" in the negotiation. Mecca was far from other centers of power and, thus, maintained its independence. The city was behind hills that protected it from the pirates of the Red Sea. It was a cosmopolitan city, flocked by believers from the surrounding areas to commemorate its sanctuary, the Kaaba.

The religious void of the time was due to continuing idolization in the region, even though Christianity and Judaism were known religions and embraced by several Arabs. The doctrine of the nomads was a kind of multi-demonism associated with the paganism of ancient Semites, and various gods were subject to a superior deity commonly called Allah. The success of Islam among the Arabs is indicative of their need for a Prophet of Arab descent for a monotheistic religion that would eliminate idolatry.

Mecca of his time, the city of Makoraba of Ptolemy, was occupied by the northern Arab tribe of Quraish, whose main occupation was trading. Quraish merchants had concluded trade agreements with the border authorities of Byzantium, Abyssinia, and Persia. The need for Islam was proven by its use as a unifying element for the enormous expansion of Arabs that followed. Islam was the common cultural expression of Arabs. However, not all Muslims are Arabs or all Arabs Muslims.

Islam is a unifying factor mainly for Arabs. However, it was not meant as a unified apolitical construction even from the beginning. Moreover, Westerners quickly took over the reins and divided the Middle East into states. Although this division is not as arbitrary as it could be seen, geography has an essential role in real diversification.

Islamic conquests

In the East, due to the wars between them, both Byzantines and Persians had been weakened. In 626, Persia besieged Byzantium unsuccessfully. In 634, twelve years after Hegira, the Byzantines were defeated by the Muslim Arabs near Jerusalem and lost the Byzantine Damascus. In the next ten years, Arabs conquered the Empire of Persia. Byzantium quickly lost Syria, Palestine, and its more productive province, Egypt.

In Islam, the world is divided into an area of Islamic peace, Dar al Islam, and an area of war, Dar al Harb. The Arab world expanded rapidly and, within three centuries, conquered a vast space more extensive than the Roman Empire. By the mid-7th century, it spread to Libya, while between 674 and 678 unsuccessfully besieged Constantinople. In the 8th century, it occupied the rest of Byzantine provinces and spread throughout North Africa, passing Gibraltar to the Iberian. The advancing Arabs were intercepted on their way to France at the Battle of Poitiers in 732. Arabs also occupied Byzantine cities in Italy and the islands of Crete and Sicily, gaining control of the sea routes in the Mediterranean. In the East, they reached the Bay of Biscay at the Indus River's estuary; in the north, they conquered Samarkand and regions up to the Chinese border.

Besides, Arabs were engaged in trade through the sea. They developed maritime art and ocean navigation using the compass as early as the 12th century while designing ports and building lighthouses. Marine commerce centers were the ports of Hormuz, Tyros, Beirut, Gaza, Accra, Alexandria, Basra, Tripoli, Tunis,

Morocco, Medusa, Cádiz, Malaga, and Seville on the Guadalquivir River. For Arabs, the economic basis of their feudalism was the money economy, not the barter economy, as in the West. Moreover, the feudal system of the West emerged for military reasons, while for Arabs, it had roots in collecting taxes. The feudal system of the Arabs was closer to that of the Byzantines than of Western Europe.[88]

The distance of the advancing Muslim Arabs from the bases of their origin, the Christian Church's reaction, and the feudal system's power resulted in impeding Arab ambitions. Crusades, Mongol raids, and the advance of Turkmens that followed forced their vast Empire into relative shrinkage. Arabs used the tactic of non-conversion to Islam by force, at least initially. They took over the administrations of the territories they occupied, but they usually did not plunder private property. Churches, monasteries, and state land were enough loot to meet their needs. They left non-Muslim smallholders and small business producers at the time in their peaceful works - for which the Arabs had no aptitude. In this way, and unlike other conquerors, Arabs managed to stabilize and hold their conquests.

Saudi Arabia

The Saud family belongs to the Anza tribe, one of the largest Arab tribes, whose members are scattered throughout the Arabian Peninsula, Iraq, and Syria. The Saud dynasty leader and the Saudi state's founder is Prince Saud Ibn (son of) Muhammad Ibn Muqrin. In the early 18th century, Saud commanded the emirate of Diraiyah, a few kilometers from the center of the current capital, Riyadh.

---

[88] L.Th. Humanidis: Ibid., p. 283

The son of Saud, Muhammad (1726 – 1765), succeeded with the help of his brothers in extending his authority to the surrounding areas. Meanwhile, further south, in the village of Najd, at a central location of the peninsula, in Uyaniah, a wealthy nobleman, Sheikh Muhammad Ibn Abd al-Wahhab, decided that he should lead a strive to return to the old Islamic values and the pure faith.

When Abd al-Wahab was forced by the political-religious authority to flee, he took refuge near the Emir of Diraiyah in 1744. The Emir provided him full support and protection for disseminating the principles of his religious reform, which envisaged a return to the old values of Islam. For his part, Abd al-Wahab would help spread the Emir's authority. This agreement concluded between the Emir and Imam Muhammad ibn Saud, on the one hand, and Sheikh Abd al-Wahab, on the other, is the cornerstone of the Saudi state. With the doctrine of Wahhabism, the Saudi state claimed the holy cities of Mecca and Medina from the Ottomans who administered them. However, this period expired in 1817, when the Ottoman Empire sent the third Egyptian Expeditionary Corps under the leadership of Ibrahim Pasha, who defeated the Saudi Arabs.

The son of Abdulrahman, Abdelaziz Ibn Abdulrahman Al-Faisal Al Saud, known just as Al Saud, managed later, in 1902, to occupy Riyadh to gradually expand its power throughout the region, ensuring stability and security among its inhabitants, the Bedouins. He made use of the opportunities afforded him by the defeat of the Ottoman Empire during the First World War, activating the forces of the Entente to stabilize the entity of the state he created. On September 22, 1932, he established the Kingdom of Saudi Arabia by royal decree.

Mecca was a place of pilgrimage even before the advent of Islam. Its inhabitants wanted to preserve their city's character and its benefits. The new religion continued the pre-Islamic tradition of pilgrimage. The "Bride of the Red Sea," Jeddah, owes its development to its position as the seaport of Mecca. However, it was a famous city. In antiquity, Alexander the Great passed from there on his way from India to Egypt.

In the southwestern part of the Arabian Peninsula, Hadhramaut, the current region of Yemen, historically bears the name of Eudemon (prosperous) Arabia. The name is due to the temperate climate prevailing in contrast to the arid, rocky, and deserted rest of Arabia. Rainfall, weather, and the sea ensured rich vegetation and prosperity. From the 12th century B.C. to the 6th century B.C., there are known civilizations, such as the ancient civilization of Saba. However, it ceased to be prosperous when it turned out to be dry from oil deposits in contrast to the eastern Arabian Peninsula. In addition, although intelligent and diligent, its people could not be administered democratically and in order.

The Geopolitics of Islam

Geographically, Islam is divided into the center and the periphery, not in economic or developmental but in historical terms. Central Islam is mainly the Arab countries, from the Middle East to the Arabian Peninsula to North Africa and Iran. Geographically, Egypt occupies a central position. Peripheric Islam includes the countries Islamized after the Middle Ages, the countries of the Indian Ocean, Central Asia, and sub-Saharan Africa. Muslims in the peripheral countries of Islam are not Arabs.[89]

---

[89] I.Th. Mazis: Geography of the Islamic movement in Middle East, 1992, p.25 (In Greek).

Politically, the geographic spread of Islam moves in a zone – subtropical, north of Ecuador – from east to west. From Indonesia, it expands to the West, Bangladesh, Pakistan, Afghanistan, the Middle East, Turkey, the Arabian Peninsula, North Africa, and the Sahel. In addition, Muslim islets exist in Central Asia (Tajikistan, Uzbekistan, Turkmenistan, Kyrgyzstan, and Kazakhstan), Europe (Albania, Bosnia), and Africa. The geopolitical exception is Israel, in a zone of mentality that is not tolerant of diversity.

In the early 21st century, Islam is flourishing and attempts to spread beyond its actual borders, having as its primary target Europe. In the so-called areas of "peace and war", a coexistence area, Dar Al Sulh, is added to propagate Islam. This area initially included countries not under Islamic sovereignty but dependent on Islam. It could now be covering Europe with its growing Muslim population through immigration. Europe is the target of two distinct groups: the Islamists, on the one hand, who are attempting terrorist acts to punish it for its colonial past, and mild Islam, on the other, which does not intend to Islamization of Europeans by force but the colonization of Europe by Muslims and their descendants. Muslims have already taken significant steps in this direction. Simultaneously, many Europeans do not seem to raise objections regarding forming a Muslim majority, driving Europe to Islamization and accepting Islam as the mainstream religion and way of life.

Islamists consider Western imperialism to be responsible for the fragmentation of the united Arab nation in nation-states by introducing borders between them, although the nation-states preexisted Islam.[90] In a

---

[90] I.Th. Mazis: Ibid., p.59.

sense, the political unity of the Islamic world could never be achieved due to the schism between Sunni and Shiites, the differences between Arab and Persian culture, the armed intervention of the Turkmens in the Middle Ages, and the extensive spread of Islam in vast geographic areas. Islamists' allegations of unity are crumbling, after all, since they are expressed in Arabic, a language not shared by all Muslims. At the same time, Muslims in the periphery have their own social formations and languages. Except for their religion, they do not have other cultural relationships with the Arabs.

THE TURKMENS AND THE OTTOMAN EMPIRE

Turkmens were a group of nomadic tribes that lived in Central Asia, near Mongolia and China. Climatic conditions and their tendency to conquer and loot as a means of living led them to migrate westward, south of the Caspian, and through Iran to reach the Middle East. The Islamized Turkmen of the Oghuz tribe defeated the Byzantines near Manzikert in 1071 and settled in Anatolia by founding the Seljuk state. They managed to survive the Tatar attacks and forced many of the region's oldest inhabitants to Islamization and Turkification. Most devastating of all, it proved to be the members of the nomadic tribes. The scorched earth policy contributed significantly to the extermination of the local Byzantine Christian population. It was supplemented by enslavements and sporadic violent Islamizations. As a result, there have sometimes been massacres of entire cities' inhabitants.
    Geography played a crucial role in the transformation of the identity of Turkmens. Everything was different at the new place they settled, as Central-Asian Turkmen got in touch with a higher civilization. Intercourse and intermarriage with the local population, together with the Islamic religion, changed the features of their race.
    The power of the Seljuk Sultanate of Rum declined in the 13th century, and Anatolia was divided into several independent Turkish principalities known as the Anatolian Beyliks. One of these Beyliks, in the region of Bithynia on the frontier of the Byzantine Empire, was led by the

Turkish tribal leader Osman I,[91] from whom the anglicized name Ottoman is derived. Ottomans are the descendants of this statelet, established by Turkmens and renegade Byzantines in 1299 A.D., and constituted the Islamic world's vanguard towards European Christianity. They dominated because of their aggressive character, discipline, organization, and orientation towards military conquests. In terms of economic organization, however, they were significantly lagging, in addition to the fact that they considered these tasks inferior to war and administration, which suited them better. Nevertheless, the Ottoman state became a coherent political expression for most of the Anatolian Turkmens of the 14th century. From there on, it succeeded by uniting them under a single administration to instill the sense of community that would characterize a nation.

When establishing the Ottoman state around Bursa, the Turkmen tribes were already long-ruled Anatolia. Dominant Seljuks were under the pressure of the Mongols. Although this battle constitutes the milestone for the Turkmen conquest of Anatolia, the gradual and violent colonization of the region continued for centuries, with ongoing raids and looting. Nevertheless, the Turkmen tribes succeeded in settling in the Anatolian peninsula despite the sporadic victories of the Byzantines. With the power of arms, the Turkmens achieved the Turkification of the region, to no small extent, imposing the supremacy of their religion. Starting at the Beylik of Karamanogullari, an early version of the Turkish language was consolidated as the official language (circa 13th century). The Ottomans'

---

[91] A Brief History of Ottoman Empire. https://www.behist.com/a-brief-history-of-ottoman-empire/

replacement of the Eastern Roman Empire was not only a geographical and political event. It altered the area's anthropogeography. Civilization, religion, language, everything in the region has changed.

The consecutive victories of the Ottomans over the Byzantines reinforced their self-confidence. They attracted other Turkish Beyliks to unite with them, securing the political unity of Turks in Anatolia. The conquests in the west, in Rumeli, against the Byzantines, in Dar al-Kufr (House of infidels) were usually the result of wars waged by Ottomans without pretext. Still, the first acquisition of European land was made without a battle. Emperor John Kantakouzinos offered a fortress in Gallipoli to Orhan to thank him for his help to the Byzantines in a war in the Balkans.

The Ottoman Empire quickly adapted to changing situations. Sultan Murad I (1362 to 1389) focused on developing institutions. He moved the state capital from Bursa to Edirne in Europe to demonstrate the shift of his interest toward the West. In 1395, after the failed talks with Byzantines in Xanthi, the Ottoman army attacked southern Greece and arrived in Attica. In 1397, it organized raids against Koroni and Methoni in south Peloponnese, which belonged to Venice, with the intent of plundering. In the era of Sultan Murad I (1362 - 1389), the Ottoman state's image was enhanced as its size had quintupled, and it became the most potent power in southeast Europe. The Ottoman state was transformed into one resembling an empire, and Murad I himself, through his character, personified this change. He fancied grandiosity and etiquette, and he saw himself as an emperor.

The conflicts of the Ottomans with the other Turkish Beylics of Anatolia ended during the time of Bayezid I (1389 – 1402). They dissolved, and their territories were annexed to the Ottoman state. Besides, the Ottomans succeeded in occupying the areas of southeastern Anatolia, expanding their borders to the Euphrates. However, the Turkish Beys of Anatolia, expelled by the Ottomans, fled to the Turkish-Tatar Timur. The latter aspired to the revival of the Mongolian Empire. During the Battle of Ankara (1402), the administrations and army of these Beys crossed to the Timur side. Eventually, Timur defeated the Ottomans. The political unity established a short time ago under the Ottoman state broke.

Although the state of Timur could not survive long after his death, the heavy defeat was a severe blow to the Ottoman state. The latter remained headless during the so-called "Fetret Period" (Sorrow period, 1402 - 1413). Moreover, it was torn apart by the aspirations to the throne of the four sons of Bayezid I. Eventually, Mehmed I (1413-1421) was the one who prevailed and succeeded in restoring the unity of the Ottoman state.

The resilience of the Ottoman state is remarkable. Throughout the defeat by Timur and their internal conflicts, the Byzantines and other Balkan countries failed to take advantage of the existing favorable circumstances to liberate their lands. Modern Turks attribute this indifference to Balkan peoples' satisfaction with Ottoman rule and order. Also, they bring forth that the land ownership system Ottomans introduced was more progressive than the pre-existing order in the Balkans. However, this claim is inaccurate – the Balkan states and Byzantium were powerless to attempt anything; neither had the will nor the financial means. On the other hand, Venetians, Genoese, or other Balkan states shared no common interests to undertake any action against the Ottomans.

The Ottoman state regained after a while its strength. The defeat by Timur was quickly forgotten. This was how the Ottoman state's persona had been shaped just before the Fall of Constantinople (1453). The Conqueror (Fatih), Mehmed II, felt strong enough to accomplish what his ancestors could not. Constantinople was not a real obstacle for the Ottoman state; geographically, it was just a thorn, but in the Ottomans' imagination, it was an old dream of greatness.

Bayezid II (1481-1512), who succeeded Mahmud II, tried to consolidate the state's power by deploying naval forces to prevent any new crusade and new conquests in the Mediterranean. As was the case with Byzantium, the involvement of the Ottoman Empire in the struggles between cities of the Italian peninsula, on their initiative, weakened them. It ended with the loss of the naval supremacy of Venice in favor of the Ottomans, the latter defeating them in several naval battles. Bayezid II, acting in moderation, did not carry out any conquering operations against Italy's cities; instead, it preferred to develop trade relations with them.

By the Alhambra Decree issued on March 31, 1492, Spain expelled the Jews from the country and confiscated their estate. As a result, a large part of the Sephardic Jews headed toward the Ottoman Empire, where they were admitted and settled in Thessaloniki, Edirne, Bursa, and Constantinople.

Yavuz Sultan Selim (1512-1520) rose to power by dethroning his father. Selim ordered the exile of Bayezid II and put his brothers and nephews to death upon his accession. Immediately afterward, he dealt with the situation in the east where the state of Safevi (current Azerbaijan region) had acquired power that could threaten the Ottoman state. Selim crashed it, reaching Tabriz.

During his return, he defeated the Beylik of Dulkadirogulları; while appreciating the supremacy of the Sultan, the Beylik of Ramazanogulları surrendered. In this way, Yavuz Sultan Selim secured the unity of Turkmen in Anatolia. Controlling the highlands of Anatolia through the significant number of Turkmen stationed there strengthened the state's defense against Timur-type attacks.

The campaign continued in Egypt with the termination of the Mamelukes' governing. After his victory at the Battle of Ridaniye (1517) against the Sultanate of Mamelukes, Sultan Selim took over the Caliphate of Islam in the name of the Ottoman dynasty and transferred the sacred trusts to Constantinople. Since then, Ottoman rulers have claimed caliphal authority. Also, controlling Mecca, the Medina, and the road to Haj, the Ottoman Empire became the ultimate protector of Islam. However, he could not seize Yemen at the time.

Despite the victory of the Ottomans on the Safevi, no peace treaty was signed between the two parties, and the adversarial suspicion continued. On the one hand, South Azerbaijan sought to occupy a part of Anatolia. On the other, the Ottomans wanted to seize Iraq and the Persian Gulf to continue their course toward the Indian Ocean. The border incidents were not missing between the two, while national identity facilitated the border guards to change sides. Finally, an Ottoman campaign in 1534 culminated with the occupation of Iraq, including Baghdad (1535). In 1555, the agreement of Amasia ended the wars against South Azerbaijan, and this region, along with its capital Tebriz, passed to the Ottoman domination. South Azerbaijan is currently an area in north-western Iran, south of Armenia, and the Republic of Azerbaijan, east of Turkey.

From 1538, three years after the conquest of Iraq, the Ottomans, wanting to enlarge their wins up to the Indian Ocean, began their operations in the region, which lasted until 1669, mainly fighting the Portuguese. They attacked with their fleet to India and Sumatra and occupied areas in East Africa, including Ethiopia. However, the efforts of the Ottomans to control the Indian Ocean have not been successful. The reasons for failure are rendered to the fact that their ships were not adequately equipped, and their crews were not sea-worthy. Moreover, they did not have any local support in India.

Sultan Suleyman I, who succeeded Selim, continued the policy of expansionism toward the West. He attacked Central Europe, defeated the Hungarians, and confronted the Habsburgs at the unsuccessful Ottoman siege of Vienna (1529), which meant the end of the Ottoman expansion in Europe. In addition, Suleyman occupied the Greek island of Rhodes and the city of Tripoli in Libya. Algeria was under the authority of the former pirate Barbarossa, who had taken it from the Spaniards. Eventually, it passed under Ottoman command when the former pirate was assigned Admiral of the Ottoman fleet. However, Suleyman's campaign to India was unsuccessful.

The "rise era" of the Ottoman Empire, during which wars increased its territory, lasted from the Fall of Constantinople until Selim II (1566-1574). It was followed by a period of stagnation. It has been a continuous war of conquest in the West and East for over a hundred years. The opponents in the West of the Ottoman Empire were non-allied, busy with the Renaissance, and failed to unite in time. To its most considerable extent, the Ottoman Empire occupied the entire Balkan Peninsula, the northern shores of the Black Sea and Crimea, the Middle East, including the Arabian Peninsula and North Africa.

Soon after his ascent to the throne, Selim II (1566-1574) campaigned against Yemen, conquering it (1568). Selim II was not as "illustrious" as his predecessors. Although, during his kingship, the Ottoman state retained its power. The Greek-inhabited islands of Chios and Cyprus (1570) and Tunisia were occupied. From Tunis, the Ottomans wanted to control all of North Africa. The Ottoman fleet dominated Africa's Mediterranean and west coast, conquering Venetian and Genoese colonies, one after the other, up to the second half of the 16th century. The Christians' ships could not travel to the Mediterranean without being the target of attacks by the Muslims. The Ottomans no longer ruled only on land but also at sea.

In the 16th century, Europe was divided because of Catholics' and Protestants' conflicts. Still, European leaders eventually realized that they had to confront the most substantial and widespread danger threatening Europe's existence: the expansion of the Muslim Ottomans. This danger was so great that even the capital of the Roman Catholic Church, Rome, was under threat. After the massacres of Christians committed in 1570, when the Ottomans took Cyprus from the Venetians, the Western powers Spain, the German Empire, the Papal state, Venice, Genoa, and Malta coalesced in an alliance. This alliance aimed to regain, by force, the domination in the Mediterranean. The Christian "Holy Alliance" (Lega Santa) organized a considerable fleet assembled in the port of Messina in Italy in September 1571. The naval battle in which the Western forces defeated the Ottoman Navy took place at the Patras Gulf entrance near Naupactus (Lepanto) on October 7, 1571.

The period of regression - not only in geographical terms - of the Ottoman Empire began with the Treaty of Karlowitz (1699). It lasted until the Yash Agreement (1792).

The Karlowitz Treaty was signed between the Ottoman Empire and the Holy Alliance (Austria, Venice, Poland, and Russia) after the defeat the Empire suffered in Zenta. It is regarded as the beginning of this period, ending with the Yash agreement between the Ottomans and Russia, establishing the border between the two states. The retreat of the Ottoman Empire was due to several factors, among which geopolitical reasons.

These factors concern the inevitable blow to the economy and the finances resulting from the Empire's character. Fundamental causes were the change of trade routes and the reduction of customs revenues, the cutback of exports and the increase in imports, and the provision of monopolistic conditions for trade and shipping to European countries. Moreover, resources were spent on wars against Austria and Iran. A further burden was the disproportionate increase in the monarchy costs. Finally, the increase in taxes led to urbanism, reducing agricultural production.

On the other hand, the discovery of new gold and silver mines demoted these metals' value, leading to the devaluation of the Ottoman currencies. Finally, external factors of the weakening of the Ottoman Empire were the economic growth achieved by Europe with the explorations and discoveries of new territories and the ideas introduced in the era of Renaissance and reform. However, because of its cultural origins, the Ottoman Empire has been unable to follow Christian Europe's progress.

The situation on the Ottoman Empire's western side differed from the eastern Anatolian side. The Aegean divided the Empire into two regions with different histories. If the Turkish conquest of Anatolia began formally after the defeat of Byzantium in Manzikert in

1071, the conquest of Greece was completed more than three centuries later, in another era. The circumstances of the relocation of Turkmen-Turks in the area were also different. It was no longer the nomads looking to settle anywhere, but it necessitated the offer of motives. Beyond coercion, providing command positions, and giving land, the Sultans had no other incentives to offer.

The local administrative institutions of the Ottoman Empire were different on the two sides of the Aegean. On the Western side, the system was somewhat more tolerable because of the Greeks' demographic superiority and the Sultan's indifference to dealing with issues that did not fall within the military or sovereign sphere. The middle, Constantinople, and its surroundings were a unique case; it was neither Anatolia nor exactly "Greek land," and it was, after all, the capital of the Ottoman state. With the Patriarchate having its base there and the prominent and robust presence of the Greeks, along with the tolerance of the Sultans, a one-of-a-kind Ottoman capital city took shape, where Christians excelled.

Any land conquered by the Ottomans was the property of the Sultan. It distributed part of it to the warriors as compensation for their services. These concessions, the timars,[92] encompassed all kinds of private or public income. Within the timar system, the state gave timar owners, including the cavalryman, the authorization to have control of arable lands cultivated by local villagers in bondage. In return, the timar owners were responsible for safeguarding order in their region and collecting taxes.

---

[92] A timar was land granted by the Ottoman Sultans between the fourteenth and sixteenth centuries, with a tax revenue annual value of less than 20 000 akche.

At the same time, the timar system provided the Sultan with armed horse riders in the event of war. The Sultan, who was deemed the sole owner of all land, had the discretion of selling Feudal-Timariotic privileges of landowning. At any rate, the Ottoman Empire's timariotic system was different from the feudal system in Europe. Turkish timar owners' power was limited and less burdensome to the villagers. It only existed to the extent that the Sultan tolerated and allowed it.

Since the 15th century, resettlements of Christian populations have taken place largely. They were between regions of the Empire and the Ottoman-occupied areas in the Balkans to areas under the control of the European Catholic States. Sometimes, they were permanent, others temporary, sometimes legal, but usually uncontrolled and involved many people.[93] In growing numbers, Greeks resettled in mountainous areas, and this trend continued within the 17th century. These movements were necessary for Greeks wanting to move away from the Muslim-inhabited centers of cities and avoid the hefty taxes imposed on farmers.[94] Christians' land ownership percentage in mountainous areas was considerably higher than in the plains dominated by Muslims. Mountainous communities developed a self-sufficient economy with agricultural and craft production. The inaccessibility of regular Ottoman troops to rocky territory provided them a setting for some autonomy and safeguard of their nationality and traditions.

---

[93] The Muslim Presence in Epirus and Western Greece, p.293.
[94] K. Moskof: National and social conscience in Greece, 1972 (in Greek).

The Balkans were an impoverished region, and the food produced locally was inadequate. The villagers, however, avoided trading with money and preferred self-sustenance with some bartering, wherever and whenever needed. The community's economic characteristics were self-sufficiency, self-consumption, low money economy, and small commercialization.[95]

Gradually, as time passed, the money economy era began, and an early form of capitalism emerged, as did the organization of a new Ottoman state. The weak Christian villagers were confronted by the landowners and the Ottoman state's central administration, who collected taxes more efficiently using modern methods. From that perspective, one could reason the emergence of mass nationalism in the Balkans in the context of these dramatic economic and social developments.[96] Greece was the first to rebel in 1821 against the Ottomans, claiming freedom, and succeeded, with its allies, Britain, Russia, and France, to gain its independence in 1832.[97]

By the 17th century, the Ottoman Empire had realized that it had begun to weaken and that the great European States had surpassed it in all areas. The Ottoman leadership introduced some reforms in response to a series of defeats. During the reign of Mahmud II, one of the most important was the abolition of the Janissaries' body. This military branch, over time, had lost its status and turned into a hotbed of constant uprisings. It had become a state in its own right.

---

[95] V. Filias: Ibid., p. 14.
[96] Mark Mazower: The Balkans, 2000, p. 39.
[97] Vassilis Moutsoglou: The Greek Revolution of 1821, the transition from slavery to freedom, Amazon, 2020.

The reform in the Empire continued in 1829 with the imposition of the European suit and the European military uniform. The Fez replaced the chariques. It was mandated for Muslims to wear red Fez and Christians black. However, women and priests were permitted to wear their traditional costumes. The westernization of Constantinople spread rapidly, starting in the district of Pera, a renowned Greek neighborhood and headquarters of many European embassies. In 1836, the Ottoman Empire established a Ministry of Foreign Affairs, in the western sense of the term. The reforms of Tanzimat proclaimed at the Garden of Roses in 1839 guaranteed the right to life for non-Muslim nationals of the Empire.

THE 19th CENTURY

The century began with the implications of the French Revolution in international relations. Napoleonic Wars were a series of Napoleon's campaigns to extend its territory or against states that had turned against him. These wars resulted in the dissolution of the Holy Roman Empire. Further, they contributed to the birth of modern nationalism in Germany and Italy, creating nation-states in the second half of the 19th century.

Napoleon took over a chaotic republic to turn it into a state with a stable economy, a structured bureaucracy, and a strong army. In 1805, Russia and Austria attacked France, but Napoleon defeated them in Austerlitz. However, Britain beat the joint French–Spanish fleet in the Battle of Trafalgar (October 21, 1805. Later, Napoleon defeated Prussia and the Russians, who attacked him in 1807. Intending to isolate Britain economically, Napoleon invaded the Iberian Peninsula in 1808 but met the reaction of the Spanish and Portuguese armies. Finally, with the support of Britain, Iberians achieved the eviction of France from the Peninsula in 1814.

Meanwhile, the ban on British ships to approach France-controlled ports has led Russia to an economic recession and subsequently to the need to violate the "Continental System." Napoleon attempted in 1808 to massively invade Russia. It resulted in the dissolution and withdrawal of the "Great French Army." Emboldened by this failure of Napoleon, Prussia, Austria, and Russia attacked and defeated France in Leipzig in 1813, invading Paris. After Napoleon's return from Elba, where he was exiled, the Allies, who in the meantime had set new frontiers in Europe with the Vienna Congress, defeated him again at Waterloo in 1814. Thus, the Empire of

Napoleon suffered a complete military defeat by the unified European forces, resulting in the restoration of the Bourbon monarchy in France.

Geographically, this was a victory for the central land Powers. Still, the Napoleonic Wars had another direct result. Being a naval power and controlling its overseas colonies, the British Empire became the world's most significant military force in the next century. Pax Britannica was thus started. From a broader perspective, the Napoleonic Wars might have been an attempt to unify Europe under the scepter of Napoleon since the continent's geography was constantly pushing toward unification.

With the Chaumont pact in March 1814, the allies Austria, Britain, Prussia, and Russia had guaranteed, collectively and individually, the future of Europe's "territorial and political status" that would result from a future agreement. However, in the aftermath of the wars against Napoleon, authoritarian regimes were established in many countries of Europe. After the Vienna Conference (1815), which attempted to establish order in Europe following the previous wars, the major European conservative Powers formed a dispute settlement system. This aimed to safeguard their powers, confront revolutionary movements, weaken nationalist forces, and secure the Balance of Power. The "Vienna System" established by the victorious Powers (against Napoleon), the Kingdom of Prussia, the Empires of Austria, Russia, and Britain, functioned for only a few years and was expressed in two forms, the Holy Alliance and the Quadruple Alliance. Although it had territories in the Balkans, the Ottoman Empire was not invited to participate in the Vienna Conference or the subsequent Vienna System regarding the European order. The reason was that it had not been involved in the Napoleonic Wars; besides, it was a Muslim State and, therefore, a "non-European Power." Consequently, the European Powers considered that it could not be part of the solution in Europe.[98]

The Holy Alliance was founded on September 26, 1815, by Russia, Prussia, and Austria at the Czar's initiative to protect the Christian social values and the traditional monarchy. It had no political significance and was merely an expression of "noble" aspirations. Nevertheless, in the coming years, the Holy Alliance embodied the odious European system of the Chancellor of Austria Metternich - with the ulterior motive of conspiring against the freedom of European peoples. Britain did not participate in the Holy Alliance; British foreign minister Lord Castlereagh described this alliance as an act of supreme mysticism and foolishness.[99] Nevertheless, Britain joined the Quadruple Alliance, which later evolved into a quintuple with the addition of France in 1818 and became politically more influential.

On the contrary, the Concert of Europe that followed the Vienna Conference did not result from contractual arrangements but was formulated with international practice through the sway of the states of the European "Directorate." Nevertheless, the most crucial decision-making criterion in foreign policy, namely, to ensure that leaders continue to hold on to power, prevailed. The "principle of legality" sanctioned at the conference in Vienna (1815) regarded the maintenance of the territorial status quo in the context of the Balance of

---

[98] S.Th. Laskaris: The diplomatic history of Greece 1821-1914 Athens 1947, p.7 (in Greek)
[99] S.Th. Laskaris, Ibid., p.7

Power. The ethnic principle was not only ignored but was systematically spurned.[100]

Through the European order, i.e., the Balance of Power system, the Congress of Vienna brought long-lasted peace to the continent. Liberalism and nationalism spread in the continent, delivering a blow to "monarchical" states and empires. On the other hand, the French occupation of Spain had weakened Spain's authority over its colonies, giving rise to revolutionary movements to create nation-states in Latin America.

During the Napoleonic Wars, the principles of enlightenment that had acquired a political influence with the French Revolution were broadly disseminated, and the national conscience of European peoples began to develop. The path towards creating independent states by nations with a commonality of language, cultural, and racial characteristics, in most respects also of religion, was now inevitable. Soon, a diversification of interests, with the awareness of a national community and the nation's shared fate, started to appear. This came about through independence struggles establishing nation-states in cases of success. Nevertheless, no proper definition of "nation" existed yet.[101]

Due to its cultural and economic development, Europe acquired world political power in the 19th century. In the first years of the century, the principle prevailing in international –European– relations was the pursuit by each state individually, exclusively of its national interest. Each state was taken as a unit. Those units were in

---

[100] Vasilis Moutsoglou: The criteria in international politics, Athens, 2015, p. 31 (in Greek)

[101] G. Zotiadis: Political and diplomatic history of the New Era, 1973 p. 81 (in Greek)

constant political and economic competition in a game perceived as a zero-total sum, i.e., one's profit was the loss of its opponent. However, after the Vienna Conference in 1815, the Balance of Power system was restored based on ethical and legal principles.

According to Richard Haas, the European Understanding (Concert European) was the most successful attempt to shape and maintain a European order.[102] The Vienna conference system has broadly defined international relations for almost a century and set the basic rules for global behavior. Moreover, it provided a model for collective security management in a multipolar world.

Gradually, before the end of the 19th century, Europe returned to the practice of exerting political sway by each state individually.[103] Germany and Russia, both continental Powers, were forced to engage in the affairs of Europe by participating in the system of Balance of Power. Britain is a naval force; it prides itself on never being possessed by a foreign army. In any case, it felt compelled to control the opposite coast and intervene whenever the composition of the forces there thought it constituted a threat.

The borders in Europe had been mutable until the end of the Second World War. However, after the Vienna Congress, the first geographical division among countries became apparent in Europe. In particular, the borders between Austria, Germany (Prussia), Russia, and Poland have changed many times.

---

[102] Richard Haas was the President of the Council on Foreign Relations, USA.
[103] H. Kissinger: Diplomacy,1994. σ.22, 30.

The case of Poland is indicative. In 1772, Poland's efforts to reform led to its First Division among Prussia, Austria, and Russia. In 1793, after the Polish-Russian War, Russia and Prussia, not accepting the existence of Poland, proceeded on the Second Division. Moreover, after an uprising, they moved on to the Third Division, effectively ending the continuance of Poland. In 1807, Napoleon re-founded the Polish state as the Duchy of Warsaw after a successful Polish uprising against Prussia. However, after the defeat of France, the Vienna Congress in 1815 distributed Poland again between Russia and Prussia, while only the Galician region and the free city of Krakow remained culturally Polish. In 1830, a new Polish uprising expelled the Russian garrison from Warsaw. Still, no party supported the Poles in the ensuing war, and consequently, they were defeated. The Prussian army suppressed a new revolution during the Spring of Nations in 1848. Russia suppressed the uprising of 1863. However, this was not an Ottoman type of harsh repression. Despite political repression, Poland proceeded with its industrialization and reforms within its occupying states, particularly in Greater Poland, Silesia, and Eastern Pomerania, which was under the control of Prussia. After World War I and a successful uprising in 1918, the Second Republic was founded in Poland.

In the Balkans, the borders began to change after 1821. For the European forces involved, the Greek Revolution was an affair in which geography and geopolitics were crucial. The system in the region was bipolar with the conflicting aspirations of Russia and Britain, with the first wanting to gain free access to the Mediterranean and the second to prevent it, using as a lever, mainly the Ottoman Empire. Britain was bound to Greece's independence only when it realized that the

Ackerman agreement constituted an approach between the Russians and the Ottomans, which should be undermined according to the British strategy. The "duty" of the Ottoman Empire from the British perspective was precisely the Ottomans' rivalry with Russia. On the other hand, through its close relations with Mehmet Ali's Egypt, France had dominated the eastern Mediterranean, creating an unacceptable situation for the British and the Russians. Ibrahim's eventual victory in the Peloponnese and his permanent stay there would give Egypt a dominant position in the region of the eastern Mediterranean.

London's foreign policy during Gladstone's ministry was characterized by some isolationism of Britain concerning European issues until the mid-1870. This policy climaxed with the lack of response to Germany's unification in 1871, overturning the Balance of Power. Disraeli, who succeeded Gladstone, worked more effectively for the British policy interests and tried to deal with Russian gains against the Ottoman Empire in the Balkans by attempting a renegotiation at the Berlin Conference.

Starting from the mid-19th century, the movement of Pan Slavism, the goal of uniting all the Slavs in the Balkans, emerged. It took various forms in various Slavic countries, resulting in the unification of their respective nations. This movement evolved similarly to Pan-Germanism and the Italian unification movement.[104]

---

[104] Italian unification, the Risorgimento, was the 19th century political and social movement that resulted in the consolidation of different states of the Italian peninsula into a single state. Precipitated by the revolutions of 1848, reached completion in 1861, when Rome was officially designated the capital of the Kingdom of Italy.

Russia used Pan-Slavism as a means of creating a unified Slavic state under Russian sovereignty. It was a pretext for the Russian conquest of the Balkan Peninsula and descent to the "warm seas," i.e., the Mediterranean. An obstacle to Russia's plans was the Ottoman Empire, assisted by the Western Powers that reached the point of warfare in 1853 with the Crimean War.

The staggering Ottoman Empire and the Balkans territories were a crucial geographic area in which competition among the principal European Powers occurred in the second half of the 19th century. However, Britain and Russia continued to have conflicting interests as far as the Balkans were concerned. Russia was interested in the region ideologically in the name of Pan-Slavism and to ensure greater control of the Mediterranean, while Britain aimed to prevent it. On the other hand, the unification of Italy and Germany obstructed the efforts of Austria-Hungary to expand its influence in Western Europe.

After the Bulgarian uprising in April 1876, Russia waged war against the Ottomans in 1877. With a rapid advance, it defeated Turkey, reaching the gates of Constantinople. With this victory and the ensuing Treaty of St. Stephen (1878), Russia occupied almost all the European possessions of the Ottoman Empire. The Ottomans were forced to acknowledge the independence of Montenegro, Romania, and Serbia. Russia created the Great Principality of Bulgaria as an autonomous vassal to the sultan state, expanding its sphere of influence and prohibiting other Powers' influence there. Furthermore, the new administration of Thessaly and Epirus would be under the control of Russia. Besides, Russia took under its control areas in the east of the Black Sea and Armenia, imposing its military superiority everywhere in the Ottoman Empire.

According to London, the Treaty had cut off the land road of the European forces to Constantinople. As a result, the influence of Britain had been reduced, even though it was the only naval force that could reach the Ottoman capital by sea. Furthermore, the British considered that the terms of the Treaty of St. Stephen, to which the Ottoman Empire had been forced to consent, left Ottoman Constantinople without a strategic depth of defense. The situation created was unacceptable to the British. Britain had already threatened Russia with a new war (after Crimea) if it occupied Constantinople. Moreover, France did not want any other power to control the eastern Mediterranean or the Middle East, where both itself and Britain had colonial and commercial interests.

All European forces wished to avoid war, but Britain believed it would be inevitable if the Treaty of St. Stephen could not be circumvented. As the strongest continental nation after the Franco-Prussian War of 1871 (in which it occupied Alsace-Lorraine), and without significant direct interests in the settlement, Germany was the only power that could mediate in the Balkan Issue. Austro-Hungary wanted to control the Balkans, while Germany wanted to prevent its allies, Austro-Hungary and Russia, from a war between them. In this direction, the German Chancellor Otto von Bismarck convened a conference in Berlin to discuss the distribution of the Ottoman Balkans between the European forces. At the same time, he tried to maintain the alliance of the Three Emperors (Germany, Austro-Hungary, Russia) to tackle European liberalism. Russia, wishing to avoid a war of European forces against it, gave in to renegotiating the

Treaty according to the British prerequisites, participating in the Berlin Congress of 1878.

The first gain of Britain, resulting from the Berlin Congress, was the downgrade of Russian sway in the Balkans. However, Russia's influence was estimated to be strong in new Bulgaria. However, further south, the belief was now that Russian power would be diminished. The Turks would control the borders in the Balkans through their vanguard. The Kingdom of Greece, according to London, with the expanded territory and increased influence in the Balkans, would ensure the limitation of Slavs. Moreover, Austria's occupation of Bosnia Herzegovina would impede any scope of Russia beyond the Balkans. It could extend a considerable economic and political influence on the Ottoman Empire.

As far as Asia's side was concerned, the British were not satisfied with the Russian profits. Russia took Batumi, the stronghold of Armenia, and succeeded in the border's transfer at the line between Kars and Erzurum. The British feared that the Christian populations of the region could turn to Russia for protection and tried to avert that "danger" with an Anglo-Turkish convention. By undertaking to protect the Asian possessions of the Sultan from any further attack and guaranteeing that the Sublime Porte would make the necessary reforms giving rights to Christians, Britain felt that it gave the "proper" response to the situation created. The Berlin Congress eventually ensured British interests, but the balance in Europe, according to the British, was not restored until after the two world wars.[105]

---

[105] The Times, July 13, 1878.

The 19th century transferred many border and geopolitical problems to the next. The 20th century was destined to resolve them in the bloodiest way.

Baghdad Railway

The conventions of 1899 and 1902 between the Ottoman Sultan and the German Eastern Railways Company on the construction of the Baghdad Railroad constituted an event that stands out because of its importance and the results it brought about in the geopolitical conception of the era. The completion of the construction of the Suez Canal in 1869 transformed the sea-terrestrial-marine medieval way, linking Europe with India to a route exclusively maritime, the realization of the dream of Spanish and Portuguese explorers. Forty years later, the construction of the Trans-Siberian Railroad in 1905 modernized the Northern Overland Route to China and India through European Russia.

Disraeli's purchase of the Suez Canal was the first step in gaining sway over Egypt. This imperialist pursuit cost Britain thousands of lives. It brought the Empire several times to the brink of war with France. It damaged Middle Eastern British diplomacy for forty years. After constructing the Trans-Siberian Railroad, a fight broke out between Russia and Japan. The same happened concerning the Baghdad Railroad and the First World War. At the time of the conclusion of the Baghdad Railway Convention in 1903, the Ottomans controlled Anatolia, the threshold of Asia towards Europe, and the Balkans, Europe's doorstep to Asia. The capital city of Constantinople was the economic and strategic center of gravity between the Black Sea and the Mediterranean. Possessing northern Syria and Mesopotamia, the Sultan controlled the central road of eastern commerce throughout its length, from the Austro-Hungarian border to the Persian Gulf's shores.

The proximity of the Ottoman territory to the Sinai Peninsula and Persia allowed Turkish attacks on the roads to Persia and the Far East. The Sultan's possessions from Macedonia to South Mesopotamia constituted a broad avenue between West and East. This position would be a source of strength for a fair and civilized state. For the Ottoman Empire, it was a source of weakness. Strategically, the Baghdad Railway crossed an area of worldwide importance. However, this area was economically one of the most critically underdeveloped regions globally. Germany's economic and diplomatic rise in the Near East and the emerging power of the Ottoman Empire due to its military cooperation with Germany were not issues other European Powers could overlook.

Russia, seeking to continue its long-term policy, objected to any upgrading of the Ottoman Empire. France was restless with the involvement of another Power in Ottoman economic affairs. It also wanted to promote the political ambitions of its then-ally, Russia. Britain feared for the security of its trade roads with India and Egypt. In this way, the Baghdad Railway exceeded the limits of Turkish-German relations and became an international diplomatic issue. It caused concern not only to Foreign Ministries but to accountants, politicians, and the military, as well as to engineers and banks. Moreover, the Ottoman Government clarified from the outset that the Baghdad railway would serve not only economic but also military purposes.

The German government showed great interest in this project from the very start. The glorious visits of the German Emperor to Constantinople and Palestine, the assignment of the German military and consular personnel to the technical committee overseeing the realization of the project in 1899. The enthusiastic support of the German Ambassador contributed to the success of the decision on the project.

Russia raised objections as early as 1899 when the Sultan announced the assignment of the project to Deutsche Bank. The Russian press complained that this railroad was opposing Russia's vital interests. It argued that the new railway line would be competitive with the railways of the Caspian and Caucasus regions. Thus, it was threatening the success of the original Persian railroad, competing even with the Trans-Siberian. It would hinder the implementation of the Armenia-Alexandretta line that would provide access to the Mediterranean for Russian goods. It would hit Russia's economic interests regarding the Persia and Afghanistan markets and offer Germany advantages. If German funds were to develop the possibilities to produce cereals in Mesopotamia, the revenues of the Russian oligarchs would lessen. Another question raised was that since the oil production capacities of the region were high, according to rumors, they would hit Russia's oil wells profits.

France's questioning of the Baghdad Railroad, in addition to economic, political, and religious reasons, extended to historical issues that affected the opposition to the German intrusion in the Near East. The Sultan's assurances that the project's contract had been entrusted to private companies and not to the German government were not convincing since Germany's state involvement was more than evident.

Although the Baghdad Railway was a project that could, in the view of its initiators, lead to the economic and political recovery of the Near East, it became a source of international competition. It also highlighted the differences between European Powers and contributed to the causes of the World War.[106]

The Macedonian question

For Bulgaria, Serbia, and Greece, the fate of the central Balkan region was a significant problem within the broader Eastern Question. Following national ethnic revolutions in the surrounding areas, Macedonia remained an Ottoman islet with a mixed population that, slowly but steadily, began to realize its ethnicity. They identified either with one of the surrounding nationalities or claimed the existence of a supposedly separate Slav Macedonian or, rather queerly, "Macedonian" ethnicity. The latter came from a part of the geographic region they inhabited.

Macedonia, in the mid-19th century, was an impoverished and ill-governed region. The Ottoman authorities neither wanted nor could impose the order. The uncontrollable killings, looting, and acts of violence were unbearable. The robbery had become a constant regime. The Christian population began to see no solution but to shake off the Ottoman yoke and be incorporated into one of the surrounding states according to ethnicity. Unfortunately, the reforms adopted by the Ottoman government in the second half of the 19th century did not improve the conditions in the region. This result was due to the inability of the Ottoman state to enforce them and the opposition of the Muslim population, who feared that they would lose the privileges they had against Christians.

The Treaty of St. Stephen in 1878 provided for a Great Bulgaria, whose boundaries included Macedonia

---

[106] Edward Mead Earl: Turkey, the great powers, and the Bagdad Railway: a study in imperialism, 1923.

and the Thracian coast in the Aegean. Bulgaria was in Russia's sphere of influence. It mobilized the European Powers, which succeeded in overturning this Treaty by signing in Berlin in July of the same year. This new settlement returned Macedonia to the Ottoman Empire. However, the message on the future of Macedonia was sent. It was received both by the region's population and the surrounding Balkan states. Those states were engaged in an intensive effort to assist their nationals in their struggle for liberation from the Ottoman Empire and their integration into the national body.

A relatively large part of Macedonia's population either did not have formed a national conscience or was of a mutable national conscience. In northern Macedonia, the Slavic linguistic idiom of the community was screened by Bulgaria as proof of Bulgarian ethnicity. At the same time, Serbs raised, albeit less successfully, the similarity with local customs as an indication of the Serb race of the population. In southern Macedonia, Macedonian Greeks constituted a more distinct ethnicity, although many spoke the Slavic idiom, in some cases exclusively. To protect themselves both from the Ottoman administration that hated the newly liberated Balkan nations and from the violent ethnic battles, the inhabitants of the region often resorted to the assertion that they were of "Macedonian" ethnicity. Since 1890, a movement featuring a separate ethnicity began to emerge among the Slavic speakers of the region.

In 1893, a group of predominantly pro-Bulgarian divergence Slav Macedonians founded IMRO, the Internal Macedonian Revolutionary Organization. It intended to shake off the Ottoman yoke. At the same time, a part of it sought the region's annexation to Bulgaria. IMRO functioned as a terrorist (with today's criteria) organization and engaged in violent incidents. In August 1903, during the feast of Prophet Elias (Ilinden), IMRO provoked a revolt called Ilinden against the Ottomans. Ilinden resulted in the slaughter of many region inhabitants by the Ottomans, regardless of nationality, but mainly Greeks. However, as a result, Russia and Austria pushed the Ottoman administration to go ahead with specific reforms to improve the living conditions in the region.

However, Serbia, Greece, and Bulgaria did not suspend their communities' plans to liberate. The local people not only did not believe that the Ottoman administration could carry out measures that would radically improve the lives of the inhabitants but considered that, in any case, they would be temporary. The Balkan states also believed that sooner or later, the Great Powers would intervene to distribute the region to the surrounding states. The terrorism of IMRO, but also the various groups of Serbian or Bulgarian tendencies, as well as the selective Ottoman administration's oppression against Greeks, not only the most hated and feared ethnicity of the Turks but also the most internationally unprotected, led Greece to reinforce their struggle by sending several former officers. Serbia and Bulgaria did the same, creating respective committees and bands. The conflict resulted in an internal war against all, including the Ottoman administration. Many people were murdered and killed, villages destroyed, and mostly Slav speakers migrated to North America.

In the meantime, the Young Turks, a radical reformist group based in the Ottoman Thessaloniki, created the concept of a new nation, the Turkish. Turkism was not considered until then as an ethnicity in the Ottoman Empire; only the notions of Islam and Ottoman existed. For the Ottoman administration, whoever was Muslim was a Turk. The Young Turks put up and opposed the Turkish nation to the different groups in Macedonia without success; frustrated, they chose for the future the way of conflict.

The Macedonian struggle was a peculiar national liberation struggle against other ethnic groups and organizations. Its primary purpose was not the liberation from the Ottomans but their prevalence in Macedonia within the Ottoman administration. This is one of the parameters that shaped the contemporary impression of Westerners regarding the concept of the Balkan and the Balkan people. The violence of the conflict, the bloody result, the disasters, the inability to understand the objectives, and the means used by the parties had an unfavorable resonance in the West, which regarded the Ottoman Empire as a relatively well-off state.

Despite their occasional communications issued, the major European Powers having minorities within their borders had never understood the vast difference between the treatment of their minorities and that of the Christian populations under the Ottoman Empire. Therefore, they could not foresee the fate of Balkan minorities under the Ottomans. Thus, they could not understand the reasons for the struggle to include as large sections of the national community as possible within the national borders of the Balkan states. On the contrary, they believed naively that the ethnic groups could prosper in the Ottoman Empire as minorities.

America

The Atlantic and Pacific Oceans define U.S. foreign policy. The two oceans that divide the USA from Eurasia and the cultural affinity with the more liberal Canada give the impression that it is a peninsula "with a single (supposedly) threat, the demography of Mexico."[107] The U.S. used this geographic "isolation" of the American continent between the two oceans to develop its political influence on a tight embrace with Latin American countries. It reached the point of imposing military dictatorships on them. According to N. Spykman, US power stems from the fact that it is the only superpower controlling the entire Western hemisphere. No other state in the world controls a whole hemisphere.

Moreover, geography does not allow the creation of large states south of Mexico and up to the Amazon. For various reasons, the large countries in the region, such as Mexico, Colombia, and Venezuela, could not develop significant force. The northern part of South America is part of the political-economic sphere of the Caribbean.

Brazil and Argentina are the two largest countries in South America. However, because of Chile's narrow strip of land with the towering Andes separating it from the rest of the continent, the reach of large parts of South America to the Pacific Ocean is limited. North America, the U.S., and Canada consider, in some way, only those two countries. They have at least one common language, English (although French is spoken in Quebec and Spanish in the USA), and shared cultural origin. South of the U.S., the Latin American countries share the Spanish language with variations (except Brazil, which retains the Portuguese). Their cultural backgrounds are a mixture of Spain, Portugal, pre-colonial America, and Africa.

In Canada, in some locations, amid land, the horizon line is visible in a circumference of 360 degrees, as in an open sea. For people from southeast European

---

[107] R. Kaplan: The Revenge of Geography p.97.

countries, it creates the illusion of being in the ocean. Further south in America, the same terrain generally continues in many areas but with a warmer climate. With the natural wealth and the liberal mentality that prevailed, the United States became the most influential country globally, offering freedom and comfort to its inhabitants, though not to all. The difference in growth and size between the U.S. and Canada is due to climatic conditions and low population density. In Canada, immigrants were not very welcome in the past. However, when Canadians realized that migration had positive economic effects, they encouraged immigration to some extent.

Canada followed a policy of multiculturalism. The result was a rapid diversification of the existing Anglo-Saxon social framework and its transformation into a patchwork of Asia, the Caribbean, and the Maghreb cultures. However, in Quebec, French culture was maintained, in part, by enforced measures.

On the contrary, the USA followed the "melting pot" policy until a certain point. This led to cultural homogenization and assimilation of immigrants.

Eventually, a unique American culture was created mainly as a myth and less as a reality. It was called the "American Way of Life." Later, a differentiation occurred, mainly by introducing Latin American culture. Finally, the mass migration of Latin Americans and Chinese to the U.S. led to the establishment of ethnic-cultural societies within the Anglo-Saxon culture, given the inability to assimilate into such different cultures.

The belief that U.S. colonists' destiny was to spread across North America (Manifest Destiny) was commonplace in the 19th century. This oncoming, "inevitable" development was thought to be due to the "special virtues" of the American people and its institutions. From this point to the transition toward the idea of an "obligatory" imperialist policy, the course would be natural. The term "Manifest Destiny" was connected in this way with the U.S. territorial spread between 1812 - when the U.S. wanted to conquer British Canada and expel the English from the American continent- and 1860. As far as the expansion to Mexico is concerned, the concept of "expansion" collided with the idea of "racial correctness" since the Mexicans were considered non-white.

The United States wedged several wars against the British, the Spanish, and the natives, aiming to conquer the whole of North America, including Cuba. The result of their territorial expansion is the current USA. By adapting the same idea, Germans presented their Manifest Destiny - through a misinterpretation of the German Geographer Friedrich Ratzel- as the right of Germany to establish colonies in Asia and Africa. Later the Nazis used this theory to base a request for a broader living space, Lebensraum.[108]

Along with its residents' mentality as colonists who initially sought just a place under the sun and freedom, the U.S. geographic position and its self-sufficiency led to a policy of isolation. Americans, as a euphemism, call this policy non-interventionism. This policy is popular among Americans and their administration, and they revert to it periodically in history. However, whenever they had interests, this policy was forgotten for the good of themselves and, sometimes, of the entire world.

The non-intervention policy of European Powers in America started in 1792, shortly after the anti-colonial

---

[108] Friedrich Ratzel (1844 –1904): He introduced the term Lebensraum with the meaning used by the Nazis.

struggle against the British Empire. During the war between France and Britain, George Washington declared the U.S.'s neutrality, claiming that the 1778 agreement was not applicable. The U.S. was the only significant non-European power of the time that could have a word in global matters. So. it had the luxury of its geographic position, not participating in the Balance of Power system. Instead, it followed a policy of isolation.

The U.S. is entrenched between the Atlantic and Pacific by a relatively friendly country in the north – Canada- and a weak state in the south –Mexico- defeated militarily in 1848. However, the Americans wanted to believe that their foreign policy reflects American society's conviction that the principles of moral behavior apply to international practice in the same way as among individuals. It was an idea opposite to the raison d'etat of Richelieu.

The history of international relations is a synthesis of nations' political, military, and economic power, proven symmetrical. Either a country manages to gather so much potential that it could overbear others by creating an empire, or no state proves so powerful that it can achieve this goal. However, America believes it has never participated in a system of Balance of Power, even though it has benefited from it.[109] These positions are incompatible with the practice followed later by the USA since it seems that the ethical factor has receded due to the necessities of the bipolar system and the aspirations for global influence.

In 1823, James Monroe formulated a doctrine according to which the U.S. would not take part in case of war between the European Powers and on issues

---

[109] H. Kissinger: Diplomacy Ibid., p.p..22,30.

regarding them. The United States would not undertake defense preparations except if its rights were jeopardized. The Monroe Doctrine was considered a policy of opposing the United States on European colonial policy by tackling, starting from 1823, any action of the European states for the control of North or South American countries as a non-friendly action against the United States. At the same time, the U.S. stated that it would not interfere in the existing colonies or the affairs of Europe. The doctrine remained in force with some changes for about a century. Still, the U.S. continued to object to non-American states' involvement in the continent's affairs. With the Monroe Doctrine, the U.S. utilized its geographic position to stay far from Eurasia and be away from the "immoral" European policy of Balance of Power. The doctrine was also the American response to the Russian (Ukase, 1821) declaration banning non-Russian vessels from approaching the shores of Russia and then Alaska. The U.S. goal was to stay out of the sphere of influence of Europeans so that the U.S. could exert its sway without European interference. Great Britain, possessing Canada in the American continent, did not want European Powers like Spain to trade with its former colonies. Thus, its naval forces imposed a blockade between the two spheres of influence.

The American Civil War (1861 – 1865) was fought between the northern states loyal to the Union and the southern states that had seceded from the Union to form the Confederate States of America. The Union never recognized statehood to the Confederation. War broke out in April 1861 when secessionist forces attacked Fort Sumter in South Carolina. However, the Union could not tolerate secession; it would fight even without the attack of the separatist forces. Eventually, on April 9, 1865, the Southern troops surrendered, and the Confederacy collapsed. Three months before the end of the war and after a great deal of political wrangling, slavery was abolished by the 13th Amendment passed by Congress on January 31, 1865, and ratified on December 6, 1865. As a result, the Union gained self-confidence, granted civil rights to the formerly enslaved people, and rebuilt the country.

The non-interventionist U.S. policy continued throughout the 19th century, while the first significant violation was the American-Spanish War (1899). Subsequently, in 1904, Theodore Roosevelt instigated the Revolution of 1904 against the Colombian government to ensure the opening of the Panama Canal. Consequently, the USA gained complete control over the Caribbean and the entire region through it.

GEOPOLITICS OF THE 20th CENTURY

The "theory of the central area (Heartland)" was formulated in 1904 by Halford John Mackinder in his book "Geographic Pillar of History." The central area of the "World Island" (Eurasia and Africa) covers the region from the Volga to the Yangtze and from the Himalayas to the Arctic Circle. According to Mackinder (1919), whoever controls Eastern Europe controls the central area, whoever controls the central area controls the "World Island", and whoever controls the "World Island" rules the world.

The Russian Empire controlled the "central area" at that time. The Arctic ice protected this area in the north and mountains and deserts in the south. Transport with westernmost Europe was difficult; winter and the lack of rail lines prevented intruders. Moreover, the Western powers, allied with the Ottoman Empire, had restricted the expansion of Russia both toward the West and the Mediterranean.

Mackinder considered that the central area could constitute the springboard for world domination in the event of Russia's invasion by a central force, i.e., Germany, or the forming of a Russian-German alliance. The latter could be achieved easily since, by 1917, both countries had authoritarian regimes. They could ally themselves against the democratic countries of Western Europe. Finally, Russia could be occupied by a Sino-Japanese empire. Accordingly, Mackinder excludes North Africa, Eastern Europe, and the Middle East from the central area.

Later, in the decade of 1970, D. Kitsikis introduced the model of the "intermediate area" covering parts of the central area. Russia, Turkey, Greece, the Middle East, North Africa, the Arabian Peninsula, and Iran were included in this area, whereas Germany-Prussia and northeast China were excluded. The model of the central area was geopolitical, while the model of the intermediate zone was geo-cultural. As to their effect, the separation criteria are like those of Huntington. The initiators of the theories considered the role of both the central and intermediate areas as crucial in examining the evolution of world history.

Nicholas John Spykman, one of the founders of the realistic classical school of American foreign policy, considered the importance attributed to Heartland by Mackinder because of its size, geographical position, and supremacy of land forces against naval forces. He claimed that Heartland could not be a focal force in Europe. Russia was then mainly an agricultural society, and the area was restrained - except for the western direction - by geographic barriers to all other courses. Besides, the real conflict was not exclusively between land and naval Powers.

Spykman thought that the Rimland, the strip of coastal land that encircles Eurasia, is more important than the central Asian zone (the so-called Heartland) to control the Eurasian continent. Spykman thought the Rimland was more critical than the Heartland's central Asian region to dominate the Eurasian continent. According to Spykman, "Who controls the Rimland rules Eurasia, who rules Eurasia controls the destinies of the world."

The "Rimland" of the Spykman theory or the "inner ring" of the Mackinder includes most of the world's population and resources. Rimland includes Anatolia, Arabia, Iran, Afghanistan, Southeast Asia, China, Korea, and eastern Siberia, leaving outside Russia and Eastern European countries. These countries are located in the intermediate zone between the land powers and naval forces. However, Spykman opposes the overall grouping of Asian states, considering that areas north of the Indian Ocean differ geographically and culturally from the Chinese regions. In any case, the countries of Rimland do not present any homogeneity. Therefore, it cannot be controlled by a single force. Rimland is located between the Heartland and the naval forces. The countries there are obliged to plan their defenses on both sides. Concerning the supremacy of the naval Powers in peace (trade) and war (navy), it was argued that Spykman's theories resemble those of the American Alfred Thayer Mahan rather than those of Mackinder. Mahan had underlined the importance of the sea for building the power of states.

The 20th century, however, began relatively quiet on the continent with minimal turbulence. Disputes existed, such as Alsace-Lorraine, which, since 1871, was dominated by Germany but vehemently claimed by France. The latter had lost it during the Franco-German War of 1870-71. Despite the quietness that prevailed in general, claims existed in many respects. The Balkan nations sought the liberation of their territories from the Ottoman Empire and Austro-Hungary. The aphorism that minorities in Europe and Anatolia would cause wars was confirmed with the Balkan Wars. One of the primary outbreaks of territorial disputes was between the Ottoman Empire and the Balkans. The Ottoman Empire's proximity to the Balkans and the Middle East qualified its position on the geopolitical scene. Germany sought and achieved an alliance with it to expand its geographic vicinity, including the Ottoman Empire. A result of the Ottoman Empire's political approach to Germany was the railway line uniting Germany with Baghdad, thus extending German sway to the Middle East.

The gunpowder that exploded was of German origin. German nationalism was based on expansionism, considering the German people as the chosen one, the fate of whom was their sovereignty all over Europe. Among the theories was the Proto-Indo-European homeland (Urheimat). German linguist Franz Bopp (1791-1867) incorporated the ideas of the English judge of the East Indies, William Jones, and developed the so-called "Indo-German theory." According to this theory, all European peoples, in addition to the supposed common language, had a common cultural cradle in the north of Europe and common ancestry. A similar theory was expressed a little later by the Turkish Republic of Mustafa Kemal. According to the Turkish doctrine of the Sun Language (Gunes Dil), all people originated from the Turkish race, and all languages from the Turkish language, the mother of all civilized languages (sic).

Mitteleuropa, meaning Middle Europe, is one of the German terms for Central Europe. The idea of Mitteleuropa began to dominate Germany after the revolutions of 1848 when both the Socialists and the National People's Party would adopt this approach. With elements of ethnocentrism and anti-Slavism, but mainly anti-Polish sentiments, Pan-Germanism was spread by the German League. In 1914, in Septemberprogramm, Mitteleuropa became part of the German sovereign policy. The plan professed to set Central Europe under the cultural and economic hegemony of the German Empire. The term Mitteleuropa describes a geographical area, but it is not exclusively geographic. According to the historian Jorg Brechtefeld, it is a political term, such as a reference to Europe or the West. The German Chancellery's plan of September 1914 (after the start of the war) provided an economic union of Central Europe. It would include France in a customs federation of Central Europe. The primary step in this process was the occupation of Belgium, which would constitute the first seaport of Mitteleuropa. Part of the different projects drawn up by the Pan-Germanists was the occupation of the area west of Alsace-Lorraine, rich in iron ore.

Since the 19th century, the German expansionist policy Drang Nach Osten, "Passion for the East," was turned against the Slavic lands east of the German state, bringing forth historical issues from the Middle Ages. The superiority of the German tribe and the German civilization was at the core of German nationalism. This policy foresaw violent population movements to open space for German colonizers targeting demographic alteration of the area.

The German idea of Lebensraum, the living space, concerns the colonization policies and procedures in parts of Europe, including a large part of Russia in the East and the current Benelux, Denmark, and Scandinavia in the West. The idea began to prevail in Germany starting in 1890, and the pursuit of this target lasted until 1945. In the First World War, it was a geopolitical goal of Imperial Germany as the nucleus of the German national expansion program. The current Turkish "Blue Sea" policy is the analog of Germany's Lebensraum in the Aegean.

Western Power's interventions in the Balkans

The Balkan Peninsula has always been a field of intervention and involvement of the Great Powers, although their character in each period is different. The Great Powers assisted in the liberation struggles of the Balkan peoples, though their interventions afterward exclusively served their interest. At the same time, the Balkan countries failed, contrary to the Ottoman Empire, to use this interest for their economic development. Since the 19th century, the Great Powers enforced their political guardianship to the Balkan states. However, the latter could eliminate, at least, their direct political consequences. The Europe of the 20th century, with a political philosophy of raid, had turned the Balkan states captive: Greece to England, Bulgaria, Romania to Russia, Serbia to Austria-Hungary, and Albania to Italy.

At the beginning of the 20th century, the Great Powers advocated their intervention policy, arguing that powerful countries with "general interests" should prevail over the "limited interests" of the small Balkan states.[110] For example, the value of commercial roads and seaports had been proven by the possibility of Serbia using the port of Greek Thessaloniki to escape the blockade imposed on it by the monopolistic interests of Austria-Hungary. However, the economic attention of the Powers did not focus on the barren Balkans. Instead, they viewed them as a bridge, a transport route, a field of transition to the wealthy East, instead of an area for economic investment. On the contrary, the Western European countries perceived the Ottoman Empire, notably Constantinople, with a broader scope for investment. They exploited it rapidly through the exclusive privileges and navigation rights they were granted. However, they created conditions of exhaustive exploitation that provoked a political response even there.

As a multinational state, Austria understood the dissolution of the Ottoman Empire as the beginning of its partition in the nations that composed it and, therefore, took an opposing stance. After founding the Balkan states,

---

[110] Jacques Ancel : Peuples et Nations des Balkans, Paris, 1930.

it tried to control Serbia and Romania through political alliances and economic agreements. The intensity of this effort eventually led to the First World War and the dissolution of the Austria-Hungary Empire. At the time, Germany did not have direct political interests in the Balkans but supported the aspirations of its ally, Austria. It apprehended the Ottoman Balkans as a business area and promoted the Eastern Railroad project that crossed the Balkans to reach Baghdad through Constantinople. However, it did not omit to exploit the Romanian market in terms of monopoly. As it had no interest in the existence of any state in the Balkans, Germany wholeheartedly supported the integrity of the Ottoman Empire. In addition to the military aid, it proceeded on several investments there. Italy had expansionist tendencies towards the Balkans, especially Albania, Greece, and Dalmatia, where its interests clashed with Austria. It succeeded in extending its influence to a significant degree in Albania, although it failed to conquer territories in the Balkans. However, in 1911-12, it defeated the Ottoman Empire and occupied the Dodecanese in the Aegean and Tripoli in Libya.

For Russia, the Balkans were an access route to the warm seas. To this end, it tried to control the Balkan countries alongside its attempt to replace the Ottoman Empire. Russia also attempted to impose a regime of free passage through the straits, only for its ships, if possible. The naval and industrial Britain was interested in acquiring naval and supply bases for its fleet and keeping the sea route free to India in the eastern Mediterranean. Its main commercial interests, however, were in the Ottoman Empire. France, like England, had political and economic interests in the Balkans; it also had several investments in the Ottoman Empire. However, by exporting its culture and ideas, it also made some investments in Greece and Serbia.

The Balkan states managed to escape the surveillance and attention of the Great Powers. They succeeded in understanding among them to implement the shared quest to liberate territories from the Ottoman Empire. As a result, Serbia, Montenegro, Greece, and Bulgaria united and crushed the Ottoman Empire during the Balkan Wars of 1912-1913. The understanding occurred because, among other reasons, they did not have to agree in advance on the subsequent distribution of their territorial gains. However, Bulgaria, which had to face the bulk of the Ottoman army, could not gain what it aspired to and resented. When it turned against its former allies during the Second Balkan War in 1913, Bulgaria was confronted by the Ottoman army again and suffered further casualties.

The pretext for the First World War was the attempt of the Central European Powers to intervene in Serbia, which led Austria to attack Serbia, seeking to cut Russia off the southern Balkans. On the other hand, however, the intervention of the countries of the Entente to force Greece into the war was brutal and armed. After the Greek-Turkish War of 1897, the Italian-Turkish War of 1911, and the two Balkan wars in 1912-1913, another war in the Balkans could be nothing unusual. However, this time, the European conditions had matured. This resulted in a more general reclassification of the balance of powers in the continent. The Balkans certainly was not the cause of the global conflict; it was the pretext.

The First World War

The Great War fundamentally changed the image of Europe, which entered the 20th century only after its end. The Second World War, a consequence of the First, ended the special conditions of the interwar era. It marked the beginning of the post-war bipolar period that lasted until 1990, when the modern era began, the circumstances of which became understood, in turn, after the first decade of the 21st century. In Europe in 1914, the doctrines of the Balance of Power, extreme nationalism, military competition, and the belief that everything was a zero-sum game were dominant. The Balkan Wars of 1912-1913 and their geographical–territorial effects showed that the Balkans' political regime and borders were unstable.

Throughout history, war was considered inevitable; peace was just the interval between the wars. Until the end of the Second World War, despite the efforts of the League of Nations during the interwar period, the law of the jungle regulated international relations. In 1913, there was peace between France and Germany. Still, no one could exclude the possibility that the two countries would be at war in the next year despite their cultural affinity.[111]

The First World War was unprecedented in the number of victims. Contrary to the Second World War, it had rather "ideological" and geopolitical than mere expansionist motivations: the ideology of obsession and a perverse geopolitical perception. In addition, the Septemberprogramm with geography as a motive to be always present and push towards expansion. Germany and Austria-Hungary sought geopolitical benefits, whereas

---

[111] Yuval Noah Harari: Homo Deus, 2016.

France, Russia, and Britain were involved in the war, partly for the sake of their alliances. However, the start of the war may have resulted from bad luck; the war at that time might not have been inevitable. It was a complex mechanism of sequential events and wrong judgments of various governments and military establishments, which did not adequately estimate or realize the ensuing risks.[112] However, regardless of the famous Christopher Clarke's observation, the states did not function as "sleepwalkers" but with clear geopolitical aspirations on the one hand and the perception of risk in case they did not defend Europe against the attack of the Central Empires, on the other.

Before the War, Europe was shaped geopolitically in three zones. In west France, Britain, and Belgium, in central Europe, Germany, Italy, and Austro-Hungary, and Russia in the East. Poland, Finland, and the Baltic states were annexed to it. The role of geography in the formation of alliances was crucial. Territorial claims were not lacking. France claimed Alsace-Lorraine, which Germany had annexed after the War of 1871. Italy coveted the region of Trentino and part of the Dalmatian coast that were under Austro-Hungarian sovereignty. Nevertheless, they were not going to go to war for their claims. On the other hand, Austria-Hungary and Russia claimed territories or influence over the Balkan states, and the war broke out.

On June 28, 1914, when Archduke Ferdinand, the successor of Austria's throne, arrived at the train station in Sarajevo, Europe still lived in peace. Nothing or almost nothing (although the spring was compressed) did reveal what was to come. A few weeks later, Europe was at war. The ensuing conflict had over fifteen million dead and

---

[112] Christopher Clark: *The Sleepwalkers: How Europe Went to War in 1914, 2013.*

three empires destroyed. It radically changed world history and European political geography a hundred years after the Vienna Conference. The Balkans, a region geographically and politically distant from the European centers of power and wealth, seem to have caused an unprecedented global drama for the era. However, it appears that the war was inevitable, even without the assassination of the Austro-Hungarian crown prince; Europeans would find another reason for wedging the war.

Austria-Hungary, i.e., Emperor Franz Joseph himself, believed that the assassination of the Archduke was organized by Serbia's chief of secret services, who supported the independence of Bosnia. The latter belonged to Austria-Hungary. However, Franz Joseph wanted the war, and the Hungarian prime minister's objections could not bend his will. After all, Austria aimed to control Serbia and, following this, Bulgaria to reach the Black Sea. For its part, Russia could not allow such a development that would cut off its way to the southern Balkans.

Germany, an ally of Austria-Hungary, was unhappy with the situation in Europe. Two hostile countries, France and Russia, allied with each other, surrounded it. Regarding Britain, an ally of France, Germany felt competitive and not only because of the colonies. There is evidence that Germany was preparing for the war, even before the conditions that caused it. Apart from its land and sea armaments, significant companies had contracted substantial loans from the U.S., a reason for American unwillingness to enter the war. Russia had to face a geographical problem: the enormous distance between the two fronts it had on the one hand with Germany on the other with Japan. Therefore, it prioritized the construction of means of transport, namely rail trains, namely the Trans-Siberian.

Austria sought and achieved the Kaiser Wilhelm of Germany's partnership in its plans against Serbia. The Austrian ultimatum to Serbia served on July 25, 1914, contained conditions contrary to international law principles considered "inviolable," such as national sovereignty. By this ultimatum, they demanded the participation of the Imperial Government of Austria-Hungary's agents in the fight against the anti-Austrian movement within the borders of Serbia.[113] France, Russia, and Serbia itself regarded the demands as a direct blow to Serbia's sovereignty and the ultimatum as a declaration of war, even though Serbian Prime Minister Pasic, to avoid conflict, tended to accept it. The mobilization of Russia led to the mobilization of Germany. France rejected Germany's request to declare neutrality, claiming its alliance with Russia bound it. Britain also rejected Germany's unofficial proposal not to intervene in exchange for the territorial integrity of France after the war. However, the war had already begun. The German appeal to Austria to stop the advance toward Belgrade remained unanswered. To deal with the vastness of Russia, Germany felt it was strategically right to attack France first, passing through Belgium. This act led Britain to declare war.

The Triple Alliance was composed initially of Germany, Austria–Hungary, and Italy (that remained neutral in 1914) together with the Ottoman Empire, and

---

[113] Although the Austrian demands violated less the sovereignty of Serbia than the terms of the Rambouillet agreement of 1999, that even Henry Kissinger described as provocative, as a pretext to bomb Serbia.

Bulgaria formed the attacking block. The Entente, France, Britain, Russia, and Serbia constituted the opposite camp. Italy joined later during the war (1915). Greece, unable to choose between the two camps or neutrality, was split and occupied by the Entente powers before joining them. However, the geopolitical benefits of such an alliance were clear from the outset. Japan sided with France, releasing Russian troops against Germany. The war continued until the final victory of one of the two blocs, both of which hoped its success would force the defeated adversary to repay the enormous debts created by the war.

The U.S. succeeded in remaining out of the war during the first three years. In addition, when later it declared War on Germany, it avoided becoming a member of the Entente. Reasons for the U.S. participation in the war were assistance to mother nation Britain, various offensive movements against U.S. ships, loans granted to Britain and France, and information on the incitement of Mexicans against them. President Wilson, referring to the reasoning for U.S. involvement in the war, presented the idea of creating a new world order, a general association of nations, the League of Nations, which would provide mutual guarantees of political independence and territorial integrity for all countries.

After the February Revolution and the October 1917 coup, and while the Great War continued, communist Russia virtually ceased to participate in the alliance of Entente. In front of the pressure of the German troops, the Bolsheviks called for a "no annexations – no compensations" treaty. They agreed on a truce on December 15 of the same year. The negotiations for a peace agreement in Brest-Litovsk run almost with no conditionalities from Russia. The talks, however, were adjourned and resumed on January 4, 1918. At the same time, a general advance of the German forces began on the entire front length. Trotsky said unilaterally on February 10, 1918, that the war was over without the conclusion of a treaty or any other consultation. However, on February 18, the Germans began new hostilities with general raids throughout the front. Under the insistence of Lenin, the negotiations were resumed and finally concluded in a peace treaty on March 3, 1918. With the Treaty of Brest-Litovsk, Russia was forced to hand over Karelia, Lithuania, and Poland to the Central Powers and agreed to evacuate Russian troops from Latvia, Estonia, Finland, and Ukraine. The "ideological" war had mutated to conquest, with geography taking over the scepter, albeit not entirely since communist propaganda had also to be dealt with.

The Treaty of Versailles (1919) that terminated the First World War included very unfavorable compensation clauses for Germany. Still, mainly, it was a partition agreement at the expense of the defeated, even though several of the regions cut off from Germany had a majority of German populations. The Treaty broke up Austria-Hungary through the detachment of Czechoslovakia and Hungary. It created Finland, Estonia, Latvia, Lithuania, and Poland, whereas Serbia expanded and became Yugoslavia. Germany handed over Alsace-Lorraine to France. Northern Schleswig, with many German cities, was accorded to Denmark. The Prussian provinces of Poznan and Eastern Prussia were given to the newly created Poland. Poland also took Upper Silesia and West Prussia and a gate to the Baltic Sea (the corridor of Dantzig). Other territories were granted to Czechoslovakia and Belgium. A stipulation of Versailles characterized the rich in coal and steel Saar region as a demilitarized zone. It removed German control of the area to weaken Germany's industries. The result was a queer geographic map, mainly in the case of Germany, split in two, with Eastern Prussia not having territorial continuity with the other part of Germany.

Joseph Stalin took over the leadership of the Soviets as Secretary-General on April 3, 1922. Thirteen days later, the Rapallo Treaty was signed between Germany, under the Weimar Republic regime, and the Soviet Union under the Genoa Treaty. The Treaty was signed on April 16, 1922, in the Italian town of Rapallo. According to the Treaty, the two countries agreed to normalize their diplomatic relations and "cooperate in the context of mutual goodwill in meeting the economic needs of both countries."[114]

Turkish troops, at the time, were fighting against a Greek expeditionary force sent to Anatolia to protect indigenous Greeks from Turkish irregular forces slaughtering them. Eventually was attracted to the center of Anatolia out of a series of mistakes. A few days after signing the Treaty, on April 29, 1922, the Soviet authorities provided Turkey with adequate weapons and ammunition for three Turkish divisions. Four days later, on May 3, 1922, the Soviet government handed over 33 million gold rubles to Turkey.[115] Therefore, the Bolsheviks' military and financial support to Mustafa Kemal's forces began almost immediately after Stalin took over the leadership of the Soviets and signed the Rapallo Treaty with the Germans. Kemal's reinforcement came from Germany through the Bolsheviks. Greece was defeated.

---

[114] German-Russian Agreement; April 16, 1922 (Treaty of Rapallo), Article 5.

[115] Kapur, H., *Soviet Russia and Asia, 1917-1927: A study of Soviet policy towards Turkey, Iran, and Afghanistan*, p. 114

The Second Republic of Poland consolidated its existence after the conflict with the Soviet Union in 1919, stopping the further spread of communism in Europe. Furthermore, Poland succeeded in merging the three regions under the sovereignty of the neighboring states after its successive partitions. Finally, with the Munich Agreement of 1938, Czechoslovakia granted Poland a small area (Zaolzie).

During the interwar period, efforts were spent for peaceful cooperation in Europe with the functioning of the League of Nations and the various treaties concluded. However, particularly in Southeast Europe, the numerous agreements concluded did not end the objectives for territorial alterations. At the end of the World War, the Balkan countries had lost much of their active population. They were financially ravaged, and the prevailing social conditions could not give solutions to the problems in the economic and social spheres. The commitment to democracy weakened through political and social action. During the First World War, the international monetary system based on the gold rule was deregulated. Efforts to reset it during the interwar period failed, intensifying polarization and social conflicts. Finally, the clash among the four empires of continental Europe (German, Hapsburg, Russian, and Ottoman) at the beginning of the century led to their fragmentation, favoring the conditions for the emergence of totalitarian rulers. Economic instability, political fragmentation, imperial aspirations, multinational populations, and demographic imbalance have been the components of the resulting explosive situation.[116]

---

[116] Niall Ferguson, The bloody 20th century

The regimes of the Balkan states reacted to divergent views and instability with a shift towards authoritarianism that was expressed as far-right, especially in Romania and Hungary. Fascism emerged. However, during the interwar period, the interest and direct interventions of the Powers in the Balkan states were lessened as the lines of conflict moved westward. The Balkan countries found the opportunity to indulge in the first attempts to cooperate peacefully.

The Second World War

The League of Nations had not been successful. German nationalism considered the situation created for the country by the Versailles Treaty. The Second World War did not begin as an ideological one but mainly as a war of Germany to conquer and eventually reshape Europe. It was a war primarily about geography and less about Nazi ideology. The winners of the First World War soon forgot the evils of the war wedged by Germany. They proceeded in concessions, bringing forth the hefty compensations imposed on Germany, the country's dismemberment, and the creation of the Danzig corridor. Therefore, it may not be entirely fair to judge Neville Chamberlain unfavorably. He attempted to avoid a bloody second war by rendering territories to Germany, even if no one could predict its vast destructive results. The allies could not realize they were preparing for a new war unless they took preventive measures in time. Knowing the philosophy of German nationalism, they should have done it, but they did not.

On the ideological field, the war on the part of the West was wholly justified. It could not be avoided except for a change in the internal political situation of Germany. However, on the other hand, the West demonstrated apathy regarding the "Night of Crystals" against Jews in Germany. After the Second World War, when Turkey committed, with the same Nazi mentality, pogrom against the Greeks of Istanbul in 1955, Western countries showed the same apathy.

The situation created by Germany's fragmentation and the segregation of Eastern Prussia was considered unacceptable for the German nation that was always driven by visions of greatness. This fact is certainly not an excuse for the emergence of a brutal regime, which many Germans have served faithfully, with murderous fury. Initially, Hitler had stated that he had no claim on the western border of Germany and that he considered Alsace-Lorraine definitively France's territory. He initially focused on Sudetenland and the oppression of the German Sudetes in Czechoslovakia. Germany also paid attention to its colonies that had lost after the previous World War. Although not openly admitted, Hitler apparently had a plan against Poland.

However, the nationalist theories of Karl Ritter's Organic Conception of the State, Living Space (Lebensraum), self-sufficiency, zones of influence (e.g., Monroe Doctrine), and the discrimination of land power - sea power, with Germany being the first (as opposed to Britain) led to an aggressive "geo-strategic" vision of the situation. The Nazis built on these theories the Aryan racism. According to some criticism by the German military general and geographer Karl Haushofer of Nazi methods, the Lebensraum is the reformed colonial imperialism and self-sufficiency. It was a new formulation of tariff protectionism. Nevertheless, as far as the borders were concerned, he claimed these were mutable. However, Haushofer supported the attack on the Soviet Union, having considered it necessary to occupy the center of the

"World Island." Eventually, however, he was executed by the S.S. for his involvement in the assassination attempt on Hitler. As it was left undisturbed, Germany could not but attack Poland to reunite with Eastern Prussia when it felt ready.

Fascist Italy was mainly interested in Ethiopia, while Japan was in Manchuria and Korea, the war with China, and its conflict with Russia. The fascist alliance aimed more at territorial gains and less at safeguarding its ideology. It was mainly against the Communist International (Anti-Comintern Pact concluded between Germany and Japan on November 25, 1936) and its opposition to democracies. The fascists considered their system was better than the others, but contrary to communism, they did not aim to disseminate, at least as a primary concern, as this is inherent in fascism.

Like Germany, disappointment in the loss of territory was also felt by the Soviet Union. However, the initiative for the proposal to sign a non-aggression pact came from Nazi Germany, whose geopolitical views were changing according to war developments. The U.S.S.R. felt abandoned by the Western powers in front of the German threat. So it accepted the proposal in the hope not only to avoid war but to annex certain territories or, with the modern terminology, to "expand its sphere of influence." In Moscow, the Soviet Union and Germany signed the Molotov-Ribbentrop pact on August 23, 1939. In addition to improving the German-Soviet economic relations and the non-aggression pact, it included specific secret appendices. There, it was stipulated that the two countries would parcel out Poland. Except for Lithuania, the Baltic States, Finland, and Romania would pass to the Soviet "sphere of influence."

Britain entered the war clearly for geopolitical reasons, with the element of the old Entente backstage. Britain could not tolerate the dominance of one superpower on the territory opposite the Channel. Indeed, it had fought for this a few years ago. Moreover, the government had explicitly stated that if Germany attacked France, Britain would react, not for sentimental reasons but because its interests dictated this. In this context, it later ignored even the competitive relations it had always maintained against Russia and eventually allied with it against Germany.

By 1937, the U.S. had limited itself to its isolation and pacifism. Still, in early 1938, it realized that it would have to take specific measures due to Japan's stance. Especially after the "U.S.S. Panay" incident, in which the American gunship docked in the Yangtze River near Nanking was hit "accidentally" by Japanese Fire (December 12, 1937), the U.S. became more decisive. The U.S. built its defense on both sides –the Atlantic and Pacific– from which it could be threatened. Particularly on the Pacific side, it had developed an "island policy," organizing its defenses based on its island – possessions, even up to the Philippines. It fortified the Hawaiian islands, especially the Pearl Harbor base, the Pago-Pago base on the island of American Samoa, two stations in Alaska, and the Aleutian Islands in the North Pacific. The Aleutian – Hawaii – Panama Canal was considered a vulnerable triangle. They could deal with Britain and France for their defense in case of a German attack on the Atlantic side. Nevertheless, the U.S. defense plans proved ineffective.

However, the U.S. initially opted for a non-interference policy. In a speech in 1940, President Roosevelt presented that those who believed that the U.S. could be a lone island in a world dominated by the philosophy of power were deluded. The war, however, was only declared after the attack on Pearl Harbour.

Hitler applied the Drang Nach Osten Policy to Germanize Central and Eastern Europe regions. To exterminate the Slavic peoples and replace them with Germans, it occupied Poland, the Baltic States, Belarus, Ukraine, and areas of European Russia. The Eastern General Plan provided soldiers – peasants in a demarcation line to enhance security. However, the plan did not go far because of the reluctance of Germans to settle in these areas.

Initially, the Western democracies did not present ideological opposition to the fascists; they did everything they could to avoid the conflict despite Hitler's contempt for "democracies." Their reaction to fascist aggression was due to geopolitical and not ideological reasons. However, the German savagery, the realization of Nazi policies by the Westerners and their criminal plans and actions, and finally, the Holocaust of the Jews turned the conflict into an ideological one.

On July 7, 1937, Japan invaded China, starting World War II in the Pacific. Under Germany's pressure, on March 14 – 15, 1939, the Slovaks declared their independence and established the Slovak Republic. The Germans occupied the rest of Czechoslovakia, violating the Munich Accord, and created the Protectorate of Bohemia and Moravia. Germany and Austria united on March 12, 1938, after the annexation of Austria into Nazi Germany, an act referred to as Anschluss Osterreichs. On March 31, 1939, France and Great Britain guaranteed the integrity of Poland's borders. On April 7 – 15, 1939, fascist Italy invaded Albania and annexed it, rendering it responsible for Mussolini's acts. On August 23, 1939, Germany and the Soviet Union signed the non-aggression pact and a secret supplementary protocol, dividing Eastern Europe into "spheres of influence." On September 1, 1939, Germany invaded Poland, starting World War II in Europe. Two days later, respecting their guarantee for the Polish border, Great Britain and France declared war on Germany. On September 17, 1939, the Soviet Union invaded Poland from the east. With a Blitzkrieg, Germany attacked Western Europe and occupied it. Churchill said Britain would fight everywhere never surrender. Italy attacked Greece on October 28, 1940, using its bridgehead in Albania.

On the part of the fascist alliance, it was purely an offensive war for conquest, a war on geographical issues. A German attack against all European countries not drafted with the fascists or not adhering to the same ideals (such as Spain) ensued. All the democratic nations of Europe had succumbed to the forces of the Axis. Between 1940 and 1941, Britain and Greece were the only countries fighting on behalf of the free world. U.S.S.R. participated in the war only after the German attack against it on June 6, 1941. The United States was forced to enter the war by counterattack when Germany and Italy declared war against it on December 11, 1941. Greece was eventually defeated by the combined forces of Germany and Italy and was occupied by both countries and their ally, Bulgaria. During the German occupation, the leftist groups in Greece dominated the partisan movements.

Germany could not win the fight in North Africa and was defeated by Russia. Although the adverse conditions in Russia were known, this fact did not hinder its conduct and eventually brought about the defeat of the Nazis. Hitler was defeated by geography and climatic conditions both in Africa and Russia. Napoleon had the same fate in his campaign against Russia for the same reasons. On the other hand, geography the sea borders of France, did not save Hitler; they did not prevent the Allied invasion of Normandy on June 6, 1944. Geography has a role, but it is not always decisive.

The use of the atomic bomb was not only a cause for the immediate surrender of Japan. It caused an international surprise at the possibilities of the new weapon, which would permanently "abolish" geo-strategy. According to the diplomatic reporter of the Reuters Agency in Washington (1945), "Following the discovery of the atomic bomb, the decisions of Potsdam, Tehran, and Yalta on military issues should be considered obsolete. Security will not depend in the future on the control of the Straits or the Canal of Suez. The occupation of a port or acquiring a border on a river or mountain will no longer provide strategic advantages.

The defeat of the Axis forces did not result in significant territorial changes. Italy lost its territories in Africa and the Dodecanese, which was liberated. At the same time, the most considerable territorial profits favored Poland, which was "transposed" toward the West. Most of the demographic and cultural changes Germany's eastern policy brought about were overthrown. The German populations east of the Oder-Neisse line, indigenous or settlers, were expelled in 1945-1948, based on the Potsdam Conference's decisions. Eastern Prussia was shared between Poland, Lithuania, and Russia, and the respective ethnicities colonized it.

This time, the Western winners of the war were lenient towards defeated Germany. In this case, they introduced a new institution, the trial of the defeated opponents, criminals. They separated the Nazi ideology and the German national idea from the German people, which was principally responsible. The communist threat and the Soviet national plan led to this development.

The departure of the Germans from the world scene left the field open for the U.S.S.R. in all the Balkans, except Greece, where the vital interests of Britain were at risk. The democratic forces of the Greek people, with the help of Britain and the U.S., managed to repel the communist attack against it. The ideological affinity of the northern Balkan states and the confrontation between the two blocs, on the one hand, imposed cooperation. On the other hand, it did not allow claims that could easily lure the world, once again, into a generalized conflict. There has been silence in Europe and the Balkans for over forty years, imposed by the Cold War and the doctrine of mutually assured destruction (MAD).

The role of the United Nations in preserving world peace or order is negligible. The two superpowers looked to their interests, and smaller countries did the same. Nuclear terror secured world peace, but the world order was not guaranteed at all; smaller-scale conflicts continued unabated.

The post-war period in the Balkans

The U.S.S.R. was able to set under its influence all Eastern Europe. However, it missed Greece, which would finally acquire its storied access to the Mediterranean. It is naïve to believe that Stalin would respect agreements with the Western block. As soon as he considered it appropriate, he allowed the Communist Party of Greece (K.K.E.) to commence martial operations against liberal and democratic Greece. Under the guidance of its General Secretary Zachariadis, the Party was ready to abstain from the 1946 elections. The goal of the Soviet Union that was initially embraced by the K.K.E[117]., among others, was an independent communist Macedonia. This communist state would cover the entire geographic region of Macedonia, despite the will of Greek Macedonians.

Moreover, the Slav-Macedonians considered the Greek Civil War, mainly against Greece, a "liberation" struggle. Independent Macedonia would cut off Greek Thrace and leave it between Bulgaria and Turkey, with communist Bulgaria possibly prevailing. Northern Greece would remain isolated and might be rendered to Albania for geographical balance. Greece would probably stay at its pre-1912 borders.

Greece was able to cope with the impending danger. The communists' plans failed because of the Allies' assistance to Greece. At the same time, Yugoslav's Tito and communist Albania interrupted their assistance to the Greek communists. For Yugoslavia, the reason for interrupting aid was the alienation between Moscow and Belgrade. Tito realized that the plan for an "independent" Macedonia (under the control of Belgrade) was no longer an object for the Greek communists.

Turkey could not be considered a reliable ally for the Western democracies (at both the World Wars was not at their side). Greece's geopolitical position as a pro-western Mediterranean country was critical. Its eventual acquisition by the central powers would lend them control of the "World Island." If Greece could not present an adequate resistance to communists and fell into the "sphere of influence of the U.S.S.R., the outcome of the Cold War might be different.

Greece has a strategic position in the center space of the three continents: Europe, Asia, and Africa. Suppose

---

[117] Greek Communist Party

the U.S.S.R. won the civil war in Greece. In that case, Turkey might have been cut off from the West, and this Euro-Asiatic country's overall national orientations would never really favor the West, even if it wanted to. It could, therefore, ally with the Soviet Union, as Turkey had done during the 1919-1922 war against Greece. The U.S.S.R. would raise a political and commercial wall between the Western world on the one hand and the Middle East and Asia on the other. The West would hardly win in these circumstances the Cold War.

The blockade of Berlin

By the agreement of Potsdam of 1945, defeated Germany had been divided into four geographic zones of occupation among the winners: the Soviet Union, the U.S., Britain, and France. Although half of France was occupied during the war, and a pro-German regime, Vichy, governed the other half during the war, France was eventually considered a winner for geopolitical reasons. According to Yalta's imperatives, the agreement had left the three sectors of Berlin – the American, the English, and the French- deep within Soviet-occupied East Germany. The first victory of democratic countries was the West's response to the blockade of West Berlin in 1948.

The currency in Germany was still the Reichsmark, which speedily collapsed due to the inflationist tactics of the Soviets. When the German Deutsche Mark was introduced in West Germany, the Soviets ruled out all land accesses to West Berlin, demanding the withdrawal of the new currency. Therefore, procuring foodstuff for the population of the three sectors of Berlin was challenging since the agreed access lanes to West Berlin were closed. Furthermore, the daily air transport of such a large food cargo could not be done with the limited number of allied aircraft.

No one, of course, wanted a Third World war. Eventually, through enormous efforts, the Western allies successfully supplied the necessary amount of food, with 1,500 flights daily carrying 4.5 thousand tons. The blockade did not bring the expected results for the Soviets; they were forced to lift it about a year later. This was the first victory for the Western Alliance.

The Middle East and imperialist policies

Their victory in WW2 gave the feeling of omnipotence to the UK, France, and the U.S. They thought they could interfere in the internal affairs of various states in Latin America, the Middle East, or even Greece, with no consequences.

The democratically elected government of Iran, headed by Prime Minister Mosaddegh, sought to audit the documents and accounts of the Anglo-Iranian Oil Company. The Iranian parliament voted to nationalize Iran's oil industry upon its refusal to cooperate. Britain reacted by instigating a worldwide boycott of Iranian oil. However, the embargo did not offer the desired results. The U.K. Prime Minister Winston Churchill and the Eisenhower administration decided to overthrow Iran's government. On the pretext of a communist takeover in Iran, they orchestrated a coup carried out by the Iranian military on August 19, 1953, overthrowing the democratic government. The consequences appeared in the long term with the Islamic Revolution of 1979.

The nationalization of the Suez Canal by the Government of Egyptian president Gamal Abdel Nasser caused the reaction of France and the United Kingdom. Israel, France, and Britain had conspired to plan out an invasion to regain Western control of the Canal and overthrow Nasser. On October 29, 1956, Israel invaded the Egyptian Sinai. On November 5, Britain and France landed paratroopers along the Suez Canal. The Egyptian forces were defeated but blocked all shipping through the Canal. Political and economic pressure from the United States and the U.S.S.R. obliged the attackers to withdraw. As a result of the conflict between France and the U.K., they were humiliated. The U.S.S.R. may have been encouraged to invade Hungary.

The bipolar system and the Cold War

According to the Marxist theory, the proletariat's dictatorship would come with the rebellion of the oppressed working class. However, in Russia, the revolution had the character of a coup d'état organized by intellectuals supported by the military. In the remaining eastern countries of Europe, the change of regimes occurred following outside military action. The Marxist way to enforce the dictatorship of the proletariat has not been observed either in China or the other countries of Southeast Asia. However, the Marxist theory and the awe of the "specter haunting Europe" contributed crucially to improving the workers' position in democratic countries. In this respect, the work of Karl Marx is rightly honored. Marx did not seem to have foreseen the situation that arose later in the countries of the "existing socialism."

The conflict between the liberal states and the Communist dictatorships dominated the second half of the 20th century. Geographically, the world was separated in political terms, as "Western" and "Eastern" with some exceptions. Most of the developing countries, democratic or supposedly democratic, who had chosen the market economy but did not want to take part in the two coalitions, were organized as "Uncommitted Nations" in the "Group of 77", actually a dormant coalition of 135 developing countries, designed to promote its members' collective economic interests and create an enhanced joint negotiating capacity in the United Nations. Geographically, these countries are placed in the south and are called somewhat disparagingly by the Westerners as "third world," perhaps not as a third faction about the two warring blocs but in connection with the "Third Order" of the era of the French Revolution.[118]

The main features of the Third World countries are their relative economic weakness and their desperate search for a solution to the primary issue of the choice of the model of development. The Uncommitted Nations have been a crucial field of controversy between the two poles of the world system, sometimes at the edge, as it happened in Cuba and the Middle East. Moreover, the first and decisive defeat of the Eastern Bloc is recorded in the domain of the Uncommitted Nations, a large part of which was gradually won over by the United States.

The Cold War era has distinctive features: the clear geographic and ideological line separating the West and East coalitions and the entrenched perception of a direct threat against the US and the West. Western Europe believed that the Soviet Union and its satellites threatened them and their interests in the Middle East and Asia. This perception of the Soviet-communist threat and the ensuing reaction of the US created a bipolar global system. This system was dominated by the two major countries that won the Second World War.

---

[118] Jean-François Couet, Régine Lignieres: Pays Sous Developpes, Hâtier, Paris, 1979.

In addition to the military threat it represented, the Eastern Coalition constituted an ideological threat to the Western World of the market economy. The two superpowers, along with several other countries, being in their geographic proximity but not always, formed two stable and powerful coalitions that clashed with violence in the political sphere.

Reacting, the West, i.e., the US, at the armed challenge in East Asia and the ideological–military challenges in Europe, declared a "war." The US response to Asia was not merely ideological but geopolitical against Soviet satellites. The fight was "warm" in Asia, Korea, and Vietnam. The West, represented mainly by the US, was defeated in both cases.

As early as 1945, the US realized that the further spread of Soviet influence should be constrained. They considered, however, that they should not recourse to a philosophy of a power balance system. However, after a few years, the side with a relatively "aggressive" attitude was the West.

On the Atlantic side, the United States allied with the weak Europe just coming out of the war, establishing the North Atlantic Treaty Organization (April 4, 1949). It became the most potent military force in world history. Turkey and Greece surrounded the USSR from the West and the south, complementing its somewhat imperfect encirclement from the east. As a reaction, the eastern states established The Council for Mutual Economic Assistance (COMECON) on January 8, 1949, and the military organization of the Warsaw Pact on May 14, 1955. In 1960, although preserving the communist regime, Albania fled the sway of the Soviet Union. Yugoslavia had dissociated its political position from the USSR. However, the West perceived both countries as members of the Eastern Bloc.

Regarding the economic-ideological dispute, the US established an international economic system that created one of the necessary conditions that led to the final prevalence of the West. The US, based on a series of commercial and financial agreements and assistance programs for its allies, such as the Marshall Plan and the establishment of organizations, such as the OECD and Breton Woods, aimed at shielding the nations against economic misery.

In any case, the war could only be "cold" because of the awareness of the destructive effects of a nuclear war. Under this perception, the US formed the doctrine of prevention of the threat and containment of the Soviet bloc with the ultimate goal, the self-collapse of the communist regime, which was considered incapable of surviving. Through a series of actions and demonstrating similar behavior, the US foreign policy set the objective of convincing Moscow, initially by diplomatic means but ultimately with the military threat, that its course could only lead to the destruction of the Soviet Union. According to the Americans, this doctrine had nothing to do with traditional diplomacy. In the present case, they estimated that no conflict of national interests might be negotiated but that it was an attempt to change the very texture of Soviet society.[119]

However, according to Kissinger, Americans realized in time that the deterrence theory erred in two respects. First, in the regard that the challenges would always be unambiguous, as it was in the Second World War, and second, the communists would passively expect

---

[119] Henry Kissinger: Ibid., p.p..446-450.

the dissolution of their system. Korea was the first case of a complex problem since it was considered in principle outside the US area of direct interest. The Suez Crisis highlighted the range of the geopolitical conflict between the two superpowers, the uprising in Hungary in 1956 and the privatism in this case of the Western world, the Berlin crisis, Cuba, and Vietnam ensued.

In the American way of thinking about international relations, the concept of international law does not seem to be the basis. Other factors such as armaments, geographic elements, size of each country, its global position, determination on foreign policy issues, and the internal aspect prevailed. The US acted with this state of mind, even though they presented their foreign policy as having moral criteria.

The US created a bow of friendly countries on the Pacific coast from Japan, South Korea, the Philippines, and, of course, Australia and New Zealand. In the Near East, they used regimes that had reasons to oppose the USSR. In this direction, the US deployed against the Eastern Coalition a series of bilateral and multilateral treaties of military alliance based on geography, such as the North Atlantic Accord, the Baghdad Pact (afterward CENTO)[120], the Pact of Southeast Asia SEATO,[121] and the ANZUS[122] to address the military threat. To exploit the non-friendly

---

[120] The Baghdad pact was established in 1955 with members Turkey, Iran, Pakistan, Iraq and Britain. Iraq withdrew in 1959. Its seat was transferred to Ankara and it was renamed CENTO, Central Treaty Organization.

[121] Southeast Asia Treaty Organization (SEATO), 1954. Members: U.S.A., France, Britain, New Zealand, Australia, Philippines, Thailand and Pakistan.

[122] The Australia, New Zealand, United states Security Treaty (ANZUS or ANZUS Treaty), 1951.

relations of communist China with the USSR, they transferred in 1971 the recognition of the Government of China from nationalist Taiwan to Beijing. Consequently, the UN Security Council seat was attributed to communist China.

With major economic problems and international commitments but with a significant geographic location and proximity to both the Atlantic and the Soviet Union, Greece and Turkey could not remain outside the scope of the world competition. Each country, for its reasons, was incorporated into the Western Alliance. The only Balkan countries drafted with the West were Greece and Turkey. Nevertheless, only a small part of Turkey is geographically in the Peninsula and Europe. Under the surface, intra-Balkan conflicts continued to exist. In the southern Balkans, the Macedonian issue in its modern version appeared in principle as a difference between Yugoslavia and Bulgaria, to become a problem between Yugoslavia and Greece. Apart from ideological differences between Greece and Albania, the lack of a peace treaty and a profound repulsion of the Albanians towards Greece hindered good neighborly relations. On the contrary, relations between Greece and Bulgaria improved dramatically. Apart from the Macedonian question, Greece maintained good ties with the Uncommitted Yugoslavia.

The US incited military coups and dictatorships to create a ring of "friendly" anti-communist governments of countries belonging to the Third World, mainly in Latin America and Greece (1967), a member of NATO. Those dictatorships were extremely harsh regarding their treatment of communists. A typical example is the anti-communist massacres in Indonesia in 1965 and 1966, with about one million people slaughtered. Those killings were tolerated by the United States, which supported the country's anti-communist military rulers. Such violence allowed right-wing authoritarian regimes to take power and hold on to it. Right-wing movements in Latin America saw Indonesia in 1965 as a horribly "successful" example.[123]

The USSR attempted to break its encirclement by seeking an outlet in the Indian Ocean via Afghanistan. However, the West reacted by using Bin Laden's radical Islamic fighters.[124] Eventually, military competition and the "Star Wars," the American missile defense system, exhausted the USSR economically, resulting in economic and political collapse. The Soviet Union, by a pointless decision, dissolved itself in 1991.

The end of the Cold War

The Cold War, quasi-geographic but mainly ideological, ended unexpectedly in 1989 when the Eastern Coalition collapsed from endogenous political, social, and

---

[123] Vincent Bevins: The Jakarta Method: Washington's Anticommunist Crusade and the Mass Murder Program That Shaped Our World, 2020

[124] In April 1978, the communist People's Democratic Party of Afghanistan (PDPA) seized power in a bloody coup d'état against then-President Daoud Khan. The PDPA proceeded on some social reforms that provoked strong opposition, while also brutally oppressing political dissidents. This unrest caused expanded into a state of the civil war by 1979, waged by Islamist mujahideen against regime forces all over the country. It turned later into a proxy war with the Pakistani government providing these rebels training centers, while the United States supported them through Pakistan, and the Soviet Union sent thousands of military advisers to support the PDPA regime.

economic reasons. Among the factors contributing to this end is the constant pressure of the West in the field of Human Rights. The image of life in the West, transmitted by mass media, also played its role. The U.S.S.R. politically and geographically dissolved when the then-leading group lost its temper under the pressure of a coup attempt. In the face of the collapse of the Berlin Wall and the Eastern Bloc, the Westerners expressed triumphant views, speaking about the "end of the (ideological) history." Still, the society of nations and peoples is not static. It has an ever-renewed purpose according to the dynamic nature of human societies, always seeking a new level of integration. As a producer of history, politics has no terminal point but only integration stations in terms of goals and results.[125] The history of politics, philosophy, ideologies, and morals is a constant process where balances are never final.

The static geopolitical situation of the Cold War, with the confrontation of the two strong coalitions under the menace of nuclear devastation, centrally or by controlled regional conflicts, ended. Mobility characterizes the new situation in geography and the hot, frozen, or creeping conflicts.

In August 1990, after misunderstanding a word from the U.S. Ambassador in Baghdad, Iraq invaded and annexed Kuwait. This illegal act led to military intervention by U.S.-led forces in the First Gulf War. The coalition forces bombed military targets and then launched a short ground assault against Iraqi forces in Southern Iraq and those occupying Kuwait, defeating them.

The United States considered that it had won the Cold War thanks to its moral, military, and economic superiority and that the world belonged to it. It thought it

---

[125] G.K. Vlahos: Political Theory (in Greek).

could run the world by diktat. As a submissive state, Russia became a friend of the West, an equal member of the G-8, the eight industrially most developed countries. NATO expanded into Eastern Europe. Europe enlarged its geographic boundaries and included countries such as Georgia and Azerbaijan. Israel claimed that it is a European country, too; it may belong to the Middle East in the classical geographic sense, but many of its citizens had European citizenship along with the Jews, and its mentality was European. After all, Turkey, a predominantly Asian country in terms of geography and culture, was accepted earlier as a European country for political reasons. Globalization made one more leap forward.

However, the end of the bipolar system did not bring about the "end of history." The U.S. dominated world politics as a single pole only for a short time. The system became multipolar. The number of communist and pro-communist countries fell drastically. The proliferation of South American and African countries with elected leaders did not signal their turn toward democracy.

Eliminating the threat represented by the competition between the two Powers allowed the manifestation of ethnic and religious conflicts, often with Western responsibility. Liberalistic movements, usually in the form of Non-governmental Organizations, in the context of individual and Human Rights, made a dynamic appearance. They mostly acted in cases where Western interests were not affected, and sometimes, they became their instrument.

The dissolution of federations such as Yugoslavia or the Soviet Union, with Western "contribution," resulted in a division of territories among the federative nations. The division was unjust as the federations were not created to be dissolved in their constituting parts. In the context of the federal structure of the U.S.S.R., Crimea, inhabited by Russians, was donated to Ukraine, and Armenian-inhabited Nagorno Karabakh was given to Azerbaijan. Some federative states in Yugoslavia were given disproportionately large areas. However, these "injustices," before the dissolution of the country's federal structure, did not have much importance. As the nucleus and custodian of the Yugoslavian state, Serbia reacted to its demise, as it was historically deterministic. It opposed the military intervention of the West militarily.

The end of the West glory of 1989 occurred when the biased U.S. policy in the Middle East led to the savage attack on civilians at the Twin Towers in New York. Geography was set aside; the asymmetric threat of terrorism concerned people in all geographic lengths and widths of the earth. The U.S. was obliged to attack Afghanistan, demanding the surrender of Bin Laden.[126] Despite the objections of their European allies, and in essence, without a justified reason, it also attacked Iraq, supposedly because Saddam possessed weapons of mass destruction.[127]

---

[126] In October 2001, the United States attacked Afghanistan to remove the Taliban from power after they refused to hand over Osama Bin Laden, the prime suspect of the September 11 attacks, who was a "guest" of the Taliban and was operating his al-Qaeda network from Afghanistan. The U.S. and U.K. forces bombed al-Qaeda training camps, but they did not hand over Bin Landen.

[127] On March 20, 2003, a United States-organized coalition invaded Iraq under the pretext that Iraq had failed to abandon its weapons of mass destruction program supposedly in violation of U.N. Resolution 687. Many European countries opposed the military action as having to do only with the U.S. plans to dominate the oil-rich

The clash of the Western and Eastern Blocs in the second half of the 20th century did not only occur in the field of economic system communism - capitalism, or the system of governance, liberal democracy, or dictatorship of the proletariat, but in the area of the formed mentality and ideology of the peoples of the two blocs. The dominant ideology in the world on the verge of the 21st century was the Western. Whether conventional or merely ideological, the Western Coalition seemed to have prevailed fully. The peoples of Western Europe and North American countries expressed themselves with ideological affinity. They are of a common culture formed in the last millennium, their same religion, origin from the same geographical area, and their joint, overwhelming victory over the Eastern Coalition in the 20th century.

The principles of ethics and justice are seemingly prevalent in Western societies. Still, these same principles, as expressed in the context of the conventional foreign policy of the Western states, appear immersed in a strong connotation of "interest", sometimes with a short-sighted perspective and narrow-hearted calculations. The "interest" is built in the context of a complex process with pluralistic and chaotic characteristics under the influence and reaction of various factors, which affect each other at multiple levels. Following a public debate with the participation of the media, the final presentation of the issues often appears as distorting the truth. Westerners' principal divergences in the perception of issues appear to be the differentiation in the standards of examination of each case, the falsification of the data, the selective

---

region, but eastern European countries condone it. United States' claim was based on documents provided by the CIA and the British government that was proved to be wrong.

memory, and especially the stereotypes rooted in the consciences.

The variance of views regarding internal and external issues led to stricter criticism since the Cold War was partly won, thanks to Western society's moral supremacy.

THE BALKANS

The geographical notion of the Balkan Peninsula does not always coincide with the perception of the term Balkans. This term has different content in every historical era, both as designation and geographic space. As a designation, it sometimes includes the notion of extreme national conflict and fragmentation, sometimes of underdevelopment and delay, sometimes of the cultural difference from "Europe," but always with a derogatory, exotic for Western Europe, and somewhat Eastern connotations. Even notions such as nationalism, liberalism, capitalism, or communism were considered by Western academics to have a different meaning in the Balkans.[128]

The Balkans, as a geopolitical term, are geographically variable. Sometimes include Hungary and Romania, sometimes exclude Greece or Slovenia. Turkey holds few Balkan territories and should be understood as an Asian country. Turkey's role in Europe passes through the Balkans; the latter is considered a bridge to the Middle East or a passageway to Russia and central Asia. According to the classical designation, supposedly, the term Balkans refers purely to geography. In that case, the Balkan

---

[128] Steven W Sowards: The Balkans, Twenty-five Lectures on Modern Balkan History, 1996.

Peninsula has the Danube River and its tributary Sava as its northern border. It includes all the countries of the former Yugoslavia, Bulgaria, Albania, Greece, and European Turkey. Still, most of Romania and Hungary remain out. Yet again, the basis of the inverted triangle of the Balkan Peninsula can only be defined conventionally, which allows the adjacent countries to promote their political self-exclusion.

In a first geopolitical-historical analysis, the Balkans could be considered the geographic region southeast of Europe, between West Europe, on the one hand, and Russia and the core of the Ottoman Empire, on the other. This area was under Ottoman dominance during the crucial centuries when Western Europe embraced values, ways of production, and economic systems that contributed to the development and introduction of the actual "European culture." Balkan countries missed these developments and were cut off from the "European trunk." In this sense, the Balkans are considered Greece, Bulgaria, Romania, Serbia, North Macedonia, Albania, and Bosnia, but not Croatia or Slovenia, the "Frankish" countries, which were already placed in the 9th century under the sway of Charlemagne and his legacy.

From a different point of view, the Balkans could be understood as the area of conflict between the Habsburg Empire and Russia, on the one hand, and the Ottoman Empire, on the other. Throughout recent history, the Balkans have been a scene of clash of the Great Powers, which used the Balkan peoples for their benefit, exploiting their national aspirations for independence. Later, they used the Balkan states to promote their goals of extending their influence in a greater European area.

In the second half of the 19th and early 20th centuries, the Balkans included the countries founded and occupied the European regions of the shrinking Ottoman Empire. Despite the increasing weakness of the Ottoman state, its retreat from the European territories where non-Turkish peoples lived did not happen in a self-inflicted natural way or only thanks to the intervention of third Powers. On the contrary, the Balkan peoples rebelled and fought hard and bloody to gain independence. Balkan nationalism was the expression of a current aiming at national integration within the framework of single-nation states. This struggle, even though it generally met the consensus of the Western peoples due to the high ideals it represented, sometimes collided with the interests of the Western states, with their governments taking an opposing stance. In this sense, the Balkans included Greece, Bulgaria, Serbia, and Romania, involved in revolutions or armed conflicts with the Ottoman Empire.

On the other hand, if the pejorative meaning of the term Balkans refers to acute national conflicts, then it should be understood only as the geographical area of Macedonia and Thrace after 1878. Suppose the term's demerit refers to underdevelopment. In that case, it fits in varying degrees to each Balkan country due to historical and geographical factors but mainly due to the Ottoman occupation. The comparison, of course, is always made with Western Europe. The accusation against these Southeast European countries is not trying adequately to overcome the difficulties and join in time, on equal terms, the level of the continent's other countries. Finally, suppose the term Balkans refers to cultural and social discrepancies. In that case, there is undoubtedly a range of differences, mainly due to historical drive. However, it could not be categorized since, for example, the cultural gap between Portugal and France is more significant than between Austria and Slovenia.

After World War II, the Balkans were mainly the countries that joined the Eastern Bloc or remained outside the Atlantic Alliance. Having adopted a Western-type democracy and having joined the Western alliance, Greece was excluded from the derogatory designation of a Balkan country; it was identified as a Mediterranean country. After the final defeat and collapse of the Eastern Coalition in 1989, the concept of the Balkans, with derogatory content, was focused on the former Soviet satellites. Romania and Bulgaria succeeded in transforming into a market economy and establishing democratic governance systems. Immediately after that, the term Balkans identified with the states of the former Yugoslavia. European Union uses the term West Balkans for the countries of the former Yugoslavia.

The Balkan states have always had significant differences despite their collective identification by this term. Even before the founding of their countries, the Balkan nations did not have the same status within the Ottoman Empire. Through the Greek Patriarch, Greeks held a special place, head of all Orthodox Christians and the Phanariotes, the Greek-Ottoman officials, and the bourgeoisie they had formed. At the same time, the Albanians did not fully realize their existence as a nation. The ideological-political division of the Balkans after the Second World War is characteristic of the variety that can hold such a small geographic region consisting of mountain ranges and valleys. Romania and Bulgaria participated in the Warsaw Pact, with Romania following seemingly a more independent policy and Bulgaria being the most loyal ally of the Soviet Union. Yugoslavia was socialist and Uncommitted, among the founders of the Uncommitted Movement and Stalinist Albania with special relations with China. At the same time, Turkey and Greece belonged to the Atlantic Alliance. Since 1981, Greece has been part of an international organization with supranational objectives, the European Communities. In the minimal - in global measures - the Balkan region, almost all ideological tendencies and currents, all geopolitical formations of the time, were represented.

Greece is geographically a Balkan country; however, its Mediterranean-archipelago dimension is also acknowledged. Before 1821, for Europeans, Greece was an idealized area of antiquity, with residents who had little to do with their glorious past. Indicative of the European spirit of the time is Elgin's thievery of the Parthenon Marbles and their transfer to Britain to "rescue" them (in fact, to sell the swag for profit). Several European intellectuals' efforts to underline the nation's continuity and the heroism of the revolution of 1821 woke up the philhellenism concerning antiquity. Still, others returned to older stereotypes expressed by Jakob Philipp Fallmerayer.[129] Racial homogeneity did not even exist in ancient Greece. Contemporary Greeks speak a modern form of the ancient Greek language.

The term Southeast Europe that Bulgaria first brought forth to get rid of the derogatory term Balkans seems to be the most successful in characterizing this geographical area and the group of the modern states of the region. The latter have indeed widely adopted this term.

---

[129] Jakob Philipp Fallmerayer (10 December 1790 – 26 April 1861) was a German journalist, politician, and historian, best known for his controversial and long-disproved discontinuity theory concerning the racial origins of the Greeks.

Political shaping of the Balkans

The geography of the region did not allow the creation of large countries. At the same time, its Ottoman past with intermingling nations at certain borders undermined peace because of the various liberation struggles. The geographic position of the Balkans between central Europe and the road to the Middle East through Anatolia has historically caused the interest of the European states.

Racially and religiously, the Balkans are diverse. Greece historically is considered as a Mediterranean rather than a Balkan country. The Albanian population is dominant in Kosovo, while in North Macedonia, this nationality has a constituent capacity. Slovenians, Croats, Serbs, Montenegrins, Bulgarians, Slav-Macedonians, and part of the population of Bosnia and Herzegovina are Slavs. Romanians have a long history and speak a kind of Latin language. In Albania, Kosovo, and Bosnia, the prevailing religion is Islamic, and a small part of Bulgaria and North Macedonia are Muslim. Serbia, Montenegro, Romania, Bulgaria, and a large part of the Slav-Macedonian population are Orthodox Christians. Croats and Slovenes are Catholics; the latter use the Latin alphabet, but Orthodox Slavs use the Cyrillic.

The principle that prevailed in the Balkans for establishing states was based on national homogeneity despite significant minorities - as opposed to general conditions in Western Europe. There, the state ideology was based on characteristics that broader population strata could assimilate, regardless of ethnicity. Indeed, in the Balkan states, political citizenship lags behind the notion of ethnic origin; identity cards are less important than the national conscience. Geography has a secondary role; the birthplace is less critical than ethnicity. The historical justification of this fact is strong. It concerns the existence of large parts of the Balkan population in the Ottoman Empire and the region's fragmentation among the new states regarding minorities.

In the early 20th century, the Balkans were considered the powder keg of Europe. The region's instability was attributed to territorial conflicts, nationalist hatred, the involvement of the Great Powers, and geography. The few relatively fertile plains separated by impassable mountains break down the unity of the region and the ethnic groups that inhabit it in contrast to the uniformity of Western Europe. The fragmentation of the area into quarreling segments is called Balkanization. This term, with pejorative content, introduced in 1912, became notorious and is used in every similar situation.

Nationalism appeared in the Balkans as a reaction to Ottoman oppression and evolved during a specific historical period. Balkan nationalism -except Romania during the inter-war period- differs from racism, fascism, or Nazism, mainly Western European or North American phenomena, and has other underlying causes. The continuing nationalist dimension to varying degrees and rhythm of the Balkan peoples results from the initial torque of ethnogenesis. It is not a pathological behavior by the standards of the West. The Kosovo Albanians did not target the prevalence of their race in a fascist way. At the same time, the Yugoslavs, during the war, did not consider doing anything more than preserving the state's territorial integrity under international law, reacting to internal "attitudes" and external military interventions. Nationalism in the Balkans is the expression of the continuation, for an extended period, of the inability to create a political balance with fixed borders.

Despite the breakup of Yugoslavia and the establishment of smaller states, the issue of ethnic minorities is still there. Croatia has Serbian, Bosnian, Hungarian, Slovenian, and Italian minorities. Serbia has a significant Hungarian minority in Vojvodina. In addition to Albanians, North Macedonia has a Turkish minority as well as Roma, Vlachs, Serbs, and those who self-identified as Bulgarians.[130] In Greece, several Muslims identify themselves as Turks. In Romania, there is a substantial minority of Hungarians in Transylvania, which is a cause for discord between Romania and Hungary. There are also Roma, German, and Ukrainian minorities.

According to a view expressed following the uprising of the ethnic Albanians of the Former Yugoslav Republic of Macedonia, the Atlantic Alliance does not help the situation in the Balkans by defending the myth of multinational states. These states are breaking up in internal wars. On the contrary, ethnically homogeneous states have better survival opportunities and harmonious coexistence with neighboring nation-states. There are several questions on the puzzle. Since communities and nations prefer to govern themselves, why the Euro-Atlantic Alliance would deprive people of what they dream and aspire to? If the Kosovo Albanians or North Macedonia want a state of their own, or if Bosnian Serbs would like to join Serbia or Croats in Croatia, why should the alliance oppose it? Finally, if a border change is required, NATO should help to bring it about.[131]

---

[130] Bulgarians consider that Slav-Macedonians are of Bulgarian ethnicity.
[131] Fareed Zakaria, Newsweek, Arab News, March 27, 2001.

The generalization of this view is based on a flimsy foundation. First, how would people genuinely express their opinions? What about the minority of minorities? Will they be expelled, ethnically cleared, as was the case of the Kosovo Serbs, where it has not been possible to be protected even by the NATO forces? When Croatia broke out of the federation, the Krajina Serbs asked for their secession from Croatia on the same terms and the annexation of the region to Serbia. Considering the diversity of minorities, it is clear that changing the borders would result in an absurd situation. In any case of border demarcation, several individuals will always be on the "wrong side." The geography of the populations is not deterministic in this case.

THE CURRENT TURBULENT FLOW OF HISTORY

The international liberal order of the past century has retreated for the benefit of a multipolar global system. The latter favors countries that depend on their power and the threat of using force in their international behavior. Globalization followed the conflicts that accompanied decolonization, and the confrontations of the superpowers by proxies shaped the new order in the international community. Globalization changed the face of the World with the emergence of China and new powers, together with the introduction of different forms and procedures. New values and morals appeared and widely have been accepted.

The 21st century began with the September 11 attack on New York. The new century brought about several changes, with technological developments, close communication, the economic crisis, and the creation of the world village. However, those were not felt until a couple of decades later. The actual World is as dangerous as in the Cold War era, although the threats are different. Terrorism has transformed the entire Earth into a quasi-battlefield in peacetime. Russia[132] and Saudi Arabia[133] proceeded with extrajudicial killings, joining the US. Natural scourges such as pandemics or climate change, horizontal threats such as illegal immigration, and cyber-attacks afflict societies. The unipolar system has ended, but the US realized the situation only a decade later. Several political or economic power poles emerged with problems created by failed governance (or the governance of failed states). The rise of China and commercial–economic wars present a different world setting. At present, everything seems relevant to everything else. According to the new geopolitical approach, irregularity is a new regularity.

Environmental protection and coping with extreme weather conditions resulting from climate change emerged as a horizontal case of high interest. The dangers of climate change, possible sea-level elevation, drought, and lack of water are looming. At the same time, the international community is not unanimous regarding understanding the danger and the responding measures. Risks are changing; in 2017, global risks were of the order: extreme weather conditions, migration, natural disasters,

---

[132] The poisoning in Britain, in 2018 of the former Russian spy Sergei Skripal and his daughter Yulia, has raised questions around the possible involvement of Moscow. Boris Johnson, the then U.K. foreign secretary, pointed to the link with the 2006 murder of ex-spy Alexander Litvinenko, which a British inquiry said was "probably" ordered by the Russian government. The poisoning of the Russian opposition politician Alexei Navalny in 2020 is another case of Russian regime's probable action.

[133] The murder in Istanbul, on October 2, 2018, of dissident Saudi journalist Jamal Khashoggi is proved to be an extrajudicial killing.

terrorist attacks, and digital data theft. In 2020, the pandemic was a higher risk, followed by its economic consequences. At the same time, there was the US-Russia conflict over Ukraine, the Turkish threat against Europe, and the financial conflict between the US and China, with Europe unable to take a decisive stance in the last two cases.

As most of it is already inhabited, the land is valuable, and therefore, geography counts. Natural disasters, wherever they occur, affect almost always populated areas. Any part of Earth is only a few hours away from any other; the range of missiles of mighty states overlaps. The adequacy of energy and water is becoming a matter of paramount importance. Oil and pipelines have become a decisive geopolitical factor.

The UN has failed in its mission. It became an instrument of the Security Council's permanent members having the right of veto, particularly the US and Russia, but not only because of this. In some cases, it acted with blindsides, sometimes from the West-NATO side, in others with Third World countries. For example, on the immigration issue, the UN favors open borders, while on security issues, it supports controlled frontiers. Based on economic figures, but with a robust political extension, the Group of 7, the seven most industrially developed states,[134] is Western-minded. It competes in some respects

---

[134] The Group of Seven (G7) is an international intergovernmental economic organization consisting of the seven largest IMF- advanced economies in the world: Canada, France, Germany, Italy, Japan, the United Kingdom, and the United States. Russia was formally joined the group in 1998, resulting in a new governmental political forum, the Group of Eight or G8. In March 2014 Russia was suspended by G7 members from the political

with the Group of BRICS[135], one of the top emerging markets, whose philosophy is of third-world origin. BRICS members are also members of the Group of 20, the forum of governments and central banks of the 20 largest economies globally (19 members + EU). The action of all these groups, but especially of the G-7, is primarily political. Financial Organizations, such as the World Trade Organization, the World Bank, and the IMF, have been technically successful.

The West remains rallying, but only to a certain extent. Even the Nobel Peace and Literature awards are instrumentalized on the altar of its aspirations. The election of President Trump and the policy that followed broke the until then solid unity. Indeed, the West is now less united than during the Cold War. However, it believes that NATO is its main defensive body against any threat, although Turkey's participation complicates issues. NATO has formulated its values and uses the European Union to promote them. In the term West, under the parameter of pursuing interests, not all countries considered Western are included. Depending on the circumstances, it is a term with variable content, including mainly the states of geographical Western Europe, the U.S.A., Canada, Australia, and others.

Despite the attempted organization of the international community in various forms of cooperation

---

forum G8 following the annexation of Crimea, this being just a pretext since Turkey, that military occupies part of Republic of Cyprus, continues to participate in G-20.

[135] BRICS is the acronym coined for an association of five major emerging national economies: Brazil, Russia, India, China and South Africa. Originally the first four were grouped as "BRIC" (or "the BRICs"), before the induction of South Africa in 2010.

in the political and economic sphere, countries with authoritarian regimes, such as Russia, China, North Korea, and Turkey, act with a mentality of pursuing individual interests. The UK, after Brexit, attempts to enter the club of the influential and independent world powers. The countries of Southeast Asia follow the same rationale – to some extent. Small countries sometimes have passive policies, such as Greece, and other times aggressive, like Israel. However, no great power is overwhelming, while Western politics appears confused.

In 2016, Trump's presidency introduced a period of fuzzy strategy with blurred aims and followed a publicly manifested introvert policy expressed by the slogan "America first." The Trump administration disdained the international organized society and the global system based on rules and international law. Trump tried to withdraw the US from international organizations that make up the cells of the international community. He was not interested in the international order. President Trump preferred to do business personally with presidents of authoritarian regimes, such as China's Xi, North Korea's Kim Yong Un, or Turkey's Erdogan, though not with great success. In particular, regarding Russian President Putin, Trump's National Security Advisor John Bolton wrote, "I would not let him alone with Putin."[136]

The US, under President Trump, manifested its intent to withdraw or withdraw from international conventions, the Pacific (Trans-Pacific Partnership), UNESCO, Paris (climate), Iran (nuclear), INF, and WHO. It did not exclude even its withdrawal from NATO[137].

---

[136] J. Bolton: The room where it happened.

[137] President Trump criticized NATO members for being "free riders," not spending adequately on their own

President Trump's justification for withdrawing the US troops from Syria was that "we will not do the work of others" and "the great nations do not make endless wars." Eventually, Syria fell under the sway of authoritarian countries such as Russia and Turkey. The US replaced NAFTA and slid into a protective regime by imposing import duties against various states and groups of countries. At the same time, the US became the World's largest oil-producing country. This led to a reclassification of the global energy order and impacted geopolitics.

At the same time, the European Union was bent under the economic crisis and illegal immigration, as well as deficiencies in organization and administration. The distance taken from the peoples of Europe, together with difficulties raised by Eastern enlargement, has contributed to the weakness of the institution. On the contrary, Brexit will disembarrass the European Union from a member state with reactive behavior, systematically undermining

---

defense budgets, but did nothing to see them carried out their obligations. At his first NATO summit in 2017, complained that too many allies were not meeting their 2014 commitment, collectively made at Cardiff, Wales, to spend 2 percent of GDP for defense by 2024, which for most Europeans meant defense in the European theater. Germany was one of the worst offenders, spending about only 1.2 percent of GDP on defense, and always under pressure from Social Democrats and other leftists to spend less. President Trump had relentlessly criticized Germany as a terrible NATO partner and attacked the Nord Stream II pipeline, which would see Germany paying Russia, NATO's adversary, substantial revenues. Trump had called NATO "obsolete" during the 2016 campaign but argued in April 2017 that the problem had been "fixed" in his presidency. (John Bolton: The room where it happened).

the Union's policies. Britain rushed to join Turkey to flank Europe geopolitically even before it left the Union.

Trends in Europe are contradictory; on the one hand, there is a tendency towards further federalism, though not stable; on the other, the tendency towards autonomy. The latter manifests itself with separatist movements, e.g., Scotland or Catalonia, and the independent policies of member-states of the European Union, such as Poland and Hungary. Due to its economic strength and political stability for a long time, Germany became a leading force in Europe. Still, it may not yet be ready to take a leading geopolitical role as its past is always there. On the other hand, France is less affected by the adverse developments in Europe. Therefore, in the future, it can return to its leading position.

The flow of developments in the second decade of this century is turbulent. It cannot be defined accurately; the next phase cannot be prefigured; determinants are not visible, sometimes even not possible. Geography is not constant anymore as technological developments and non-institutional and non-legal factors outmatch it. There is a continuing world war in cyberspace with propaganda and fake news; an incredible quantity of information is spreading at high speed through social media. Asymmetric threats and terrorism became commonplace, while simultaneously, warm local wars were held, mainly through representatives.

In business, automation, digitalization, and artificial intelligence endanger, at least initially, millions of jobs. Developments in medicine and biology can prolong life for many years or end up in a more sophisticated type of human being. In politics, traditional right-left controversy is neutralized, and new groupings appear. Various nationalisms reappeared. In the West, populism,

Far-Right, and anarchy in multiple forms took power from leaders sending contradictory messages or making abrupt turns in politics. In this sense, the Far-Right is not an extreme of the well-known liberal right and is not related to it. Money magnates or leftists, populists, or incoherent leaders contribute to the instability and volatility of politics. Immigration generates reactions in both the US and Europe. In the latter, reactions are caused by Muslim immigrants who do not want to adapt to European ways of life or proceed to acts of terrorism. Christian secularism clashes with Muslim religiousness. The generated widespread opposition extends to all Muslim immigrants, including the legal and lawful ones.

All these are aspects of a rapidly changing new state of affairs worldwide. The news, unexpected every time, differentiates the international order at an accelerated rate. The distribution of power and influence in the international scene alternates continuously in different directions. The global system is mutating. Countries considered regional Powers follow a downward course. At the same time, new forces attempt to replace them in an environment of asymmetric growth.[138]

The warm arc of crises is identified, up to a point, with the ancient "ecumene." Starting from the unstable former Yugoslavia, the arc crosses the Aegean with Turkey's threats, covers Turkey, the occupied north Cyprus, Syria, Lebanon, Iraq, the Kurdish region, Palestine, and Sinai, and reaches Pakistan and Afghanistan. It continues in Kashmir and Tibet and, further north, Nagorno-Karabakh, Chechnya, and the Muslim Uyghurs in China. In the adjacent area of this arc lies the crisis in

---

[138] N. Kotzias, MFA, Parliamentary committee, December 14, 2017

Ukraine, the Arabian Peninsula with Yemen, and, potentially, Egypt and Libya.

Overall, journalistic irony against democratically elected Western countries' leaders introduces new morals, even though sometimes the leaders themselves give causes for being ridiculed. Several times, journalism does not help public opinion formulate an accurate and integral picture of the situation by expressing personal views.[139] According to Secretary-General of the Organization of American States Luis Almagro, the difference between Obama and Trump was in rhetoric. Obama did not follow the anti-immigrant tactics of Trump; however, under Obama's control, a considerable number of expulsions took place " (Davos, January 24, 2018). Black people were also subject to police brutality during President Obama's term. A robust activist front with a liberalistic approach is formed in Western countries. It ranges itself with an excessive "political correctness," expressing in a militant way its views pertaining primarily to anarchism.

The leaders' public debate in Davos in 2018 focused on the controversy of populism versus globalization. The leaders of Germany, France, and Italy referred to the dangers that a return to nationalism and protectionism would entail. According to the President of China, protectionism resembles being locked in a dark room. India's Prime Minister voiced concern because the states increasingly focus on themselves (America First – D. Trump). It seems, he said, as if we had a reverse phenomenon from globalization, and this phenomenon

---

[139] The arbitrary interruption of President Trump's speech, after the 2020 presidential election, by some TV stations constitutes undemocratic behavior.

has no less adverse consequences than terrorism or climate change.

Nevertheless, he did not mention the negative impact of globalization on Western countries. Accordingly, the Director-General of the International Organization for Migration claimed that migration had been a positive force for the World's societies and economies. He pointed out that immigration is not an issue to be resolved but a human reality that should be arranged humanely and responsibly. However, this, he said, does not happen in Western countries. However, he did not criticize the non-western and wealthy Muslim countries, which promote migration to Western countries and hinder immigration to them. Others expressed themselves with stereotypes: Britain's defense minister "warned" that Russia is preparing attacks against his country with "thousands of dead."

The international situation after 9/11

Following the terrorist attack of September 11, 2001, stunning humanity realized that it was confronted with unforeseen and asymmetric threats directed against international stability. Moreover, the economic impact of terrorist actions was apparent. The destructive agenda of the forces of terrorism created the need to increase international cooperation and, in a long-term perspective, to proceed to an effort that could address the problem. In addition, there was a need to deprive the terrorists of shelter. Nevertheless, it was emphasized that states should respect the rules on human rights and international legitimacy in tackling terrorism. Any exemption from this rule should take account of the principle of proportionality. The leading causes of terrorism are fundamentalism and extreme nationalism. Still, it was argued that other aspects should also be considered.

At an ASEM[140] meeting of the time, the repercussions of the resurgence of terrorism were discussed. It was emphasized that Islamists' prevalence would prove very dangerous since fundamentalists aspire to create an Islamic arc. This would include Indonesia, the Philippines, and Malaysia, aiming at Singapore, thus affecting China. It was argued that poverty, although not a cause for terrorism, prepared the ground and created the framework for the growth of terrorism, as it happened in Afghanistan, Yemen, and Somalia. The fight against poverty was, therefore, a priority. Among European and Asian leaders, the problem of terrorist financing and the need to impose barriers to the movement of relevant funds were also discussed.

Although disapproving of the U.S.'s invasion of Iraq, Europeans expressed the view that the international alliance had to be maintained and that no unilateral action should be allowed to break it. Terrorists should be prevented from having access to weapons of mass destruction. Still, it should be borne in mind that the international community is organized under the United Nations principles that do not allow arbitrary actions. However, Britain, Spain, and Italy supported the U.S. positions concerning Iraq.

The view of the center-left leaders was also that terrorism is a crime and should be combated effectively as a crime. This struggle, however, could not succeed if the causes of this phenomenon, extremism, blind hatred, inequality, injustice, poverty, and wars, were not met. Leaders pointed out that Palestine was always an open

---

[140] Asian – European leaders meeting

wound. The protagonists of the dispute should be persuaded to overcome their contradictions to find a solution; otherwise, terrorism would be regenerated. There should be an overall deal, and the issues needed to be settled without giving rise to new fronts. The need to reduce the distance between the perceptions prevailing in Europe and Asia has been highlighted. The necessity of mutual understanding and eliminating stereotypes and feelings leading to xenophobia and racism was emphasized. Along the same line, the need for sustainable development and protection of the environment to ensure growth throughout the world to tackle terrorism was underscored.

According to the Muslim-Asian viewpoint, injustice is being perpetrated in Palestine. Lands belonging to Muslim Arabs were taken, and any protest was dealt with by bullets and violence; the world and Europe remained silent on this situation. Furthermore, it was shown that after the outbreak of the September 11 terrorist act, Muslims worldwide were treated as potential terrorists and subjected to degrading procedures.

The 4th Generation Wars

After the Hot and Cold Wars, evolution led to 3rd generation of weapon systems. Type 3.0 weapons use state-of-the-art technology and aim to hit the enemy behind the line through high-speed missiles. In addition, they use methods of concealment and surprise or even fully autonomous A.I. systems.

The 4th generation war, in which non-direct lethal weapons are used, has appeared in recent decades. The term was initially used in 1980 by a group of U.S. analysts. This type of war is a tactic characterized by the abandonment of the dividing lines between war and politics, soldiers and civilians. At a conference in 2018, Manwaring argued that a fourth-generation war could be an option for destabilizing the adversary. Wars 4.0 are waged through non-hot military action, such as social engineering, propaganda, and disinformation. The 4th generation war goes beyond the narrow military conduct and confrontation limits. It enters politics, diplomacy, sociology, and the national economy.

The "insidious" wars 4.0, as shown by recent developments, e.g., on the front of Ukraine with Russia and Turkey with Greece, have replaced the older type of "cold war". In the current period, among others, conflicts exist between the West (Europe and the U.S.) with Russia, the U.S., and the Pacific countries with China. The Syrian front has not calmed down since the Western target of ousting Assad has not succeeded and continues with a combination of weapons. The U.S. conflict with Iran over its nuclear program, instigated by Israel, also remains at the heart of a years-long battle unfolding with 3.0- and 4.0- generation weapons.

According to internationalists, the outcome of War 4.0 may mean a change in the international map. Although they may not bring about changes in political boundaries in most cases, without this being excluded, changes are taking place in economic zones, spheres of influence, international economic relations, energy interdependence, and culture. Geopolitical changes also concern the concept of globalization, whose negative sides begin to become visible.

Regarding changes to the political map, China has targeted Taiwan and Turkey, the Greek islands of the eastern Aegean and western Thrace. Previously, Turkey occupied a large part of Cyprus in a heated war, and Russia occupied Crimea, although these cases are not identical.

With a combination of hot and "insidious" wars, Turkey has also brought parts of northern Syria under its control. Slovenia regained territory that Tito had attributed to Croatia through the former's condition for the latter's accession to the E.U.

The Algerian internationalist A. Chikhaoui states that the "insidious" wars that sometimes escape attention have replaced the Cold War of the last century. Type 4.0 wars, he writes, are only the culmination of a strategic war with zero direct human casualties but with visible results. The classic armed war mutates into a new type that develops slowly and progressively in space and time. This is the Smart Power, a combination of armed violence and soft power.

Smart Power uses many methods, from Turkey's war of announcements and threats against Greece to the heated proxy war, as was the case in Syria and Yemen. In these, the aggressor and his target are not on the battlefield. The multiple instruments used range from European sanctions to the increase in energy prices by Arabs and Russians. The methods are many, and new ones constantly appear, depending on the opportunities presented.

For example, Turkey's involvement in Syria and its use of the EEZs' distribution in the eastern Mediterranean is a fourth-generation war. Also, International satellite television stations were used in War 4.0 to produce political developments within targeted countries. Qatar, in particular, has been accused of using the Al Jazeera T.V. station during the Arab Spring to stimulate the crowds. However, other international satellite television stations also carry out sharp propaganda and a 4th generation war favoring political interests.

The Smart Force exploits violent extremist organizations for the purposes of the state against those it considers to be opponents. Acts of terrorism are also sometimes an instrument of fourth-generation warfare. The aim is to dismantle the hostile state and create successive and lasting crises within it. The "colored" revolutions caused in countries bordering Russia, including Ukraine, fall into this category. Moreover, even the distortion of historical memory is being employed: The invocation of the indisputable then, even by Western media, of foreign interference in the coup d'état of Ukraine's elected government in 2014 today appears as fascist propaganda.

Private multinational structures with an economical size larger than several states cannot be controlled and may operate in many directions. Social media is also taking similar action. Cyberattacks are among the most commonly used weapons. These instruments are primarily used by powerful countries, mainly the U.S., Russia, China, and perhaps North Korea.

The perpetrators of the "insidious" wars can be Non-Governmental Organizations (NGOs) or Non-Governmental Individuals (NGOs), Think Tanks, as well as commercial companies. Irregular migration was a powerful weapon of 4.0 generation warfare, aiming to damage the social structure of the opponent and the economy, as well as to derail social resources and alienate the urban environment. The role of some NGOs in Turkey's success of this weapon has been catalytic. On the contrary, the state instrumentalization of immigration by both Turkey and Belarus has failed.

It follows from the above that a series of 4.0 generation wars between many different poles of power is already underway worldwide.

The post-Cold War era

Following the Western victory in the Cold War, the USSR, at the instigation of the West, dissolved itself, mainly because of economic reasons. After its defeat in the Cold War, it was natural for the USSR to have substantial financial challenges. Still, neither unsurmountable problems nor substantive separatist movements could have imposed the division of the unified federation. Most federated states, including Ukraine and Belarus, did not seek secession. Baltic States, Armenia, and a few more could split peacefully. After the end of the Cold War, Russia followed a defeatist policy liable to the West in the first decade. The latter, especially after Putin took power, did everything possible not to let Russia regain its strength.

Russia, reacting to the Western stance and seeking to increase its sway in countries of its surroundings, created the "Euro-Asian Economic Union." The relevant founding treaty entered into force at the beginning of 2015. It is a transnational economic organization with an international legal personality. It has financial and institutional structures that include Russia and countries that emerged from the breakdown of the Soviet Union with a pro-Russian orientation. Russia occupies a dominant economic role in the Union. Apart from the Russian Federation, members of the Union are Kazakhstan, Belarus, Armenia, and Kyrgyzstan. Russia aims to transform this Union into a supranational political organization. Therefore, part of Russia's plans is to restore, in a way, the territorial unity of the land of the former Soviet Union, dominated by Russia. The defense of Belorussian dictator Lukashenko is indicative of this stance.

The West, chiefly the U.S., responding to the attempts of Russia to recover, followed an active policy, intending to subvert the pro-Russian governments of the former Soviet Union federative states. It received the East European countries not only in NATO but also in the European Union, bringing about a blow to this supranational Organization, as these countries were unprepared for accession. The West followed a similar tactic in the Balkans by breaking down Yugoslavia and influencing as many countries as possible. It detached Kosovo from Serbia by bombing it and showed favor to Albania's aspirations and the then Former Yugoslav Republic of Macedonia (FYROM) for extending its influence on them too. Several Western countries pressed Greece to give up its rights on the issue of the name of the FYROM. The latter eventually joined NATO under the name North Macedonia. All Balkan countries except Kosovo, Serbia, and Bosnia-Herzegovina have eventually joined NATO.

After the dissolution of the Soviet Union, the United States, with the occasional help of Britain and other E.U. countries, attempted to detach the countries of the former USSR from Russia's influence. Based on its economic rise and political stability secured by Putin's authoritarian governance, Russia decided to react to the repeated efforts of the West to change the regimes of countries of its influence. Ukraine was the last straw. Russia was expelled from the "Western group" when it incorporated Crimea into the Russian Federation in 2014. Moscow believes its comeback with leadership claims on international matters is the reason for the positions taken against it. However, it is a fact that a significant part of the West prefers that Russia remain pinned down in its weak place of the 1990s.

Western incitements in Georgia and Ukraine

NATO granted privileged partnerships and agreements in Georgia, Ukraine, and Armenia, violating Moscow's red lines. Russia claims that NATO promised not to proceed with such an enlargement. In Georgia, the "Revolution of Roses," with Western support, overturned in 2003 the regime of Shevardnadze, leaving the country in the hands of the American-bred leader of the revolution, Saakashvili. In February 2008, Georgia was designated as a candidate for NATO membership. On August 8, 2008, Georgian troops invaded South Ossetia to overthrow the de facto government and reintegrate the region into Georgia. On the pretext of killing soldiers of the Russian peacekeeping force stationed in the area, Moscow blamed Georgia for genocide and invaded South Ossetia and a part of the territory of Georgia. The clashes that followed and Russia's bombing led to the destruction of the Georgian army and the coercion of the government to surrender. Russians took back the positions they held before 1999. The intervention in Georgia has prompted an escalation in the relations between Russia and the USA.

Ukraine has never asked for secession from Russia, which was made under Yeltsin to be pleasant to the West. Pro-Russian Viktor Yanukovych was elected President of Ukraine in 2004, but the elections were considered rigged. The pro-Western opposition under Viktor Yushchenko and Yulia Timoshenko led a revolution called the "Orange Revolution" that succeeded in the expulsion of Yanukovych. The opposition took power. Western governments and NGOs funded the movement, while Western communications consultants have trained activists of the Orange Revolution. A British newspaper quoted as instigators of the U.S. State Dpt., USAID, the

National Democratic Institute for International Affairs, the International Republican Institute, the NGO Freedom House, and the Open Society Institute of George Soros.

Yanukovych, however, returned to power in 2006 as Prime Minister of the Alliance of National Unity. He tried to resolve the country's economic problems through a partnership with Europe, negotiating an association agreement with the E.U. At the same time, he wanted to maintain its economic relations with Russia as the long-term ties could not be interrupted. After all, Europe had no surplus of financial resources to make them available for rescuing the country. Ukraine's bid to join the West was based solely on the latter's strategic objectives. In any case, signing the Association Agreement with the E.U. would exclude Ukraine's accession to the Russian-inspired Euro-Asian Economic Union.

On that basis, Yanukovych did not finally sign the Association agreement's text agreement negotiated with the E.U., guaranteeing generous financial assistance from Russia. This withdrawal of Yanukovych caused extensive demonstrations in Kyiv that began in November 2013. Civil disobedience evolved into mutiny by Western incitement, at least through statements of sympathy to demonstrators and other public expressions establishing apparent Western involvement. The request of the organized and armed demonstrators, among whom several extremist nationalists, was the expulsion of the elected President. The rebels seized public buildings and created a climate of terror that forced President Yanukovych to leave Kyiv. They occupied the Parliament, which, under such circumstances, declared the President fallen and arbitrarily appointed a new president and government, following the instructions of the West. Brussels and Washington, accepting as legitimate the new Prime

Minister and the Foreign Minister of Ukraine, confirmed their involvement in the case.

The new government began armed persecution against the Russian speakers of Ukraine, who were forced to defend themselves armed.

As a response, Russia deployed its army in Crimea, mainly inhabited by Russians. The Soviet leadership had granted Crimea to Ukraine in the context of the Soviet Union. As illegal (to say the least) Western involvement in the Kyiv coup was, the deployment of Russian troops in Crimea that followed on March 2. 2014, was equally illegal. The referendum on 16.3.14 for independence and the accession of Crimea to the Russian Federation violated international law and the Constitution of Ukraine. The President of Russia made a parallel with the Kosovo case. As a response, western countries expelled Russia from the Group of Eight.

Following these events, the Russian residents of the eastern provinces of Ukraine requested their region's secession from the central government, creating two enclaves in Donetsk and Luhansk.

The Minsk Agreements attempted to end the war in the eastern provinces of Ukraine, which had become autonomous as the Democratic Republic of Donetsk and the Luhansk People's Republic. The Minsk Protocol was drawn up by the Trilateral Contact Group, Ukraine, Russia, and the OSCE (Organisation for Security and Cooperation in Europe), mediated by France and Germany, the Normandy Format. The Protocol was signed in Minsk in 2014 by the Trilateral Contact Group and the heads of the two People's Republics without any status being granted.

This agreement failed to achieve a ceasefire and was followed by a new deal, Minsk II, in 2015, which was also unable to stop hostilities. However, members of the

Normandy Format agreed that this would remain the basis of any dispute settlement in the future.

After the secession of Crimea and the creation of the two enclaves, the fact is that a large proportion of the Ukrainian people could not vote for the government of Ukraine.

With the Minsk agreements (2014 and 2015), the Ukrainian government and the eastern provinces' administrations undertook to cease hostilities. However, in 2021, the Ukrainian government under Zelinsky expressed the intention to retake the eastern provinces of Donetsk and Luhansk. The Ukrainian army advanced there. In response, Russia sent a message of deterrence through a military buildup on the border near Ukraine's eastern provinces.

The U.S. saw an opportunity to capitalize on this military buildup by projecting that Russia intends to attack Ukraine. Although Russia maintained that it had no intention of invading Ukraine, the US continued to blame it and threaten economic sanctions in the event of an invasion. Most of the other Europeans, except the UK, were more restrained.

Russia took the opportunity to remind that NATO had undertaken not to expand into Eastern Europe, an obligation it did not honor. It demanded guarantees from NATO that it would not extend to Ukraine. Although unable to undertake such an obligation, NATO did not seem to have intended to expand into Ukraine.

Russia argued that it had been agreed that security in Europe was unified and, therefore, its security should be ensured, not just that of other Europeans. In this context, and alluding to the Cuban missile crisis, it demanded the non-deployment of nuclear weapons in Ukraine.

Russia's invasion of Ukraine, also called a "special military operation" in Ukraine, is a conflict between Russia and Ukraine, effectively the culmination of the ongoing Russian-Ukrainian conflict since 2014. It was launched on February 24, 2022, at the behest of the President of the Russian Federation Vladimir Putin, Russian troops to advance into Ukrainian territory. On February 21, 2022, Russia officially recognized the Donetsk People's Republic and the Lugansk People's Republic as autonomous states of Donbas. The invasion began on February 24, 2022, when Putin announced a *special military operation* to demilitarize *and* denazify *Ukraine, saying he was responding to a request from the two people's republics to defend them.* [141]

Legal aspects of the Russian invasion of Ukraine

1. The Budapest Memorandum of 5 December 1994 on security guarantees, under which Ukraine became a party to the Non-Proliferation Treaty (NPT) and surrendered its nuclear arsenal, provided security guarantees to that country. In particular, the US, Russian Federation, and the UK reaffirmed their obligation to respect Ukraine's independence and sovereignty within its existing borders. These three countries reaffirmed their obligation to refrain from threatening or using force against the territorial integrity or political independence of Ukraine and that none of their weapons will be used

---

[141] Wikipedia

against Ukraine, except in the case of self-defense.[142] The three countries reaffirmed their commitment not to use nuclear weapons against an NPT member state. In the event of the use or threat of the use of nuclear weapons, the three countries would seek immediate UNHCR action to help Ukraine. Russia has, therefore, violated this agreement on several occasions.

2. The Rome Statute of the International Criminal Court provides that its jurisdiction extends to the territory of the Member States, as well as, by special agreement, to the territory of any other State (Article 4). The Court has already received petitions from 41 States on the subject of Ukraine. Russia and Ukraine are not members of the Court. However, the offenses under investigation were committed on the territory of Ukraine, and Ukraine requested the Court's intervention. The main offense is Russia's Crime of Aggression (Article 8 bis 3), which was clearly committed.

Other offenses that can be considered are Genocide (Article 6) and War Crimes (Article 8), particularly strikes against civilian targets by Russian forces.

3. The UNSC, which is the main instrument for ensuring international peace and security, was neutralized because of Russia's membership as a permanent member. However, on several occasions, there have been other Permanent Members who have violated UN principles.

A reading of the UN and NPT charters is enough to show that international peace and security are at the

---

[142] The "nuclear" message from Russia to the rest of the world | Politics | ResPublica. https://respublica.edu.mk/blog-en/politics/the-nuclear-message-from-russia-to-the-rest-of-the-world/?lang=en

mercy of nuclear powers that are at the same time permanent members of the UNSC with veto power, not all collectively, but individually.

The UN has become a kind of League (as it was just before World War II), and a bold geopolitical realignment is necessary to return the organization to the pursuit of ensuring international peace and security.

The failure of the U.N.

It has been observed that even the reference to the U.N. causes boredom. And not unjustly. Many political observers have identified its inability to resolve crises and respond to situations. Nevertheless, some add that the U.N. is useful as a forum (albeit meaningless) for discussions and a meeting place for leaders to exchange views. If that were the case, it would perhaps be more successful and, in any case, more pleasing to organize annual diplomatic dances in Vienna on the model of 1815.

The historical failures of the Organization are numerous. The U.N. has become unreliable, repeatedly demonstrating its inability to meet the purposes for which it was set up. The case of Ukraine could be the last straw.

However, the U.N. cannot be an outdated Organization. On the contrary, the international situation constantly demonstrates the need for an organization to promote the principles and objectives stated in the U.N. Charter. The problem is how the agency operates as defined by its truly outdated way of action. Reform proposals are being made, but the emphasis is on increasing the number of permanent members of the Security Council.

As it turned out, the greatest danger to international peace comes from the Permanent Members of the Security Council, in particular, mainly from the U.S. and Russia, and to a lesser extent from China. Indeed, these Permanent Members of the UNSC, the USA, Russia, and China, refuse to accede to the Rome Convention on the International Criminal Court (1998). All the Permanent Members of the UNSC are nuclear powers. However, instead of finding ways for total denuclearization, they sought to prevent (rightly) other countries from acquiring nukes through the Non-Proliferation Treaty. Thus, the nuclear Powers can act illegally, attack and invade other countries, and distribute the world into zones of influence.

Moreover, promises not to use (and threaten not to use) nuclear weapons by nuclear Powers against non-nuclear countries were wiped out following Russia's threats on the occasion of its invasion of Ukraine and the possibility of Finland and Sweden joining NATO.

However, the U.N.'s inaction is mainly due to the veto right enjoyed by the permanent members of the UNSC. The UN Charter has entrusted exclusively to the UNSC the task of preserving peace in the event of a threat against it. The U.N. General Assembly (by a two-thirds majority) can only make "proposals" to safeguard the peace. Therefore, if the interests of even one Permanent Member are affected, no decision to preserve peace can be taken.

There are many unfortunate moments in the U.N.'s history. The problems are ongoing, from the election of a Nazi Secretary-General to resolving international disputes with plans that trample on its principles. Weak states did not find a supporter at the U.N. when they were wronged.

The UN Secretary-General went so far as to seemingly justify the murderous act of a terrorist organization, Hamas, that took place on October 7, 2023, by connecting it with the just affair of the Palestinians. The position that Hamas has anything to do with Palestinian rights grossly wrongs the Palestinians.

International peace was rarely safeguarded through interventions by the Organization, which usually remains a spectator. The powerful member-states of the Organization seek reforms not primarily to improve its operation but to strengthen their position within it. The search for reform is limited to their intended appointment as permanent members of the UNSC.

The U.N. has failed to protect states like Cyprus or Ukraine from invaders. In particular, it proposed plans that favored the invader (e.g., Cyprus, Annan Plan). Moreover, it did not have the means to prevent posting illegal agreements that violated its principles for maintaining international peace (e.g., the Turkish-Libyan pact). Its member-states systematically ignore many of its decisions that remain unexecuted (e.g., Western Sahara). In contrast, the current international situation is reminiscent of the interwar period.

Many member-states of the UNO say that the time has come to replace the U.N. statute. It is challenging, of course, but not impossible. Indeed, many U.N. member-states do not have nuclear weapons. Those states will benefit significantly from an organization that will effectively safeguard international peace. They can make the change if they have a strong will. They do have the democratic power.

The East-West confrontation

Many Western analysts interpret international issues and developments as a constant confrontation between the West and the East. They believe that Russia's foreign policy aims at the strategic division of the Western

Alliance and the weakening of the European Union, undermining, thus, the democratic acquis of the West. It is certain that between Moscow and Washington, as well as between Moscow and Brussels, there are divergences of opinions. West accuses Russia of being authoritarian and nationalist, and the latter speaks about the alleged reactionary interests of Western policy. Russia is pursuing a policy of serving its interests in the "near abroad." In Russia's political language, the term "near abroad" refers mainly to the independent republics that emerged after the dissolution of the Soviet Union, as well as to countries geographically nearby. In Syria, Russia supported Assad against the aspirations of Turkey to occupy part of Syria and rout out the Kurds, a U.S. ally. However, unlike the Soviet Union, Russia does not aim to export any political system abroad; it just tries to reposition itself on the map of global diplomacy. The U.S. believes that Russia would like to restore its territorial status to the extent of the Soviet Union. President Putin admitted that if there were something he would want to change in history, it would be the non-division of the Soviet Union.

Russia turned to Asia and China as a counterweight to its continued alienation by the E.U. and the U.S.. Nevertheless, its links in energy and trade and political reasoning do not allow Russia to overturn its orientation radically. Its economy remains poorly globalized, and its state institutions seem not to be functioning democratically. However, Russia is dynamically involved in international schemes that cast doubt on the West's importance, both at the level of geography (e.g., Shanghai cooperation) and economy (e.g., BRICS).

The Kremlin has specific geopolitical plans. Its opposition to the Western involvement in Ukraine and its intervention in Syria aimed at Russia's readmission in the international political arena as a "superpower." With the image of its stable political system and liberal economy, Russia sought to restore its position in the international scene with the same status as in the Cold War era. However, Russia does not seek international sovereignty in the model of the Soviet Union, but its recognition as the second pole of global scope. Russia's geopolitical interests now include the Arctic zone, the Pacific Ocean, the Baltic, the Atlantic, the arc Balkans, Turkey, the Middle East, and the last connected with Russia's fixed goal, the Mediterranean.

The Collective Security Treaty Organization (CSTO) is an intergovernmental military alliance.[143] It consists of some post-Soviet states under the leading role of Russia. Stipulations of this new Treaty replaced the United Armed Forces of the Commonwealth of Independent States. Six post-Soviet states belonging to the Commonwealth of Independent States, Russia, Armenia, Kazakhstan, Kyrgyzstan, Tajikistan, and Uzbekistan, signed a collective security treaty on May 15, 1992, the CST. The terms of the Tashkent Pact or Tashkent Treaty are also used with the title Collective Security Treaty.

Azerbaijan, Belarus, and Georgia signed the agreement in 1993, and the Treaty took effect in 1994. In 1999, six of the nine, namely Russia, Armenia, Kazakhstan, Kyrgyzstan, Tajikistan, and Belarus, agreed to renew the Treaty for five more years. In 2002, those six created the Collective Security Treaty Organization, CSTO, as a military

---

[143] Collective Security Treaty Organization. https://lotusarise.com/collective-security-treaty-organization-upsc/

alliance. According to the Treaty, the signatories would not join other military alliances, e.g., NATO.

Kazakhstan used CSTO to invite a peace force to restrain insurgents in Almaty in January 2022.

The United States, aiming to restore its position as the sole, undisputed superpower, attempted a return to the Cold War era. According to the U.S. strategic doctrine of 2017, Russia and China are competitive countries and opponents. According to the U.S. National security strategy of the Trump administration, Russia and China are revisionist geopolitical adversaries to the United States. Russia and China challenge American power, influence, and interests while degrading American security and prosperity. The U.S. claimed that Russia had used firearms and tanks in Georgia and Ukraine together with a combination of political destabilization, bribery, propaganda, cyber-attacks, and economic pressure in all the countries that constituted the Soviet Union or were under its control in the Warsaw Pact.

The U.S. also accused Russia of occasionally intervening even in NATO countries – including the U.S. presidential elections of 2016. As far as the Middle East is concerned, it accused Russia of carrying out a "military intervention" in Syria, fighting alongside its ally and client Assad. In the context of this policy, the United States declared in 2019 its intention to abandon the Treaty on Intermediate-Range Nuclear Forces Treaty (INF). As a reason, the U.S. claimed that the Novator 9M729 missile manufactured by Russia breached the Treaty.

In May 2020, President Trump said he had decided the U.S. to withdraw from another significant arms control accord, the Open Skies Treaty. This Treaty was signed three decades ago to allow nations to fly over each other's territory to ensure they are not preparing for military action. Regarding the New START agreement limiting the United States and Russia's nuclear missiles, President Trump insisted that China should join a U.S.-Russia limit on nuclear arsenals.

Putin rejected the new American strategic doctrine as an imperialist relic of a raving superpower that continues to act unilaterally on the global stage. However, the new "second Cold War" has no ideological basis. The conflict, as Trump put it, is national. It resembles 19th-century competition policies between nation-states, with President Putin and Trump being responsible. This conflict is just as dangerous for the world as was the past one. However, after its mistakes in Iraq, Georgia, Libya, Syria, and Ukraine, including Iran (by their withdrawal from the nuclear agreement in 2018), Tump's U.S. was in a global retreat, defeated diplomatically, including in their strategic conflict with North Korea. Russia and China seek geopolitical expansion following a nationalist competition and power policy. Russia tries to take back the territories it once possessed, such as Crimea, South Ossetia, and Abkhazia. At the same time, China attempts to consolidate its gains in the southern Chinese sea.

Donald Trump's election to the United States presidency 2016 brought about a turn to the U.S. policy towards nationalism. Although for Russia and China, the international community sees the political advocacy of their national interests as a fact, the U.S. is seen differently. In its rhetoric, the U.S. used to manifest a "moral" approach, support of democracy, law, freedom, and not just military and economic power. However, if it solicits a difficult international policy decision, it honestly clarifies that it was about defending American interests. From the outset, President Trump was sincere in saying that the basis of his policy is "America first." In this context, and among others, the U.S. conflicted with Mexico "that does not control its southern borders, resulting in illegal immigration from southern American countries to the United States."

The modulators of the U.S. foreign policy, expressing the U.S. international targets veritably, publicly refer to global hegemony to enforce the "correct side of history." In this context, they do not recognize as legitimate any attempt to increase Russia's or China's sway, political or economic, and consider it imperative to prevent this development. From Brzezinski and Kissinger to the most contemporary analysts, the political goal has always been to hit Russia. On the other hand, the economic rise of China added this country to the list of "enemies," together with smaller countries that do not fall within the sphere of influence of the United States. As a result, Trump wedged a trade war against all, but mainly against China.

The U.S. considers Europe as a foreland opened in the Atlantic. A small continent that dominated world affairs in the last centuries of the second millennium is perceived mainly as an economic power. The institutions of the European Union are not strong enough to make it a coherent political force with a unified foreign policy and defense policy that could protect its borders and give Europe a word in international matters, which is fortunate for the United States. However, Europe's usefulness for the U.S. focuses on confining Russia.

There were, however, voices of prudence in the U.S., especially from the part of Democrats. According to James Jones, it is a historical fact that all the great nations and empires have a beginning and an end. However, a naïve belief prevails among some Americans about the fate of their country: that the U.S.'s supremacy is assured forever.[144] According to Jake Sullivan, an active, proactive, and ultimately successful foreign policy must combine patriotism – a participatory urban spirit and a clear sense of national interest. The best kind of internationalism is the perception that when the neighbor's house is on fire, one grabs a bucket of water and runs to quench it. Moreover, it should reject the worst kind of nationalism – aggression without the perception of the consequences and hatred resulting solely from the identity of the other.[145] Other analysts likened the modern era to the politics of the 19th century when the imperial forces concluded alliances that eventually led the world into conflict. The post-Cold War order of the 20th century cannot be restored, but the world is not yet on the threshold of a systemic crisis.[146]

The press blamed President Trump, among other internal issues, for his unstable and non-serious behavior, harming the U.S. effort for global political sovereignty. Trump has simultaneously weakened the United States' international prestige and accelerated the rise of the country's most crucial economic competitor, China. The co-author of the book "Why Countries Fail," Daron Acemoglu, believes that the battle between the Sino-Russian axis and Western democratic institutions will be the decisive struggle of the present century. In the view of other American experts, the chaotic approach of Trump in Foreign Affairs serves both Russia and China, reducing the

---

[144] James Jones, retired U.S. general, former national security adviser to President Barack Obama.

[145] Jake Sullivan, a former Obama administration official and Hillary Clinton adviser.

[146] Richard Haass, President of the Council on Foreign Relations.

prestige and influence of the U.S. in many aspects of the international setting.

China's growing influence

China was an impoverished country due to its centralized economy, operating according to the classical communist model. Although its authoritarian regime was maintained, the party's leadership perceived that it could end the misery of the people by liberalizing the economy. The liberalization decision coincided with increased globalization. Through its low labor cost and the significant number of talented scientists and entrepreneurs that emerged in the new system, China managed in a relatively short time to become a considerable economic power. China most benefitted from globalization; substantial financial resources were transferred from Europe and America. Moreover, it holds significant dollar and U.S. bond reserves.

As part of its effort to increase its international influence, it launched the One Belt One Road (OBOR) initiative in 2013. OBOR is the focal point of China's foreign policy. As far as the "road" is concerned, the action takes its name from the ancient Silk Road, aiming to strengthen the cooperation between China and the countries it crosses. OBOR is not just a road but a series of land and sea trade routes that unite China with Europe, the rest of Asia, Africa, and America. In 2018, the Chinese government announced the start of a new road, the Ice Silk Road. China could be linked with Europe and the Atlantic through a ferry crossing from the North Pole, which became possible due to the partial melting of arctic ice. OBOR refers to investments in more than 60 countries. This network aims to interconnect China with its trading partners through their borrowing from China to construct large infrastructure projects by Chinese companies. With this initiative, China is aiming in the short term to exploit its manufacturing and industrial potential abroad at times when its economy is slowing down. In the long term, China considers that OBOR will help the internationalization of its companies and give Beijing the possibility of regulating world trade.

According to some Western analysts, China aims to politicalize the economy by mutually serving both politics and economics. They claim that Beijing seeks to export a "Chinese model" of state capitalism, combining selected market mechanisms with totalitarian control by a single-party state. The United States considers that China develops economic ties with other countries to shape their interests parallel with China's. Thus, it aims to prevent criticism in matters of concern, e.g., Human Rights.

China strongly opposes protectionism in other countries. Still, it imposes import tariffs on ready-made products. China's average tariffs are three times more than the American and twice as much as the European. However, it does not impose taxes on raw materials that lack, thus keeping the cost of production at a low level. Moreover, China does not only export goods but undertakes the implementation of projects with Chinese workers, proceeds in investments, and grants loans, extending its economic and political influence worldwide. It focuses mainly on the rapidly developing countries that want to remain outside the Russian or U.S. bloc.

Several countries are willing to participate in the China initiative, mainly because it offers more favorable loan terms. However, some states consider Chinese investments to be economically unprofitable or a new kind of colonialism. At the same time, China uses the links created for future military purposes. Its penetration in

Africa is substantive, while China's growing influence in Latin America is notable. China has made significant investments in Brazil and has granted considerable loans to Venezuela and Ecuador, importing at the same time raw materials from Chile. The melting of the Arctic ice led China to elaborate grandiose plans to create an "Ice Silk Road." China exports goods worth about 4 trillion dollars annually, 90% of which are transported by sea. Saving a part of the transport costs would significantly benefit Chinese exporters. Bilateral agreements on infrastructure cooperation, such as on three airports in Greenland and a railway line in Finland, highlight China's growing geopolitical ambition in the region, always in the plan Road and Zone. Beijing works with countries bordering the Arctic Ocean to construct infrastructure (ports, roads, railways, bridges) and communication facilities to exploit the Arctic Road fully.

Similarly, Beijing attempts to build unique relations with the Nordic countries. China's interests compete with those of the USA, Canada, Russia, and Denmark, countries with territorial claims and settled geopolitically interests in the Arctic. Especially in Canada, there is the question of using the Northwest Passage.

The shift of focus to Asia

Unlike Europe or partly Africa, where the countries pursue models of an institutional union, Asian nations consider cooperation based on state units to be more efficient. This is combined with collaboration in international economic organizations.

This kind of cooperation is due to the political architecture of the continent, with the assertive China and Russia potentially dominating. As a Pacific coastal country, the U.S. is involved in Asia's economic and political system, as is the European Union, a robust commercial partner. With the United States' participation, the economic cooperation between Asia and the Pacific is well established. The Asia-Pacific Economic Cooperation (APEC) is a group of 21 members formed in 1989 to promote free trade and sustainable development in the Pacific Rim economies.[147]

The cooperation in the Pacific (Trans-Pacific Partnership – TPP) aimed at tackling China in the face of its growing economic influence through a structured trade bloc that would exempt it. Following the U.S. withdrawal from TPP in 2017, the remaining 11 Pacific Coast countries signed a trade agreement in early 2018. There are no clauses of U.S. interests in the new deal, such as those relating to intellectual property protection. The new deal was named Comprehensive and Progressive Trans-Pacific Partnership (CPTPP) with the addition of the term "progressive."[148] In response, President Trump announced increased duties on steel and aluminum imports. The U.S. preferred to renegotiate its trade agreement with Canada and Mexico. It intended to conclude specific bilateral agreements with the states rather than participate in collective agreements, in which their role would be

---

[147] The founding members of APEC were Australia, Brunei, Canada, Indonesia, Japan, Korea, Malaysia, New Zealand, the Philippines, Singapore, Thailand, and the U.S. Since its launch, China, Hong Kong, Taiwan, Mexico, Papua New Guinea, Chile, Peru, Russia, and Vietnam have joined its ranks. (Asia-Pacific Economic Cooperation (APEC) – god. https://goldoildrugs.com/investments-glossary/asia-pacific-economic-cooperation-apec/)

[148] The 11 countries participating in CPTPP are Australia, Brunei, Canada, Chile, Japan, Malaysia, Mexico, New Zealand, Peru, Singapore, and Vietnam.

limited. However, this development harmed the U.S., not only its strategic interests but also its finances, since CPTPP was discriminatory against the USA.

A series of regional systems that overlap each other determine Asia's geopolitics. There is a system operating in competitive terms in the north, having as a core South Korea and Japan, surrounded by three powers, the two Asian, China (together with North Korea) and Russia, and one off-continent, the USA. Relations between China and Russia could be parallel to the relationships between Germany and France, with the first part of these bipolar being economically strong and the second with more significant political potential. The dividing line, which sets North Korea with the support of China and Russia and, on the other, South Korea and Japan with U.S. support, has not changed despite the occasional fluctuations.

In Southeast Asia, cooperation is based on the economy. It is partly directed against China, not politically or militarily, but economically. The common denominator is the collective defense against the enormous Chinese economy, which threatens their economies. India is a large and powerful nuclear power that forms the opposite pole of Pakistan, the Indian subsystem. Countries east of Turkey and south of Russia belong to another political system. Turkey, together with the Middle East, is considered geopolitically outside Asia. The USA and Australia are involved in all these systems both politically and strategically, but mainly economically. The European Union plays a purely economic role with a political voice of low intensity and reach.

Since President Obama's era, U.S. interests have turned toward Asia. However, the economic-political value of Asia became apparent a long time ago, in the early 21st century, with the enormous economic rise of China and

North Korea's - dangerous for the global peace - nuclear program. The latter causes worries, even after seemingly finding a modus vivendi with President Trump. Many analysts predict that the communist in command and the liberal economy of China will have an even more influential role in the global economy in the future, acquiring the protagonist's part. For the time being, China does not seem to be raising claims of being a great power in international politics. However, American analysts believe this will happen soon, provoking the U.S.

However, it is not only China attracting interest. Several Asian countries are also making considerable strides forward in many areas. In Southeast Asia, Malaysia, the Philippines, Indonesia, Thailand (called "The New Asian Tigers"), and Vietnam, with high economic growth rates, despite the existence of the loose "Association of South Asian Countries (ASEAN)," have their own regional and broader ambitions. On the other end of the continent lies the largest (in population) democracy globally (with weaknesses, of course), India and Pakistan, both nuclear powers. Besides Western-minded Japan, Australia and New Zealand are potent players in the region surrounding the continent.

The Indian Ocean has been a field of competition between the Soviet Union and the U.S. since 1970. The U.S. considered the two oceans, the Indian and the Pacific, as a single operational theatre under the United States Indo-Pacific Command, the term "Indo-Pacific region" being the U.S.'s geopolitical view of Asia. The "Indian-Pacific" is a geographical maritime region that includes the tropical waters of the Indian Ocean, the western and central parts of the Pacific, and the seas that unite these two regions. For foreign policy purposes, the U.S. and Australia use the term "Indo-Pacific" instead of "Asia-Pacific." The latter generally has a similar approach to the U.S. in its "Indo-Pacific" strategy since Canberra uses the Indian and Pacific oceans for its maritime transport. The term Indian-Pacific extends the expression "Asia-Pacific," including the Indian subcontinent, mainly to restore balance to China's growing economic and military power. Besides, the U.S. – Australia – Japan subsystem included India in the discussions relating to the Asian security dimension. After getting over their hesitations regarding the sensitivities of China, the four states have been conducting, since 2014, annual naval drills covering the entire region of Asia, from the Bay of Bengal to the western Pacific.

The Maldives is the central part of a chain of 1,200 islands extending from the southwest coast of India to the Lakshadweep Islands to the south. It is formed in a vertical series of atoll-shaped islands. They ended up at the British Indian Ocean region, the Chagos Archipelago, and the American military base, Diego Garcia, in the middle of the Indian Ocean. Geographically located in the periphery of a circle forming the African Horn, the Arabian Peninsula, southern Iran, and the west coast of India, the Maldives is on the sea route connecting East Asia with the Mediterranean via Suez. China, Saudi Arabia, and India are trying to extend their influence on the geopolitically weighty state of Maldives.

India has been the "invisible hand" in this island country because of its many interventions in the past. It sent Indian parachutists in 1988 to prevent a coup against the actual President. The Indian Navy provided drinking water to the capital, Male, in December 2014 when the desalination system collapsed. However, a political change removed the reconstruction project of the capital's airport from India, handing it over to China, which displeased New Delhi, a traditional geopolitical rival of Beijing. At the same time, Maldives concluded a free trade agreement with China, which opened an embassy in Male and enacted legislation to serve Chinese interests. The overwhelming proportion of the foreign debt of Maldives is due to China. Saudi Arabia sought to secure routes for the marine oil trade in East Asia, particularly with China, and cooperated with the Chinese in many business projects. Riyadh reportedly leased for 99 years a cluster of 19 islands 210 kilometers south of Male, an investment of $10 billion, thus triplicating the country's GDP. At the same time, it reconstructed ten mosques in the context of religious diplomacy. Japan is also trying to promote an initiative called "Strategy for a Free and Open Indian and Pacific Oceans."

Institutional defense partnerships in the area are only bilateral and connect the U.S. with Australia, Japan, the Philippines, and South Korea. The United States also has defense cooperation with other Asian countries. Still, bilateral cooperation between the Asian states with Japan and Australia is not yet strong. In general, Asian countries are temperate in institutionalizing their collaborations. During the Cold War, India favored the Soviet Union, unlike Pakistan, which favored China. The situation began to change somewhat in 2005 when the U.S. implied that it recognized the right of India to possess nuclear weapons. China's pressure on the common border and its relations with Pakistan is the main reason gradually driving India towards a closer understanding with the U.S., Australia, and Japan.

China is said to have seized about 35 square km. of disputed territories in the Himalayas, an event that analysts describe as a "territorial version of China's actions in the South China Sea. On June 17, 2020, hundreds of Indian and Chinese soldiers engaged in a deadly conflict in a river valley that's part of the disputed region of Ladakh. Indian authorities reported at least 20 soldiers killed; it was the first time since 1975 that any Indian soldiers were slain in border skirmishes with China.

Incidents in the Himalayas are a show of force by Beijing, which at the same time has confronted Malaysian and Vietnamese ships in the South China Sea. Simultaneously, it sent an aircraft carrier to the Taiwan Strait and acted unilaterally in 2020, abolishing Hong Kong's semi-autonomy with the security law. The bloody conflict of June of the same year in the Himalayas is not only part of the Sino-Indian border tensions, but it is placed among the broader geopolitical upheavals in the region.

China's influence in the periphery of India is increasing. India's number one enemy, Pakistan, Nepal, Sri Lanka (both previously in the Indian sway), Bhutan, and Bangladesh, are leaning towards Beijing. At the same time, Chinese warships entered the Indian Ocean. In response, Delhi is leaning toward the U.S., with which it signed a $3.5 billion arms deal. The U.S. is also approaching other competitors of China, such as Vietnam. A quartet of China-sceptic countries known as the "Quad," comprising the U.S., Australia, India, and Japan, are meeting regularly and are expected to conduct joint naval exercises. In 2021, the U.S., Australia, and the United Kingdom formalized their partnership (AUKUS). Australia signed a deal with the U.S. to construct nuclear submarines, canceling a respective agreement with France.

China was always concerned and tried to avoid its geopolitical surroundings by forces leaning toward the West. Its relations with India have never been close. It was, therefore, not concerned with the U.S. approach to India, perhaps because of its strong ties with Russia. Moreover, efforts to improve China's relations with Southeast Asian countries have yielded profits. Ultimately, the term "Indian-Pacific" used by the U.S. may mean just a move to address China's regional power. Countries in the area may regard China, to a degree, as an opponent to their interests. Still, Asian solidarity prevails as perhaps they fear the U.S. more than China. In any case, China does not conceal its opposition to the system of American alliances in the Asia-Pacific region. China indicated that it would seek a new type of international network through the debate on the international order. China is implementing a new kind of capitalism that does not depend on economic liberalization and political democracy. Through this, it tries to become an even more robust economy.

The endeavor of India, Japan, and the U.S. to connect the Pacific and Indian Oceans could be an alternative to China's Belt and Road Initiative and enhance the bargaining power of small countries vis-a-vis Beijing.[149] In a speech to the Indian Parliament on the "confluence of two seas," Japan's prime minister Abe brought forth that Japan and India, two marine democracies that are like-minded, should reinforce the freedoms and prosperity in "Greater Asia." The latter, according to Abe, should be affiliated with the USA, Australia, the Philippines, and New Zealand in a network of free movement of persons, goods, and capital. As Tetsuo Kotani put it, this strategy reflects Tokyo's geo-economic views on the region, with the participation of Africa. The militarization of China, the South China Sea, the strengthening of its military base in Djibouti, and its solid naval presence in the Indian Ocean worried Japan, seeking free navigation in the region. Japan's cooperation strategy with India, Australia, and the

---

[149] Raja Mohan, director, Carnegie India, Delhi

U.S. may offset the growing Chinese geopolitical influence in Eurasia and Africa.

Japan has a vital role in Asia's politics alongside like-minded countries. However, as a loser of World War II, it has adhered to a low-profile policy for many years. As one of the strongest economies in the world and despite the reservations of some of its people, it can no longer avoid claiming a more substantial role on the international stage. However, Japan is concerned about its conflict with North Korea, a nuclear power. Simultaneously, regarding its relations with China, besides economic competition, there are disputes on several rocky islands and maritime zones. Based on its industrial strength and strategic relationship with the U.S., Japan tries to create grids of cooperation with countries in the region and, more broadly, attempt to increase its economic and political influence in Asia.

Another action by Japan called the "Initiative for Cooperation in the Western Balkans" was intended to promote talks with various Balkan countries. Japan argues it is willing to support E.U. candidate countries to encourage economic and social reforms. It also appears ready to convey expertise through specialists and seminars in various fields, such as preventing natural disasters and promoting investment and trade. Besides, the E.U. and Japan have signed an Economic Partnership agreement.

Despite its overall commitment to India, Japan, and Australia, the U.S. has always taken a different approach as far as China is concerned. Trump's policy referred to it as a strategic competitor in the political, economic, and military fields and a revisionist force. Although they do not oppose this U.S. policy, Japan, India, Australia, Southeast Asian countries, and South Korea do not seem ready to indulge in a similar form to U.S. competition with China.

The South China Sea is essential, as merchandise of value over 5 trillion dollars passes annually. Due to this, many states reject China's maritime claims in the South China Sea and seek free navigation there. Some, including the U.S., resort to special "free navigation" operations. The coastal states, Taiwan, Brunei, Malaysia, Indonesia, Philippines, and Vietnam, claim the extension of their EEZ, the "ownership" of Spratly and Paracel Islands, and changing the boundaries in the Gulf of Tonkin. In 2016, a ruling of the Arbitral Tribunal in the context of UNCLOS, Annex VII, opposed China's claims against the Philippines. Still, China stated that it did not recognize the jurisdiction of the Court and insisted on bilateral negotiations.

The grid of international cooperation in Asia

One of the most active organizations in Asia is ASEAN. It pursues a global role by promoting cooperation in Asia, worldwide peace and stability, non-interference in internal affairs, and mutual respect.[150] The Association of Southeast Asian Nations – ASEAN is a regional, transnational organization focusing on the importance of Asia and cooperation in economy, politics, education, and culture to integrate these domains at a continental level. With its activities in these fields and the solidarity its members show, ASEAN has become a partner of the international community by participating in various foreign affairs. However, it is not a supranational organization like the European Union since the Member-

---

[150] ASEAN members are Brunei, Cambodia, Indonesia, Laos, Malaysia, Myanmar (formerly Burma), the Philippines, Singapore, Thailand, and Vietnam.

states do not want to cede powers to the association. Various formats are created with non-members, such as the ASEAN Free Trade Area and ASEAN Plus-Three, with the participation of Japan, China, and South Korea. Other forms are the East Asia Summit with the members of ASEAN Plus-Three and India, Australia, New Zealand, USA, and Russia. The ASEAN Regional Forum is a multilateral dialogue forum dealing with security issues in the Asia-Pacific region, involving Bangladesh, Canada, Mongolia, North Korea, Pakistan, Sri Lanka, and the European Union. The latter has a bilateral dialogue with ASEAN. The ASEAN member-states cover an area corresponding to 3% of the world's total land area, and the territorial waters of the member-states cover three times the size of the land with the appropriate economic significance. The population of its member-states amounts to 8.8% of the world population. Based on the total GDP of its member-states, ASEAN, as a unity, would be the world's 6th largest economy.

The Shanghai Cooperation Organization (SCO) is a significant political organization. In 1996, China and the three former Soviet republics of Central Asia (Kazakhstan, Kyrgyzstan, and Tajikistan), with the participation of Russia, discussed in Shanghai the settlement of the border between them after the dissolution of the Soviet Union and signed the relevant Treaty. "The Shanghai Five" agreed to join forces and deal with common issues related to their interests. In 2001, with the participation of Uzbekistan, the intergovernmental regional Shanghai Cooperation Organization or Shanghai Accord, as it has prevailed, was established.[151] The territory of the SCO member-states

---

[151] Members of the SCO are China, Russia, the Asian countries former members of the USSR (Kazakhstan,

comprises 60% of Eurasia, and their population covers a quarter of the world's population. Together with the observer–countries, the agency exceeds half of the world's population. No member of the SCO can have the leadership of such a vast region, with states of various political systems and various Asian cultures. As the Asian political mentality does not favor the transfer of powers to international organizations, Shanghai Cooperation operates based on the coordinated actions of its member-states. The territory of the member-states of the Shanghai Cooperation Organization appears to coincide with the "Heartland" of Mackinder, as described in the "Geographical Pillar of History" (1904). However, despite the ambitious institutionalized objectives, in the case of the Shanghai Organization, no single power controls the entire space, nor does the Organization itself, under its statute, operate in a coordinated manner as a single political or economic force. According to its statute, the goals of the pact are to strengthen mutual trust and good neighborly and friendly relations among member-states, to develop cooperation in political affairs, economy, trade, science and technology, education and culture, energy, environmental protection, and the preservation of regional peace, security, and stability. The main instruments of the Organization are the Council of Heads of State, with annual rotating meetings, and the Council of Foreign Ministers.

  The Cooperation between China and Central and Eastern European Countries (CEEC) «17+1" partnership links 16 post-communist countries in Central and Eastern

---

Kyrgyzstan, Tajikistan, and Uzbekistan), India and Pakistan.
A second ring covers countries with observer status or members of the dialogue.

Europe, plus Greece and the People's Republic of China. This cooperation is seen as the Chinese platform in Eastern Europe to implement the ambitious International Chinese initiative, "One Zone, One Road," the primary focus of China's foreign policy. The "17+1" platform crosses the E.U. border, including 12 E.U. members[152] and five non-EU Balkan members.[153] This system organizes 17 bilateral relations in a multilateral relationship that facilitates Beijing. Bilateral initiatives allow China to bypass existing alliances and include these countries in a "Sino-centric" system. The idea behind the "17+1" was for Europe's eastern countries to take advantage of China's economic dynamics, notably attracting investments. However, the overall level of Chinese investments in the region, except for Greece, remains low compared to China's investments in Western Europe. It offers Beijing another advantage: instead of negotiating collectively, the 17 countries end up competing against each other for what will become the "China Gate to Europe." According to Western analysts, the "17+1" initiative is a political project aimed at shaping the economy – and by extension, the policies – of the countries participating in the Beijing political planning model, i.e., aims at politicizing the economy. Chinese politicians and entrepreneurs conclude agreements with local counterparts, circumventing the standard E.U. control mechanisms. They add that China's model conflicts with the E.U.'s, based on arrangements to ensure fair and open competition. The Chinese model rejects the

---

[152] Bulgaria, Croatia, Czech Republic, Estonia, Hungary, Latvia, Lithuania, Poland, Romania, Slovakia, Slovenia, Greece
[153] Serbia, North Macedonia, Albania, Bosnia and Herzegovina, Montenegro

regulation of this type in favor of an ad hoc negotiation – preferably at the bilateral political level, which results in the finding of funds without transparency.

The Asia-Europe Meeting (ASEM) is a forum for dialogue between the European Union states, the ASEAN states, and some individual states in Asia and Europe. It discusses issues such as the international political situation and economic cooperation, including regional economic and financial priorities in coherence with the global economic situation, as well as social, cultural, and educational issues, such as the development of human resources and educational exchanges, the cultivation of mutual understanding, poverty reduction and increased employment. Political dialogue is conducted through meetings at the Heads of State and Governments level. Therefore, a tribune is provided for a meaningful exchange of views among the states of the two continents. Special meetings for discussing economic, social, cultural, and educational issues are also organized at a ministerial level. Globalization has evolved into a broad, interdisciplinary question, leading to a generalized public debate, with civil society holding the principal word.

AFRICA AND AMERICA

The two regions have similarities as well as differences. They have various advantages and different handicaps. They are both southern continents; they have been "discovered" relatively lately.

Sub-Saharan Africa

Africa may be wronged regarding its size in maps with a Mercator projection. However, the continent's problems are not related to maps but to politics and management. The geographic isolation of sub-Saharan Africa historically did not allow for commensurate development with Eurasia, while colonialism prevented autonomous development in both the economic and cultural sectors. Sub-Saharan Africa has been geographically wronged regarding coasts, ports, arable land, and fauna that are useful to humans compared to Eurasia and North America. Further, colonialism deprived Africans not only of the wealth of their countries but also of any possibility to follow the other free nations of the planet on the road to prosperity and growth.

Sub-Saharan Africa had an intricate 20th century. Despite being acquitted of colonialism, it failed to create conditions of peace and prosperity. The borders of the states follow the lines of former colonies, including many, sometimes mutually hated, nation tribes, or sometimes breaking up nations by dividing them into more countries. Many states could not exercise sovereignty over their entire territory. At the same time, the concept of citizenship was subordinate to the notion of being a member of a nation or tribe, resulting in interracial quarrels and massacres that, in many cases, were indifferent to the international Community.

The Nigerian Civil War (also known as the Biafran War) was fought between the government of Nigeria and the secessionist state of Biafra[154] from 1967 to 1970, resulting in about 100,000 military casualties and between 500,000 and 3 million Biafran civilians dying of starvation. In Rwanda, the Tutsi-led Rwandan Patriotic Front launched a civil war in 1990. Social tensions erupted in 1994 and drove to genocide; Hutu extremists killed an estimated 500,000–1,000,000 Tutsi and moderate Hutu. The RPF ended the genocide with a military victory.

During the Cold War, African states became a competition field for the two superpowers, trying to broaden their sway in their geopolitical interests. The West supported even authoritarian regimes if they were politically on its side. In the Horn of Africa and the former Portuguese colonies of Angola and Mozambique, hundreds of thousands of people were killed in conflicts related to the Cold War. After the end of the Cold War, Africa partly lost the political interest of both the U.S. and Russia. Financial aid declined, and specific regimes holding power because of their political orientation toppled. However, France continued to retain its influence in West Africa.

At the beginning of the 21st century, Africa was able to upgrade its importance thanks to higher growth rates. China, Brazil, and India showed economic interest in the continent. The period of the civil wars finished.

---

[154] Cryptograms from the Biafran War broken – Cipherbrain. https://scienceblogs.de/klausis-krypto-kolumne/2019/12/28/cryptograms-from-the-biafran-war-broken/

Democracy has been restored in many countries; corruption has declined. Significant reforms have brought economic growth, and African countries have begun exploiting their natural wealth to raise their citizens' welfare and not enrich colonialism or corrupt politicians. Nevertheless, they have a long way to go.[155]

Like the European ones, African states believe in the institutional integration of the continent, at least more than Latin American or Asian countries; the "spirit of Africa" possesses them. The African Union (A.U.) is a continental body consisting of 55 member-states of the African Continent. It was officially launched in 2002 as a successor to the Organization of African Unity (OAU, 1963-1999). Due to the Western Sahara conflict, Morocco was accepted only in 2017, while the Government of Western Sahara continues to remain a member of it. The central institutions of the Union are the Assembly of African Unity, which meets at the level of state and government twice a year, and the Committee of the National Union, which is established in Addis Ababa and performs secretarial tasks.

The African Economic Community is based on geographic and economic pillars such as the Saharan and Sahel, East Africa, Central African countries, and the Community of West African countries. It operates on the European Union's standards and achieves a relatively large coherence and solidarity among African countries.

The Economic Community of West African States (Economic Community of West African States-ECOWAS) is a successful regional organization founded in 1975 in Nigeria. The Organization aims to achieve economic integration and balanced growth to form a single

---

[155] A. Houliaras, S. Petropoulos: Africa and Others, 2016. (In Greek).

economic zone in West Africa, acting in the fields of society and politics.

Latin America

Although they speak the same language (except Brazil), Latin American peoples are not linked with strong supranational institutions, while the prevailing spirit is competition. Due to the quasi-colonial interventions of the U.S., their suspicion of it is justified. In particular, the Chavez - Maduro's Venezuela, the Ortega's Nicaragua, partly Morales' Bolivia and Cuba of the descendants of Castro, appear as being the most opposing to the U.S.

The Organization of American States (OAS), founded in 1948, includes all South and North American states and is based in Washington. It aims at regional solidarity and cooperation among member-states. Although the Cuban government remains a member of the Organization, it is excluded from its procedures. In 2017, Venezuela declared its withdrawal from the Organization. Many South American countries and the European Union demonstrated in 2019 their solidarity with the Venezuelan people, calling for free elections.

Among others, globalization helped these countries regain their independence, cooperate, and exclude the U.S. from this cooperation.

Mercosur is a trade bloc of South American states founded in 1991 with the Asuncion agreement. Its motto is "Our North is the South." Together with the Andean Community, they constitute elements of South America's integration process under the Union of the South American States (USAN). The Union is a regional intergovernmental organization that once comprised twelve South American countries. Still, as of 2019, most of them have withdrawn.

The Lima Group is a multilateral international body established to find a peaceful exit to the Crisis in Venezuela. The country faced a socioeconomic crisis during the Presidency of Nicolas Maduro because of his policies and the non-democratic procedures. The group, consisting of representatives of 12 countries, met in the Peruvian capital of Lima. It issued the so-called Lima Declaration on 8 August 2017. The group demands the release of political prisoners and the end of human rights violations. Furthermore, it offers humanitarian aid and criticizes the breakdown of the democratic order in Venezuela under the Bolivarian Government of Venezuela, asking for free elections.

THE MIDDLE EAST

After the Iranian revolution of 1979, Islam, which has always been a political parameter, emerged as a critical component of political developments. Islam began to occupy an increasingly important position within the Muslim states, affecting their societies and gradually eliminating their Western characteristics at an increasing pace. The power of jihadism was raised. Western involvement in the Middle East and Libya has primarily contributed to the region's situation, especially with the U.S. offensive in Iraq and during the Arab Spring. The Westerners claimed they were striving for democracy and human rights when they were mainly interested in geopolitical power and influence. As the Arabs put it, it is just oil and Israel. They repeatedly intervened to kick -and sometimes kill- objectionable leaders and establish friendly regimes. Although they do not accept it, Westerners have failed, attributing it to the assertion that "exporting ideas toward the East is impossible."

The U.S. played a detrimental role in the Middle East. Beyond its one-sided pro-Israeli stance and its involvement in Syria against the country's Government, it took the side of Saudi Arabia in its row with Iran. The United States announced on May 8, 2018, amid the Syria crisis, its withdrawal from the Joint Comprehensive Plan of Action (JCPOA), also known as the "Iran nuclear deal," concluded in 2015. The withdrawal of the U.S. caused concerns in Iran due to its impact on the economy. The European allies of the U.S. were against this move and did not follow it. There were questions about constraining Iran after the U.S. withdrawal and preserving trans-Atlantic unity. On January 3, 2020, the U.S. killed General Soleimani of Iran's Islamic Revolutionary Guard Corps (IRGC) near Baghdad while meeting the Iraqi Prime Minister. The U.S. undertook the responsibility for this killing that violated international law,[156] the penal laws of Iraq and the U.S., and the U.S. administrative powers.[157] This killing was not of the same character as the justified killings of terrorists.

Beyond Westerners, the region's countries are also responsible for the existing unsatisfactory situation. Contrary to the United Nations principles of non-discrimination based on race or religion, the Middle East region is organized in two circles based precisely on such discrimination. The Organization of Islamic Cooperation (OIC), extending beyond the Middle East, has as members the Islamic states. At the same time, the Arab League is based on race, having Arab nations as members. Nevertheless, the U.N. recognizes both organizations even though the OIC circumvents its charter.

The OIC has 57 member-states with 1.6 billion Muslims, and after the U.N., it is the most populous international Organization. It is organized into three geographic-racial groups: African, Arabic, and Asian. At the same time, the only European country member of the Organization is (Islamic) Albania. According to its statute, the Organization is the collective voice of the Muslim world. It allegedly works to secure and protect the interests of Muslims worldwide. The Organization was founded in 1970 as the Organization of Islamic Conference

---

[156] An agreement signed in 2008 prohibits the U.S. from launching attacks on other countries from Iraqi territory.

[157] Since the airstrike was orchestrated without the specific authorization of Congress, there were several legal questions.

after a fire at the Al-Aqsa Mosque in Jerusalem, considered a Jewish act. Among the reasons for its establishment, the Islamic countries presented the void created by the dissolution of the Ottoman Empire (sic). In 2011, it was renamed "Organization of Islamic Cooperation." Its purpose was primarily to promote Palestinian rights and protect Jerusalem from Israel. It evolved as a body to defend Muslim states' interests and Muslims everywhere, mostly against non-Muslim countries. Islamism has a different approach than the West to human rights and religious freedom, democracy, and secularism, creating controversies. The Organization of Islamic Cooperation has the Islamic religion as the sole criterion of all its decisions and actions. For example, in the case of East Timor, it decided contrary to the U.N. positions that members of the Organization had consented in that forum's context, supporting Muslim Indonesia. In the "Dialogue of Civilizations," the OIC asked the E.U. to be its interlocutor. However, the Union is not an organization in the Christian context.

The Arab League, founded in 1945 in Egypt, is considered a regional organization. Still, its name shows it is based on race. The geographic size of the Arab League is vast. Still, the element that gives it power is the possibility to make joint political decisions. As far as Muslim countries are concerned, the League favors Sunnis against Shiites. Decisions on Palestine are made relatively quickly, although there are variations. Decisions concerning relations among its members or in connection with Western countries are more complex to make. The League geographically extends across two continents, Africa and Asia. It includes countries of the southern and eastern Mediterranean and their hinterland in great depth with ramifications in east Africa, also covering the entire

Arabian Peninsula and reaching up to the Indian Ocean. A large part of the territory of the Arab League is constituted of deserts, but there are many fertile areas. Culturally, the Arab League countries could be classified into the groups of Maghreb, Mashreq, and Arabian Peninsula; geographically, it is distinguished in North Africa, the Middle East, the African Horn (Djibouti, Somalia), and the Indian Ocean (Comoros).

The first political breakup of the League occurred regarding the Palestinian Question and the decision of Egypt and Jordan to conclude the Camp David agreements with Israel. On December 5, 1977, following Sadat's visit to the Israeli-occupied Jerusalem, Algeria, Syria, Iraq, Libya, and Yemen, and PLO formed the Front for Resistance and Confrontation, "Front de la Fermeté," to fight what they described as "high treason," the Egyptian peace initiatives with Israel. As a result, Egypt was suspended from the Arab League in 1979. Despite the time passed and the return of Egypt, the split, under some parameters, remains. A second breakup occurred with the Arab Spring and its military-political aftermath, the NATO offensive in Libya, in which Qatar got involved. Also, the intra-Sunni conflicts regarding the Muslim Brotherhood in Egypt, the Shia insurgency in Bahrain (2011), the situation in Syria with the non-Sunni Government expelled from the Arab League (2011), and the conflict between Saudi Arabia and Qatar (2017), played a role.

The permanent dispute concerns the leadership of the "Arab nation." Traditionally, the most populous Arab country, which geographically occupies a central position, Egypt, was considered the leader of the Arab countries. However, this position was challenged after the Camp David agreements (1978). Libya's Gaddafi and Algeria implicitly claimed Arab leadership. President Erdogan's

Turkey also tried to interfere in Arab cases, allied with the Muslim Brotherhood; the Arab countries, however, refused Turkey's involvement. After the Arab Spring, Qatar began to play an extremely active and aggressive role. Several Arab states expressed intense discontent on this, particularly Saudi Arabia, initially because of its relations with the Muslim Brotherhood and later because of its connections with Iran.

Many Arab states did not appreciate the interventive role of Qatar in the developments in the Arab world. Arab countries accuse Qatar of excessive ambitions for hegemony over the Arab world, using as a weapon the Al Jazeera T.V. channel, its petrodollars, and U.S. support. Qatar was alleged to be a mediator in Darfur (Sudan), a financier of the Islamist Ennahda party in Tunisia, a negotiator in Yemen and Mali, president "without tact and diplomacy" at sessions in Arab institutions, "friend in arms" of the rebels in Syria, Islamization agent in the suburbs of Paris, an accomplice of Turkey in breaking the U.N. arms embargo to Libya and above all, a propaganda mechanism through Al Jazeera. The weight is too much for a peninsula with two million inhabitants, which considers it secure because it hosts the more significant off-border U.S. military base.

According to a part of the Arab world, Qatar uses religion to lure populations towards political Islamism, whose adverse effects have been visible in Egypt, Tunisia, Syria, and Libya. The regimes of the Arab world used to close their eyes to the financing by Qatar of radical Islamic currents in the face of promises of investment that were never realized. Qatar reportedly has supported Mali's violent jihadists through the Qatar Red Crescent that settled in Gao in northern Mali. It has been the "charitable arm" of the terrorist organization Mujao. Qatar was also accused of financial assistance allegedly to have provided to the extreme groups in Niger. Through Qatar Charity, Wahhabism expanded throughout West Africa to Senegal.

The way the Qatari T.V. channel Al Jazeera presented the news on the uprisings of the Arab Spring was seen as an attempt to manipulate public opinion. Besides, the high aspirations of Qatar did not cause much sympathy, particularly in the Maghreb, Egypt, or the Gulf countries. However, other Arab channels also do not avoid propaganda. For example, Saudi television networks systematically promote the propagation of Salafism. According to various Arab regimes that oppose this propaganda, some Arab states encourage it to "divide Islamists and weaken the Muslim Brotherhood."[158]

Although an Islamic Wahhabist country, Saudi Arabia is opposed to Islamist action, believing that the greatest danger to the monarchy is the Islamist organizations. In this context, he showed rivalry with the Muslim Brotherhood. He provided considerable financial assistance to Egypt after the June 30, 2013 revolution. However, concerning Syria, it joined the other Gulf countries in favor of Egypt's (Islamist) opposition. However, with a royal decree issued in 2014, it threatened to imprison its nationals who fought abroad. In this way, it intended to limit the number of Saudi jihadists in Syria, fearing that they would pose a danger to the regime in their return.

On the other hand, Qatar actively supports the Islamic groups and the objectives they pursue. Sometimes,

---

[158] Bechir Nafi, researcher at the Centre for Studies Al Jazeera Headquartered in Qatar, referring to Islamic rivalries in the Arab-Muslim world.

it even transcends the limits, causing reactions. The sermon, in February 2014, of an Egyptian clergy in a mosque in Doha, in which he blamed the Emirate as a country opposed to Islamic law because it supported the Muslim Brotherhood, caused a diplomatic incident between Egypt and Qatar. However, sermons in favor of the Muslim Brotherhood were also heard in Saudi Arabia, requesting to end this country's financial assistance to Egypt.

On March 5, 2014, Saudi Arabia, Bahrain, and the United Arab Emirates withdrew their ambassadors from Qatar, denouncing the latter as interfering in their internal affairs and not respecting the agreement signed in November 2013. According to that agreement, Qatar had agreed not to support any individual or a group threatening the security of the members of the Gulf Cooperation Council. The main reason for this was the support provided by Qatar to the Muslim Brotherhood, a movement banned in Egypt and the UAE. After two years, Saudi Arabia and some other pro-western Gulf countries eventually understood that they had allied with Al Qaida through Al Nusra in Syria and cut their relations. Qatar refused to follow them.

On the contrary, It continued to support this extremist Organization and other similar organizations in the region. Qatar was also accused of supporting Houthi rebels in Yemen. Al Jazeera's journalists were indicted in Egypt because they assisted the Muslim Brotherhood, which was declared a terrorist organization. At the same time, a Qatari national was tried in the UAE on the charge of supporting the Islamic political Organization Al Islah.

Together with cooperation in exploiting hydrocarbons with Iran, the rivalry with the other Gulf states led Qatar to approach Iran. Regardless of what

American President Trump was seeking with his anti-Iranian and supportive Saudi Arabia statements, during his visit to Riyadh in 2017, other Arab countries took advantage of the U.S. position to promote their agenda. Besides the "war" against Shiites in its territory, Saudi Arabia has a dispute with Shiite Iran over three islands in the Persian Gulf.

The Saudi Arabia-Qatar conflict for regional influence over the Gulf Cooperation Council continued with the so-called Second Arab Cold War. In June 2017, Saudi Arabia, the UAE, Bahrain, Egypt, the Maldives, Mauritania, Senegal, Djibouti, Comoros, Jordan, the Libyan Government in Tobruk, and the Government of Yemen under Hadi discontinued their diplomatic relations with Qatar. They also prohibited overflights in their airspace and the crossings from their territorial waters. The justification for this action was Qatar's support of Islamist groups and the unflattering reportage of Al Jazeera regarding Gulf countries.

The civil war in Yemen should be viewed in the context of the political conflict between Sunni Saudi Arabia and Shiite Iran. The battle between the Yemeni Government under Abdrabbuh Mansur Hadi, allied with Saudi Arabia, and the Houthi armed movement supported by Iran began in 2015. Under the official name Ansar Allah, the Houthi movement -Supporters of Allah– is an Islamic politico-religious militant movement under Hussein Badreddin al-Houthi based in Sa'dah in northern Yemen. The forces of Ansar Allah, controlling the capital Sana' and forces loyal to former President Ali Abdullah Saleh, clashed with troops of the new Hadi government based in Aden. The terrorist organizations Al-Qaeda in the Arabian Peninsula (AQAP) and the "Islamic State of Iraq and Levante" also participated in the clashes. The fighting with

270

the murderous raids of the Saudi Air Force led civilians on the Houthi side to misery.

The Palestinian issue

A large part of the Arab world does not accept a Jewish state at the heart of the region, considered Muslim. Otherwise, Arabs would welcome the simultaneous establishment of an Israeli and a Palestinian state from the outset (1947). The existence of Israel is ensured only by the power of arms. Israel, therefore, considers that it is in a continuous state of defense and bases its foreign policy on this doctrine. With the help of the U.S., Israel has succeeded in signing the Camp David agreements on its state of existence with Egypt and Jordan eleven years after their defeat in the Six-Day War (1967).

Clashes between Israelis and Palestinians have been constant, and both parties are to blame for the situation. Hamas is a Palestinian Sunni-Islamic fundamentalist militant organization. It has a social service wing, through which it became popular among poor Palestinians, and a military wing. It has been the de facto governing authority of the Gaza Strip since its takeover of that area in 2007. During this period, it fought several wars with Israel.[159] The United States and the European Union consider, either in whole or in part, Hamas as a terrorist organization. On the other hand, Iran, Russia, China, and Turkey are some countries that view Hamas positively.

After the commencement of the civil war in Syria in 2011, Israel regarded Iran as its greatest enemy, which, although not neighboring or Arab, has opposed Israel's

---

[159] IsraelPalestine For Thinkers: #13 Accord and Discord IsraelandYou. https://www.israelandyou.com/accord-and-discord/

existence since the Iranian Revolution of 1979 because of its religion. Therefore, in a geopolitical approach, Israel considers forming a Shia arc in its north, by Iran –Iraq – Syria – Hezbollah (Lebanon), as dangerous for its existence. In this respect, it had the tacit consent of the Sunni states of the Arabian Peninsula, except Qatar, which follows a peculiar policy.

Hezbollah, "Party of Allah," is a Shiite Islamist political party and militant group based in Lebanon. Hezbollah's paramilitary wing is the Jihad Council, and its political wing is the Loyalty to the Resistance Bloc party in the Lebanese parliament.[160] The military branch is considered a terrorist organization by the Arab League, the U.S., and the European Union. In addition, Hezbollah is viewed as the hand of Shiite Iran in the region.

However, the international community considers that Palestinians are entitled to an independent state. After the declaration of Algeria in 1988, it seemed that both parties accepted the two-state solution (Israel – Palestine) instead of Palestinians remaining as a minority under the occupation of Israel (single-state solution). Israel's policy on the Palestinians has not been fair; for decades, it has sought territorial expansion at their expense with the construction of settlements and the building of a wall to the detriment of their land.

In the two-state solution, the most critical issues are geographical, apart from political problems. Both consider Jerusalem the capital of their states. Besides, the non-functionality of a country divided into two geographic regions, on the one hand around the Jordan – the so-called

---

[160] Israel | Sandeep Bhalla's Blog. https://sandeepbhalla.com/tag/israel/

West Bank, and on the other hand, the Gaza Strip, with the territory of Israel separating them, is obvious.

President Trump took an extremely pro-Israeli stance, moving the U.S. Embassy in Israel to Jerusalem, recognizing it as Israel's capital. The European allies of the U.S. were against this move. The annexation by Israel of territory in the West Bank was effectively encouraged by the United States' controversial "peace" proposal that President Trump unveiled in January 2020. This plan could withdraw the possibility of the two-state solution.

The announced Israel – United Arab Emirates deal in August 2020 might put Israeli annexation of West Bank lands on hold as a condition of normalizing relations.[161] Palestinians and Turkey denounced the agreement. By that deal, Arab countries recognizing Israel became three: Egypt, Jordan, and UAE. Bahrein followed.

Syria

The West created the problem in Syria for its benefit. It tried to exploit the Arab Spring to replace the pro-Russian Assad with a West-friendly Sunni government, whether Islamist or not. After Yugoslavia's breakup, Syria was Russia's last bridgehead in the Mediterranean. Russia did not care about democracy or legality: It just wanted to keep its bases in Syria. However, the difference between East and West is supposed to be morality.

The relations between Syria and Lebanon were among the reasons for the West's discontent with Syria. The area's geography, as it was mapped out by the Anglo-French agreement (Sykes-Picot agreement) after the First

---

[161] Current Affairs [14th August 2020] - All Important Events covered. https://testbook.com/blog/important-current-affairs-14th-august-2020-with-pdf/

World War and Syria's will to have the upper hand, caused its involvement in Lebanese affairs angered the West, particularly France. The Golan Heights of high strategic importance at the border annexed by Israel prevented, among others, a modus vivendi between Syria and Israel. The hostile stance of Syria towards Israel was also a cause for the vexation of the West.

Assad is Alevite, closer to the Shiites, which triggered the reaction of the overwhelming majority of Sunni Arab states. The control of the Shia Hezbollah in Lebanon was an additional issue that provoked the response of Israel and the West. Turkey should have been the only one who had no problems with Assad. Instead, its anti-Assad position was formed during the developments, primarily for political reasons, precisely the Kurdish Question.

At the beginning of 2011, a current asking for democracy and reforms appeared in many Arab countries - the Arab Spring. Unfortunately, the situation was quickly diverted in favor of the Islamists, who rushed to take advantage of the developments to advance their theocratic system. Tunisia and Egypt fell in danger of becoming Islamist countries. In Egypt, a demonstration of a million citizens was required to overturn Islamist President Morsi. Libya was destroyed. The staunch republican stance of Tunisians rescued the country from falling to Islamists. The Assad regime was authoritarian, albeit not typically, like most of the governments in the region. However, it had ensured, if not the total acceptance, at least the tolerance of most of the Syrian people. Regarding freedoms, secularism, tolerance for Christians, and living standards, Syria was in a much better position than many other countries in the Arab world.

The protest events in the context of the Arab Spring in Syria began on March 15, 2011, but failed to produce an outcome. Nevertheless, the demonstrations, having requested the removal of Assad, took a more violent character since armed Islamists replaced the protesters who lacked the sympathy of most Syrians. In front of this situation, Western powers organized a military force, initially based in Turkey, to attack the regime.[162] Disgruntled military, liberated political prisoners, and al-Qaeda formed a guerrilla group, later reorganized as the Free Syrian Army,[163] that began armed and bloody attacks, starting at the Turkish border, in June 2011. The (Suni) Arab League expelled Alevite Assad's Syria from the Organization.

The rebels were supported and equipped by the West and the Sunni Arab countries. The situation quickly got into the hands of al-Qaeda, which proclaimed "with the help of the United States," [164] jihad in Syria. Eventually, another Islamist terrorist organization, ISIS, prevailed among the rebels in order not only to overthrow Assad but

---

[162] According to Arab press reports (November 23, 2011), members of the French Secret Service, the CIA, the German BND and the Israeli Mossad organized in Turkey the "dissenting" Syrians, who were in fact Islamist terrorists who had come from Libya, Chechnya, Afghanistan and elsewhere.

[163] The Free Syrian Army (FSA) is a loose faction in the Syrian Civil War founded on 29 July 2011by officers of the Syrian Armed Forces whose stated goal was to bring down the government of Bashar al-Assad. A formal organization at its founding, its structure gradually dissipated by late 2012, and the FSA identity has since been used by various opposition groups.

[164] In the words of Al Zawahiri, chief of Al Qaida

to transform Syria into an Islamic state. However, blinded by its strong wish to overthrow pro-Russian Assad, the West supported the so-called "moderate" rebels who did not represent even a tenth of the Islamist, anti-Assad rebellion. According to the Arabs with a republican (secular) approach, it was neither the first nor the second time the U.S. allied with Al Qaida or the jihadists. After Afghanistan, the Algerians point out that the U.S. and many NATO members had virtually helped Islamic terrorism in Algeria through their administrative support to Saudi Arabia and the Gulf states cooperating with the terrorists. A third case of the West-al-Qaida military alliance took place in Libya. It resulted in the brutal killing of Gaddafi. Unfortunately, in Syria, the West once more was on the wrong side of history.

According to Arab press reports echoing a portion of progressive Arab public opinion, the armed uprisings, at least in Libya and Syria, were not spontaneous but a result of Islamist instigation. The diplomatic solutions to expel Assad ended in 2012 after the Russian and Chinese veto in the U.N. Security Council. Since an external armed intervention could not acquire a U.N. qualification after the events in Libya, the countries supportive of the rebels insisted on the military neutralization of Assad. The fights resulted in a sad humanitarian situation, and the security of the citizens fell to a nadir. The persistence in this direction caused thousands of victims. Still, the international broadcasting media, Western and Sunni Arabic, had no compunction about presenting the Syrian regime as solely responsible for the humanitarian disaster.

The terrorist organization "Islamic State," posing as a state, occupied much of Syria and western Iraq, having as their main rival the Syrian Kurds, whereas the Syrian national army had to confront the Western-backed rebels.

Kurds, backed by the U.S., managed to defeat the Islamists; however, they did not achieve their goal of establishing an autonomous-independent state in the northern zone of Syria, Rojava. Following the unification of the Rojava enclaves in the east and the center, efforts to annex the third enclave in Afrin failed after the military intervention of Turkey, reacting to the establishment of a Kurdish state on its southern border.

The reason that the drama of Syria lasted for a long time is the insistence of the West to overthrow Assad. The various peace plans failed as the Westerners insisted on the prior ousting of Assad in the assumption of his defeat. Nevertheless, Assad had most of the Syrian people with him, claiming he did not refuse to confirm it with democratic elections.

In the Middle East, two broad coalitions were formed around the end of 2017. The first included Russia, Iran, the Assad regime, Hezbollah, and the Shiites of Iraq. The second was composed of the U.S. and other Western powers, Israel, the Kurds, Saudi Arabia, and other Arabian Gulf countries. At the same time, Turkey remained a wandering political player, changing objectives and camps. The Kurds, backed by the U.S. and France to a lesser extent, fought ISIS and their rival Assad. Turkey fought Assad and the Kurds who opposed him, and Israel also fought against Assad. Russia aligned with Assad, and Baghdad fought the ISIS and the Kurds. Sunnis from the Arab states fought Shiites, Shiites from Iran fought the Sunnis of ISIS and Israel, whereas al-Qaeda fought everybody. The Free Syrian Army, a Western construction, was just a decorative player. In early 2018, Turkey attacked the Syrian region of Afrin against the U.S. allies Kurds. It also confronted military bodies friendly to Assad, made up of Iranians hostile to the Iranian state.

However, the camps were only two: On the one hand, the authoritarian but legitimate, elected Syrian leader Assad with his allies; on the other, the alliance of the few rebels who fought for their personal ends and the Jihadist terrorists who sought to overthrow Syria's secular system and establish an Islamic regime and their allies, the West. The latter sought to overthrow the Assad regime and replace it with a pro-Western government. At the same time, Sunni Arab states were trying to oust Assad and replace him with a Sunni leader, authoritarian or not, indifferent to them.

The U.S. decision to set up on the Syrian-Turkish border a force of thirty thousand soldiers from the YPG Kurdish militia in Syria provoked Ankara's wrath, which considers YPG the revolutionary PKK's extension in Syria. The U.S. target was both confrontation with ISIS and opposition to Damascus. This border army's geographic boundaries of action would include a triangle extending from the north to the Syrian-Turkish border and along the eastern bank of the Euphrates River to the south-eastern Syrian-Iraqi frontier line. The northeastern part of Syria was a de facto semi-autonomous region already under the control of an Arab-Kurdish coalition. The U.S. also aimed to prevent the return to Syria of ISIS's jihadists, who fled to Iraq after their defeat by the Kurds. Damascus, for its part, was opposed to the U.S.'s plan since they considered it as promoting the division of Syria.

Turkey intervened in Syria against the Kurdish army in Afrin and created a situation in which, in simplistic terms, the enemies of Damascus Turks attacked the enemies of Damascus Kurds. The latter fought the enemies of Damascus jihadists, while the enemies of Damascus and friends of Kurds, Americans, were seemingly confronted with their NATO allies, the Turks. The partner of Damascus,

Russia, tolerated the Turkish offensive against the hostile Damascus Kurds. Since the beginning of 2019, the U.S. withdrew from Syria, and countries in the Arab world began to recognize the Assad regime. Turkey found the opportunity to consider that the time had come to attack the Kurds as the U.S. abandoned its Kurdish allies at the mercy of Turkey. After years of battles and disasters, with the military involvement of Arab countries, the USA, Russia, France, and Turkey, as well as various terrorist organizations with different opponents, millions of dead and displaced persons, the result was the prevalence of legitimacy, with President Assad in power. Syria recovered its sovereignty; the West and its allies eventually lost the initiative to move.

A German regional court became the first to judge the Syrian regime for war crimes in 2020.[165] German prosecutors in the German town of Koblenz, 2,000 miles away from the war-torn country, brought charges against two Syrian nationals who had claimed asylum in Germany. According to observers, the case "marks the first time an independent court will issue findings on President Bashar al-Assad's tools of suppression during the mass demonstrations of 2011 and the civil war that followed". That is, a German court considered the jihadists, i.e., the terrorist organizations "Islamic State" and "Al Qaeda," together with a band of insurgents motivated by foreigners, as a belligerent legal party.

North-East Africa

After the unrest of the Arab Spring period and the Syrian adventure, the geopolitical tug of war was transferred to East Africa. Turkey, with Qatar on the one

---

[165] Washington Post April 24, 2020

hand and Saudi Arabia, the United Arab Emirates, and Egypt on the other, each with their specific aspirations, have been thrown into the struggle to increase their sway. Thus, the political developments of the Middle East passed into the Horn of Africa, militarizing and polarizing it, with the building of a grid of proxies to exert pressure on their opponents.

The growing influence and resources of the Gulf oil-producing countries sometimes help achieve compromises in East Africa. For example, the acceptance of the agreement of Algiers of 2000 from the two sides in July 2018 ended a two-decade war situation for border disputes between Ethiopia and Eritrea. The mediation efforts of the African Union and the United Arab Emirates facilitated the deal.

Somalia is one of Africa's most homogeneous countries in terms of culture, ethnicity, religion, and language. About 85% of the population are Somalis residing mainly in the north, while minorities inhabit the south. The official languages are Somali and Arabic, both of which belong to African-Asian languages. Most of the population is Muslim - Sunni. The climate is hot all year round.

Nevertheless, the Middle East exports its vast geopolitical differences beyond the Red Sea. In countries such as Somalia, the Middle East's involvement, together with the action of the local al-Qaeda, Al-Shabaab, has made the already volatile local policies even more explosive. In August 2014, the Somali Government launched the operation "Indian Ocean" against pockets of insurgents that lasted for many years. In October 2017, two successive bomb blasts killed more than 500 people in Capital Mogadishu. Moreover, Somalia's political relations are strained with Kenya. Still, there is cooperation in tackling the action of Al-Shabaab, from which both countries are suffering.

In the Sudan region, the Declaration of the Independence of South Sudan in 2011, with the referendum held following the 2005 Comprehensive Peace Agreement (CPA), which ended the second civil war, did not result in complete pacification. The underlying tension between the Republic of Sudan and South Sudan is caused, besides their different religion, by geography. South Sudan has oil fields, but it is a landlocked country depending on the (northern) Sudan for the passage of pipelines, taxed heavily from the latter. Sudan and South Sudan, with their size and geographical proximity, both carry a critical geopolitical role.

In Ethiopia, the Grand Ethiopian Renaissance Dam (GERD), the largest dam in Africa with a hydroelectric station on the Blue Nile River, can transform the economy of Ethiopia and bring rapid development in the agricultural sector of neighboring Sudan. However, in Egypt, downstream of the Nile, serious problems could be created when Ethiopia runs the dam and diverts the Nile's waters to fill its vast reservoir since 95% of the population lives on the Nile's shores or its delta. A solution could be the two countries' cooperation, feasible at a technical level but politically difficult to achieve. Otherwise, the risk of mass immigration that will affect Europe, too, is probable.

Several mediators have attempted to facilitate negotiations and encourage Egypt and Ethiopia to compromise. The United States, maintaining friendly relations with the two countries, tried to help but was accused by Ethiopians of bias in Egypt's favor. On the contrary, the Egyptians accused the African Union (based in Addis Ababa) of taking Ethiopia's side. Finally, the two countries reached an interim agreement, allowing more negotiation time. Ethiopia has agreed primarily not to start filling the water reservoir until reaching a comprehensive agreement. Nevertheless, in July 2020, Ethiopia began to fill the reservoir, provoking reactions, among others, of the U.S.

President Abdel Fattah el-Sissi of Egypt and Prime Minister Abyei Ahmed of Ethiopia have substantial internal restrictions that do not allow concessions in negotiations. The Sisi regime in Egypt faces serious problems both in external relations (Libya, Israel's politics in the Occupied Territories) and, above all, at home. After the decision of the Egyptian parliament, the concession of two Red Sea uninhabited (except for a few peacekeeping forces) islands, Tiran and Sanafir, at the entrance of Akaba Bay to Saudi Arabia in 2017 created problems for the regime. It sparked protests, with President Sissi being accused of "selling" the islands in return for Saudi aid. In September 2019, thousands accused Sisi of corruption and called for his resignation.

On the other hand, Ethiopia faces significant internal problems with an armed insurgency in Oromia, clashes in various parts of the country, millions of internal refugees, and political uncertainty. The previously popular Prime Minister Abiy Ahmed Ali, who acted resiliently at the peace deal with Eritrea that assured him the 2019 Nobel Peace Prize, has little room for maneuvering the Nile issue. The dam, which cost over 4 billion euros and was financed by issuing bonds bought by hundreds of thousands of Ethiopians, is a critical element for national pride. Any retreat to Egypt's demands risks being considered treason.[166]

---

[166] Asterios Houliaras

The protracted conflict in northern Ethiopia between the Government and the Tigray rebels has killed thousands of people and left millions in desperate need of food and other assistance.

The conflict over the Nile Dam, the Tigray crisis, the resurgence of violence in Sudan and Somalia, instability in Egypt, mass migration, and threats to the Red Sea are among the potential dangers in the region that can lead to conflicts.

The MENA region

The MENA Region covers the Middle East and North Africa; it is part of the ancient Oikumene, surrounding the Mediterranean from the south and the east. Due to its geopolitical position, character, energy sources, and vicinity with Europe, MENA was at the center of interest of Europe and the U.S. for a long time. The U.S.'s approach was based not only on its existing military power -the most potent armed forces in the world- but also on its readiness to use them. Beyond this, Americans attempted to organize and activate civil society, sometimes as a counterweight against non-friendly local Governments, in the context of democracy and market economy. Europe's approach is more state-centric and is based on financial support and cooperation to implement programs of common interest. The strategic parameter certainly exists, but it is not utilized in Europe. The European interest in improving the standard of living and the population's situation, both through the development of democratic institutions and their economic potential, is sincere. The American interest focuses on collective security and cooperation in combating terrorism.

The MENA region is dominated by internal, socio-economic, and religious conflicts, transnational disputes over territories, resources, and borders, regional violence with security implications, as well as the militarization of political causes of conflict. Therefore, the various cooperation initiatives developed by both European and international stakeholders have considered addressing this situation.

The United States, particularly after 9/11, felt that it should pay more attention to its cooperation with the MENA region countries at a level different from that of the state. The U.S.- Middle East Partnership Initiative of the State Department (MEPI) has assisted since 2002 the 18 countries of the region where it operated. It offered training and support to groups and individuals who "strive to create positive societal changes." In 2003, the U.S. launched the "Broader Middle East policy," an area in which they included Turkey, the Middle East, the Arabian Peninsula, Pakistan, Afghanistan, and all of North Africa to Mauritania. The U.S.'s expressed aim was to establish or consolidate democratic institutions based on the market economy. It was a strategy for increasing its sway, which in part had succeeded without offering additional special funds.

There have been initiatives on the part of the Atlantic Alliance as well. NATO's Mediterranean dialogue began in 1994. It covered seven Mediterranean countries: Algeria, Egypt, Israel, Jordan, Mauritania, and Tunisia. Geographically, it equals the total of the Maghreb countries except for Morocco, as Algeria could not participate in a military dialogue with it. The triangle of Camp David, i.e., Egypt, Israel, and Jordan, participated also. The discussions reflected the Alliance's view that Europe's security was linked to the Mediterranean. It was an attempt by NATO after the Cold War to adapt to the new situation. Given that during the Cold War period, at least Algeria, Libya, Syria, and Yemen were considered part of the USSR's sphere of influence, this outcome was a success for the United States.

The positions taken by the West are not free from the burden of history, considering that geography is constant. As presented, the objectives of NATO's Mediterranean Dialogue are the contribution to regional cooperation and stability, better understanding, and dissolving any doubts relating to the North Atlantic Treaty. Southern Mediterranean partners do not accept Israel's cooperation forms with the dialogue states (NATO + 7). Some Arab countries proposed forms of cooperation in the context of "changing geometry," i.e. (NATO + n) where n, any number of Mediterranean states...excluding Israel.

The NATO "Istanbul Initiative" was launched in 2004 to contribute to long-term global and regional security. It would offer practical bilateral security cooperation with the North Atlantic Treaty Organization to countries in the broader Middle East region. Among the countries of the Gulf Cooperation Council invited, Bahrain, Qatar, Kuwait, and the United Arab Emirates joined, while Saudi Arabia and Oman merely "showed interest." However, the end of the Arab Spring brought about conflicts among the once fraternal countries, with issues of rivalry, mainly the leadership of the Arab states and the protection from terrorist Islamism.

The Euro-Mediterranean cooperation, known as the Barcelona Process, was established in 1995 at the Conference of the Euro-Mediterranean foreign ministers in Barcelona as a culmination of previous European initiatives for cooperation with the countries of MENA, such as the Global Mediterranean Policy (1972-1992) and the new Mediterranean policy (1992-1995). Israel's participation in the Barcelona Process eventually caused the Arabs to undermine this initiative, resulting in its inactivation. The process was succeeded in 2008 by the Union for the Mediterranean (UfM). This cooperation included 28 member-states of the European Union and 15 Mediterranean states. The proposal to confine participation to the Mediterranean countries was rejected due to objections raised by non-Mediterranean E.U. member-states. The UfM aimed to promote stability and prosperity in the Mediterranean region through cooperation in various projects. Still, again, the presence of Israel led different Arab countries to be reluctant to participate, while Gaddafi's Libya never joined the cooperation.

Within the framework of the "European Neighbourhood Policy," it was considered useful to include together with the eastern European countries and the Mediterranean neighbors of Europe.[167] This policy was added to the concluded Association Agreements, but less than a process that could lead to accession to the Union. The initiative of the Euro-Mediterranean neighborhood has been Europe's response to the American scheme of the Broader Middle East.

Turkey

Turkey, by geography, is a bridge linking two continents. Still, it could be considered mainly a country of Middle East mentality. Turkey's contemporary attitude and international behavior are non-European. Its geographical position defines Turkey's place on the global

---

[167] Forms of regional cooperation within the framework of the area were the schemes between Europe and the countries of the Eastern Partnership, including Armenia, Azerbaijan, Belarus, Georgia, Moldova, and Ukraine.

geopolitical scene as a barrier to Russia's descent into the Mediterranean. Turkey is making the most of the West's anti-Russian policy to gain benefits and avoid sanctions for its systematic violation of Human Rights and the rules of International Law. It invaded Syria and Iraq, bombarded Iraqi Kurds (e.g., on June 15, 2020), and continuously violated Greece's airspace and continental shelf and Cyprus' Economic Zone. It sent mercenaries to Libya (spring 2020) with no consequences. Westerners even forgive Turkey's often anti-Western policy by succumbing to its implicit blackmail on abandoning the Western coalition. Turkey's continuing aggression against its neighbors is characteristic, apparent from the Ottoman Empire's early years. Turkey has always sought alliances in line with its specific interests without considering ideological or moral factors, hence the nickname "the evasive neutral."[168]

The sense of loss of the Ottoman Empire's greatness, and especially the largest part of its territory, is the element that affects the mindset of contemporary Turkey's leaders. They do not consider that this territory was conquered by military means and kept through harsh measures. The success of the recovery of the Sancak of Hatay (1936) and the invasion and occupation of a large part of Cyprus (1974) gave Turkey the impression that it could continue in the same way in its neighborhood.[169] Furthermore, it signed an agreement with Libya's disputed

---

[168] Frank G. Weber: The Evasive Neutral, Germany, Britain, and the Quest for a Turkish Alliance in the Second World War

[169] That is to the Greek islands in the Aegean, with claims in their territorial zone and airspace, but also with the "invention" of grey zones to raise claims on several Greek islands.

P.M. Saraj to provide military assistance during Libya's civil war despite the U.N.'s arms embargo on Libya. It concluded a deal with Libya, violating the international law to share with this country part of the Exclusive Economic Zone of Greece as defined by the U.N. Convention on the Law of the Sea. Turkey is, of course, a big country. Still, there is a mismatch in what it really is, what various Western countries consider it, and what its elite and politicians think it is. Several of the problems that arise are the result of this mismatch. Moreover, its peculiar views on international law, accepted only by Turkey, create additional questions.

Turkey's geographical position, with eastern Thrace typically in Europe and its more significant part, Anatolia, also conventionally in Asia or the Middle East, raises doubts about its cultural-geographical identity. Still, Turkey thinks it belongs to Europe. Closer to reality, a north-south dividing line from the Black Sea to the Mediterranean, passing west of Ankara, would set Anatolia's eastern part as Asiatic and western part as European. Western Turkey differs in many ways from the east part, including the way of life and the way it votes. In any case, Turkey knows the value of its geographical location and does not stop selling it in many directions at a substantial political price.

The Ottoman Empire, and afterward the Turkish state, was considered a barrier to Slavic expansion to the south, followed by supposedly undertaking the same role against the Soviet Union and contemporary Russia. Turkey has succeeded in selling this role to the West, even though it has historically always been ethnocentric, weighing things constantly according to its narrow national interest. In WW I, Turkey took the opposite side of the West, and it remained neutral in WW II, bargaining with both sides.

Turkey also presented itself as a barrier to protect Europe from the Islamist threat. Nevertheless, since it lacked content, this claim faded as an argument supporting Turkey by the West. However, its role in creating the refugee-migration crisis of 2015 highlighted the risks involved in its proximity to Europe. In this case, Turkey has succeeded in being seen as a country that provides asylum to war refugees. It offered refuge in camps near the Syrian border to millions of Syrians who fled their homes. On the other hand, most of them were not refugees but potential immigrants to Europe. It instrumentalized them to hit Europe.

Westerners sometimes saw Turkey as the Western outpost in the Middle East. Turkey did not seek this role and tried to shake off any suspicion that it had adopted it. Moreover, despite its military might, it cannot undertake a leadership role since its influence on the region's countries is minimal. Turkey is mistrusted by its neighbors because of its revisionist and aggressive behavior. However, its military might and readiness to use it abroad more than any other country in the region represent a danger.

The elements involved historically in shaping the internal situation in modern Turkey were the opposition Islamists – secularists in the sense of Kemalist reforms, the army's attempt to influence things in this context, the conflict between the state and the leftist movements as well as the involvement of extreme nationalists, and finally the conflict of the Turkish Government with the Kurds. These elements remain for a long in political and social life as established characteristics, which have become an expression of the personality of the modern state of Turkey. Many faithful Muslim people never embraced Ataturk's changes imposed on traditional life in attire and customs. The reactions of the ordinary people were not so much related to state secularism as to those elements that directly affected life, and they were accepted only because of violence and pressure. Politicians can only take this trend into account. The army considered the guardian of the Kemalist principles, did not fail to react whenever it thought there was a considerable divergence from Kemalist principles. It also acted when the often-armed leftist movements disrupted public order. Nevertheless, Erdogan's era changed all these and drove Turkey to Islamism.

The Kurds, Turkey's wretched and repressed ethnic minority inhabiting southeast Anatolia, have repeatedly rebelled against the Turkish state, which quelled the revolutions harshly. For a long time, Turkey did not recognize the minority rights of Kurds, considering them as Turks and not allowing the Kurdish language and their cultural manifestations. Turkey's public opinion usually favors the Government's actions, even if they distort the facts.[170]

The population of Turkey amounted to 13.5 million in 1927, increasing at a rate of over 10% every five years. In 1955, it had already reached 24 million, with a growth of 10-15% every five years, reaching 35 million in

---

[170]Thus, "the Armenian genocide did not take place; on the contrary, it is the Armenians who slaughtered the Turkish villagers." "It is the Greeks who, leaving Smyrna, set it on fire so as not to leave their homes to the Turks." "Cyprus is Turkish" But also more recently: "The Turkish minority in Thrace is being oppressed, while the Greeks in Istanbul enjoy all rights. Those who left Turkey (i.e. all of them) simply found better economic conditions elsewhere." "It is the Greeks who are blocking the passage of refugees resulting in their drowning", etc.

1970. There was a debate on whether the population should grow at this speed or whether measures to limit such a rapid increase should be imposed. The conclusion was that the population was a power factor for a country and that Turkey could sustain a much larger population. Population growth continued at the same rate, reaching 68 million in 2000. However, the per capita income with rapid population growth could not follow similar rates to Europe's. Except whatever was caused by Islamists, Kurds, or leftists, the unrest in Turkey was due to this fact. However, Turkey's strong population potential and a sense of order that occurred when radical leftist activism declined have helped Turkey's economic growth. Turkey's economy is now among the world's twenty largest economies, a development indicative of Turkey's success as an economically competitive state. Along with the continued migration of Turks to Europe, the population continued to grow, albeit at a lower rate, but more than 1% per year, reaching 80 million in 2014.

Turkey's relative political shift to the West is rewarded by individual countries, such as Germany and the U.S., and international organizations, such as NATO. As it evolves throughout its history, the essence of Turkey's peculiar personality is no longer understood by the West, which now seems to perceive only the persona presented by Turkey. The latter, which has made a great effort in public relations, is aware of the West's views and, therefore, behaves accordingly. Nevertheless, it succeeds in being respected by Russia because of its geographical interests and by the states of the Middle East because of its military might. In this context, Turkey is successful in shaping its international image.

Islamism is not a religion but a political ideology, aiming at the imposition of Islamic rules, or in any case, what its adepts see as the Islamic rules. According to Islamism, the state's laws must come from Sharia and be applied following traditional Islamic standards. However, the Islamists themselves regard the term "Islamist" as being used by third parties to describe their movement disparagingly. On the other hand, democracy is not a religion; it can not be equal to Islam but a way of collective decision-making on matters of general interest. Thus, the conflict is not between democracy and Islam, perceived as concepts, but between democracy and Islamism.

Concepts such as "Political Islam" and «Moderate Islam" should be further analyzed. Islam plays a central role in Islamic societies. In Islam, religion, community, politics, and the private sphere are interconnected. Islam, at its base, is not just a religion but a way of life. It is, therefore, above everything, and in this theoretical conception, it is contrary to the democratic and liberal principles that govern modern Western - and not only - societies. "There is no Political or Moderate Islam, just Islam," as many Muslims put forward.

The Kemalist revolution overturned the concept of Islam, eliminating it from any activity other than the religious, establishing a secular state. That was not done easily or merely using persuasion. However, the Kemalist regime had vast power reserves and, therefore, had no hesitation in resorting to harsh measures. After Kemal's death, the strict ban on any exploitation of religious sentiment in politics continued. At the same time, any officer's relations with Islam automatically drove him out of the army or service. In a sense, the relationship between Kemalists and Islam was equivalent to the relationship between the U.S. Government and Communists in McCarthy's time. That was the starting point of a march that led to Erdogan's "Moderate Islam," a term made to lure Europeans. Erdogan's Islam, sometimes seen as a model for Arab countries, has started from the almost absolute Islamic zero of Kemal, whereas the current situation of the Arab states is predominantly Islamic. The starting point is always the one that sets the course to go.

The sixteen stars surrounding the Turkish Republic's current emblem symbolize the 16 Turkish states and empires that "Turks" founded during history. The Turks also include the evil Empire of Attila, the Hun in these empires. However, they argue that the latter was not vicious and no more violent than other empires of the time. In this way, the history of "Turks" extends for two millennia. Turks attribute this success to the superiority of their culture, in relation, for example, to Mongols who have managed to establish only one empire, that of Cengiz Han, and leave nothing behind. The Turks believe that they have survived by fighting the Mongolian storm and effectively addressing the crusades in the long run. When savagery dominated the world, the Turks thought they behaved to the conquered peoples with goodwill.

The Turks' views of their nation are essential because they contribute to understanding their formed personality and high self-esteem, which is vital for people. In a more objective approach, Turkey, as the successor of the Ottoman state, was a country with Islamic culture and, perhaps at a time, the country with the most Islamic culture. Since the Tanzimat, the era of reforms, the Ottoman society began to question the superiority of its culture and seek the causes of its downward trajectory in its inherent problems. Turkey, a country with eastern Islamic culture, suddenly (in historical measures), after the beginning of the 20th century, changed course and attempted to adopt the Western culture with a secular regime. The shift has been successful to some extent. The country grew relatively close to the average of European states in various fields.

The Justice and Development Party's (AKP) rise to power called into question these achievements related to the direction of culture, but the economic surge of Turkey continued. A setback in the secular state and a shift towards Islam gave Turkey the advantage to turn the Organization of Islamic Cooperation into a herald-forwarding Turkish position. When Huntington's "Clash of Civilizations" theory became fashionable, Turkey took advantage of the event to be seen as a country representing the Islamic states and participating in European conferences on the opposite side of the table from where Ataturk would sit. Erdogan played a leading role in the attempt for an "Alliance of Civilizations" (2005), aiming to avoid using historical monuments for political purposes. Nevertheless, Erdogan converted the cathedral of Hagia Sophia of Constantinople from a museum to a mosque in 2020.[171] Erdogan's Turkey skates on thin ice, but it does have a settled culture based on Turkish nationalism.

The main characteristic of Turkey's personality is the ethnocentrism that has emerged in the foreground, mainly with the Young Turks movement and the "Committee of the Union and Progress" that expressed it. The newfound Turkish nationalism proceeded with German instigation to the Armenian genocide and later to the genocide of Greeks in Pontos. During Kemal's time, it was the axis around which the whole country was turning. However, it is complemented by extroversion toward Europe, visible for a long time during the Ottoman Empire. Thus, it derived know-how in the military sector and

---

[171] Converted from a mosque to a museum by Ataturk

administration, arts, and science in return for concessions in various commercial areas, including transport.

Modern Turkey has made two main choices about its membership in international organizations that reflect sides of its personality. In the 1950s, when it joined the Western coalition, it admittedly considered the danger against its territorial integrity by the Soviet Union. Later, the second domain it chose was that of the Islamic World. It has participated in the Organization of the Islamic Conference (OIC) since its inception in 1969. Still, it showed particular interest in the Organization only after Islamist Erbakan joined the Government, but mainly in 1983 after the election of the pro-Islamist Ozal. Turkey made it clear that it would not make any concessions on staying in the Western Camp despite pressure from the other states – members of the Islamic Conference. NATO or the E.U. have not objected to Turkey's membership in an organization like the OIC. The latter often takes anti-Western positions and sometimes takes opposing stances in U.N. resolutions.

Personality is also judged by the country's behavior in the situations presented. In principle, Turkey did not miss any opportunities offered to it. Its reaction to the junta coup in Cyprus and the Imia cases is typical. Turkey invaded Cyprus in 1974 and holds 40% of the island under its military occupation. It raised claims using its military force on the Greek island of Imia. It has shown courage in not responding to the U.S. request to use its territory in the offensive against Iraq. During the Arab Spring, it did not hesitate to change its positions concerning Israel and the NATO bombing in Libya (2011) when it felt this was of interest. The tolerance and the facilitation of irregular migration from Turkey to Greece served the plans of Turkey and other Islamic countries to strengthen the Muslim element in Greece and Europe. Turkey's public opinion has converged with the Government even in these steep turns. Turkey considers itself a powerful country and respects power.

Brzezinski refers to Turkey as a first-class geopolitical pivot (1997), considering that it should be attracted to the West. On the contrary, according to its ranking on the "eastern" side of its dividing line, Huntington believes that Turkey must remain there and take over the leadership of the Islamic world. Both make a partial mistake. Turkey's value for the West is zero geopolitically if the latter does not have the Balkans. Nor can Turkey, a non-Arab country, take over the Islamic world's leadership. The Arabs do not intend to hand it over to anyone, despite Turkey's attempt during the Arab Spring, in line with the Western calls. On the other hand, a geopolitical arc formed by Turkey – Russia – and Iran could cut Europe off from the rest of Asia.

Turkey is indeed a significant country, militarily strong and with dynamic people. However, another element enhancing Turkey's geopolitical and strategic value is Western analysts' mistake about its supposedly high strategic value and political will to defend Western interests. Turkey is not a European country, as it made Westerners believe. The two countries reacted differently to the Western approach of Greece and Turkey, through the Huntington theory's prism being on the same side (!). In the face of the idea of conflict of civilizations, Turkey adopted the stance: "Good, so we are opponents and will behave accordingly, preserving our interests (i.e., staying in NATO). NATO's approach was "better keep Turkey in, as a rebel, than out, as an adversary."

The idea, however, that "Turkey is a crucial country holding the fate of the region, but also influencing global stability" dates to the classical Anglo-Saxon geopolitical norms. According to these, Turkey was a bridge between Europe and Asia regarding trade and strategy and a barrier that prevented Russia's descent into the warm seas. Turkey's geopolitical value has increased since the disintegration of the Soviet Union and the nationalist conflicts that occurred in the region. With the prevalence of the Justice and Development Party, Turkey directed its priorities toward Islam, nationalism, and the armed confrontation with the Kurds.

In any case, Anatolia and the Straits are important geopolitical areas for both the Western coalition and Russia. Turkey succeeded in maneuvering each time according to its interests, sometimes siding with the West, sometimes with Russia. Although a NATO member, Turkey approached Russia in 2016. It procured the S-400 missile system agreement, concluded a deal with Russia to build a nuclear plant in Akkuyu, and persisted in making the "Turkish Stream" pipeline. As a result, Europe's energy dependence on Russia and Turkey would continue.

In the Middle East and, more broadly, the two non-Arab countries in the region, Turkey and Iran, neighboring and with many similar characteristics, form a strategic wall from the Balkans to the Persian Gulf. They could confine the Arab Countries in the south and Russia with other Asian countries in the north and east. Turkey controls the flows of the Tigris and Euphrates River waters, with limits that cannot be exceeded without risking hostilities that could lead to war. Works in southeast Anatolia, especially at the Ataturk dam, affect the water flow, but not critically.

Politically and economically, Turkey is turned toward the West as its interest lies there primarily. However, Turkey is not a homogeneous country; there are considerable variations between its western and eastern regions, including the ethnic composition. A high rate of Kurds live in south-eastern Anatolia. Turkey's aggression is mainly directed toward the West. At the same time, the political and military confrontation and the incidents in the southeast had a rather occasional and defensive character. Westerners close their eyes to Turkey's aggression towards the Aegean and Cyprus and focus on its neighborhood in the Middle East and its oil. Turkey is aware it has gained great strategic importance as an alternative route to Europe with gas pipelines passing from its territory. Therefore, it does whatever it can so that no other pipeline alternative exists in the eastern Mediterranean.

The policy of Young Turks to expand to the ancient Turkish homeland in the center of Asia, in Turan, was restored in the late 20th century with President Ozal, who wanted to create a bow of influence from the Adriatic to the Caucasus and extend it to the Muslim countries in the south. The foreign policy proposal of Professor Ahmet Davutoglu is part of the effort to present Turkey as a great power and ensure a new global role for it. Davutoglu was appointed to the post of Foreign Minister by Erdogan in 2009. He supported the idea that Turkey would become a predominant regional power, merging geographical determinism with its cultural sway and history. The policy of Davutoglu was based on four pillars: Indivisible security, Dialogue, Economic solidarity, and Cultural harmonization with mutual respect. Davutoglu argues that his policy aims "to integrate into a regional unity, different nations with different beliefs and develop cultural understanding among the various tribes. Furthermore, to resolve the crises that arise, through cooperation and dialogue."

Davutoglu introduced the concept of strategic depth. He claimed Turkey should not follow a unilateral and one-dimensional policy because of its geography, history, and cultural heritage. Calculating its interests, it should set itself geopolitically, always in the center. Therefore, the ultimate aim of Turkish foreign policy cannot be merely to integrate Turkey into the community of the Western states. The term "zero-problem policy" is an invention of Davutoglu. However, its explanations conclude that the policy of zero problems would be realized by imposing Turkey's will on its neighbors. As it turned out, the condition of zero issues with the neighbors was not matched in practice since Turkey continuously conflicts with most of its neighbors.

In any case, Turkey, for the last 50 years, has followed a revisionist policy regarding the Lausanne Treaty and refuses to accept the UNCLOS stipulations. It continues its occupation of part of Cyprus. It proceeded to hostile actions against Greece in the Aegean – casus belli for the eventual lawful expansion of Greece's territorial zone and daily air and sea violations. However, neither Syria nor Israel nor Egypt are friendly countries to Turkey. At the same time, Syria and Iraq, with their Kurdish nationals on Turkey's southern border, are also non-friendly. In the east, Armenia is hostile to Turkey. Finally, its land outlet to Europe passes through Greece and Bulgaria, the only friendly country around Turkey. Turkey maintains unfriendly relations with most Arab countries and maintains tricky ties with Iran and Russia in the broader region.

In this context, it could be assumed that Turkey raises all the issues against Greece to apply its doctrine of "Blue Homeland," a claim like Germany's Nazi dogma of Lebensraum. The evidence shows that Turkey is seeking to occupy territory – the islands in the eastern Aegean, after caging them in its sovereign rights, space, sea, and air. Otherwise, it would have sought friendly relations with Greece and resolved the Cyprus issue.

Another issue is the views according to which Turkey represents the Islamic world in the European Union's face. In the Alliance of Civilizations of 2005 forum, Turkey represented the Islamic culture. However, such a position did not accommodate the multifaceted policy proposed by Davutoglu, having Turkey in the center and not on any side. In Davutoglu's view, Turkey represents the geography of the Middle East in the E.U., and its accession to the Union would facilitate a rapprochement between the West and the Islamic world.

Turkey has been financially and militarily invigorated compared to the past, but contradictions in its foreign policy create questions. Nevertheless, President Erdogan remembers the geographic past to note that, of the 18 million square kilometers of the Ottoman Empire, modern Turkey ended up with only 780 thousand square kilometers. Turkey fails to pave the way for E.U. membership, which is, of course, a result of the wrong way in which it appreciates itself, as demonstrated by the abovementioned views of an illusion of grandeur. As a result, Turkey seems to "confine" itself to the perception of self-sufficient regional power.

The withdrawal of the U.S. from the MENA region during the Trump Presidency and the E.U.'s lack of any geopolitical power allowed Turkey to invade various countries.

Besides its geopolitical goals to dominate the east Mediterranean, Ankara tries to become the pivot of an alliance of Muslim countries having a significant role in the Islamic-Sunni world. Its partnership with Qatar, Pakistan,

Malaysia, Saraj's Libya, and the "Muslim Brothers" aims to create a new axis that will dominate conservative Sunni Islam. Its rival is the Arab-Sunni axis of Saudi Arabia, the UAE, and Egypt. Besides, Turkey seeks in every way to harm what it calls the "axis of evil" France, Egypt, UAE, Greece, and Cyprus.[172]

---

[172] Study of ELISME: http://www.elisme.gr/images/pdffiles/Turkey_in_Libya.pdf, June 2020 (in Greek)

THE MAGHREB

The Maghreb region, "West" in Arabic, refers to the Arab countries of the Western Mediterranean. Its eastern part is sometimes called Mashreq (east). The Maghreb border is geographically undefined, but politically, it is a structured area that includes Libya, Tunisia, Algeria, Morocco, and Mauritania. Thus, geography is defined politically. Despite this identity, it is very little integrated. Relations between states are called "brotherly" but governed mainly by conditions of harsh political competition. Trade between Maghreb countries is low; they prefer bilateral trade with third countries, notably Europe.

The Maghreb countries are typically organized in UMA (Arab Maghreb Union). Still, the agency is virtually powerless and unable to act because of the Algerian-Moroccan rivalry, which is not confined to the Western Sahara conflict. Also, Algeria's relations with Libya historically were not tranquil. During the Gaddafi period, the Colonel's involvement in the Sahel affairs created adverse situations. After his fall, bad relations continued due to the NTC's stiffness[173] regarding Algeria and the activity of terrorist cells on the territory of Libya that threatened neighboring countries. Tunisia maintains rather good relations with its two neighbors, Libya and Algeria. Still, it tries to keep the balance, also maintaining good relations with Morocco.

---

[173] The National Transitional Council of Libya was the de facto government of Libya for a period of ten months during and after the Libyan Civil War.

Morocco and Tunisia traditionally maintain excellent relations with Europe; Algeria is equivocal, while Libya has always maintained distances. Gaddafi's Libya did not have good relationships with other Arab countries of the Mediterranean as they "could not perceive the greatness of Colonel Gaddafi." Therefore, he had turned south to sub-Saharan Africa, where they appreciated his money better. Mauritania is an Arab country with relatively weaker political institutions. Its participation in Euro-Mediterranean processes results from the advocacy of European Mediterranean states.

The Maghreb countries, Morocco, Algeria, and Tunisia, have participated in the Euro-Mediterranean process from the outset; Libya has had observer status since 1999. Mauritania entered Euro-Mediterranean regional cooperation in 2007. South Mediterranean countries cooperate with the European Union's member-states in the "Union for the Mediterranean" (UfM). Nevertheless, they consider it non-operational because of Israel's participation. The organization to which the Maghreb countries attach great importance is the Cooperation of the Western Mediterranean, known as the "5+5 Initiative", with the participation of Maghreb countries and their southwestern European counterparts.

Western Sahara

Spain, which occupied the region as a colonial power, leaving the area only in 1975, distributed Western Sahara between Mauritania in the south and Morocco in the north. However, according to the U.N., this action cannot be considered decolonization. On November 6, 1975, on the initiative of King Hassan, a great course was organized, the "Green Course," with the participation of hundreds of thousands of Moroccan soldiers holding the flag of Morocco toward Western Sahara for its "peaceful occupation." At the same time, the Moroccan army seized militarily strategic points in Western Sahara.

Morocco raised various allegations. It claims the region had always been part of Morocco. However, that distribution violated the United Nations' decision. The historical claims of both Mauritania and Morocco were insufficient to justify the annexation of territories of Western Sahara. Meanwhile, the region's inhabitants, the Sahrawi, organized the Polisario Front (Frente Popular para la Liberacion de Saguia el Hamra y Rio de Oro) and asked for the independence of the region. After a hard struggle of the Polisario Front against the conquerors, Mauritania receded and abandoned the territories of the part granted, which Morocco rushed to occupy, building a fence surrounding the whole area in 1979. The U.N. has never acknowledged the legitimacy of Western Sahara's attachment to Morocco and regards the region as "non-self-governing."

Algeria, as a matter of principle, supported the anti-colonial struggle of the Polisario Front and acknowledged the "Sahrawi Arab Democratic Republic" (SADR) founded on behalf of the Front and has its seat, formally, in a small part of the territory of Western Sahara, not occupied by Morocco, near Tindouf in Algeria. The SADR maintains diplomatic relations with 40 U.N. states and is a full member of the African Union. Algeria's commitment to the principle of self-determination is well-established and sincere. Indeed, Algeria has come to the point of cooling off its relations with Indonesia, despite its strong support during Algeria's fight for independence, due to the issue of East Timor.[174]

The Algerian state has granted the Polisario Front an area in the province of Tindouf to establish the Sahrawi refugee camps, on which the SADR exercises de facto power. Morocco argues that Tindouf refugees are "Moroccans," detained there against their will, with "slavery practices." In any case, Morocco considers that these refugees should freely choose their future, either by migrating to Morocco or anywhere else abroad.

However, as it concerns Algeria's pursuit of an independent Western Sahara, it could be argued that such a development would also be problematic for Algeria. Although it has natural resources (ores and minerals), the Western Sahara region is deserted. It remains an extraordinarily underdeveloped and impoverished region without state institutions and infrastructure. Even though every decolonized state should have the right to fail, it is indeed challenging for an independent state to be established and operate there without great external help and selfless support. It is doubtful that Algeria wanted to, but even then, whether it could bear such a role. Algeria has vast land in the desert, and its natural resources are exploited mainly through the know-how of third countries. Principles govern its external policy, but Algeria's primary concern is always safeguarding the state's interests (primarily the economy).

---

[174] The issue of independence of East Timor is similar to that of Western Sahara.

Sahara

The Sahara Desert, a vast wasteland that cannot be adequately supervised, is occasionally a zone of transit and refuge for all kinds of outlaws. It is an area of opaque acts and actions and, therefore, a field of various international anti-terrorism initiatives. The prevailing logic was the assumption of responsibility in addressing the problems of the Saharan countries and their surroundings, with the international community's help, which would provide the necessary means for this purpose. On the other hand, state borders can not be clearly demarcated in the desert. The post-colonial distribution of land to states violated the traditional boundaries. For the people there, used to nomadic life and the free movement of caravans, passports, and border controls are devoid of any practical meaning. The lines drawn by the colonial powers on the maps are not visible to the Saharan people on the sand.

The region's countries have tried to introduce European-borne concepts of state and sovereignty without much success. This fact is the reason for their inability to enforce the rule of law. Mali and Niger tried to suppress the Tuareg movement through transactions with terrorists and outlaws. However, Algeria and Mauritania opposed this practice, like that of Tuareg in the Toubou movement in northern Chad.

The failure of the states of the region is due to colonialism that dissolved the traditional hierarchies. The unorganized decolonization and the prevailing system of tribes and factions are additional handicaps. This has led to artificial divisions and inequalities imposed by newly founded states' immature leaderships, leading to militarization and consequent poverty. The risks to the international community were about the creation of a safe haven for cross-border terrorism, proceeding with terrorist attacks, kidnapping for ransom, piracy, and operation of terrorist training camps. As a result, a grey area of smuggling drugs, arms, cars, and other materials was created. Simultaneously, the desert was used to route illegal immigration and human trafficking to North Africa and the European coasts. The states' inability to exercise control has led them to resort to "dealing" with both terrorists and Western countries, as evidenced by their contradictory policies.

The security deficit in the Sahara results from the geographical conditions and the virtually non-existent cooperation of the region's countries. Besides, the mentality of its inhabitants and the inactivity characterizing them create additional problems. High unemployment rates are due to underdevelopment, lack of administrative structures, education, capital, and know-how. Moreover, various historical and social reasons led the region's people to perceive criminal acts peculiarly. For example, they may consider the abduction of people or theft of cars or animals as acts of bravery.

Western Sahel Geopolitics

The Sahel region is the sparsely populated geographical area between the Sahara of the Arab Maghreb and "deep Africa." It is the transitional zone extending from the Atlantic Ocean to the Red Sea and from the Sahara in the north to the Sudanese savannah in the south. It is a relatively anhydrous plain with few mountains, plateaus and steppes, and scarce savannah-type vegetation. It has different flora and fauna that separate it from the rest of the area. Rainfall is minimal but provides for primitive cultivation.

The word "Sahel" is of Arabic origin and traditionally means the Sahara's boundary or southern rim. Politically, it refers to all the states participating in the transnational "Permanent Interstate Committee for Drought Control in the Sahel," founded in 1971 and geographically comprising many countries in the wider region. However, geopolitically is confined to Mauritania, Mali, southern Algeria, Niger, Chad, and Sudan, although, in the context of the effects of the Arab Spring, reference is made only to the first four countries. This geopolitically defined region contains many sources of insecurity that have created various crises, ranging from Darfur-type conflicts to the Tuareg movement. It presents broad-spectrum risks, from AQMI's[175] terrorism to the smuggling of arms and drugs and from human trafficking to illegal immigration. The region had become a hotbed for the development of terrorism and criminality, which threatened not only the countries of the broader area but also Europe. Therefore, it was reasonable to draw international attention.

The weak link in the chain has always been Mali, where corruption thrived. The officials' transactions with terrorists and cocaine barons had broad repercussions. Drugs in considerable quantities arrived by planes from South America with the final destination, Europe. Mali, a vast landlocked country in northwest Africa, is geographically divided into two parts: the north, a sparsely populated and difficult-to-control massive area in the Sahara, and the southern, smaller but more populated and with a better climate. A relatively narrow strip of land connects the two regions.

---

[175] Al-Qaida au Maghreb islamique

Northern Mali is one of the regions with the lowest social development index, abandoned by the Government in Bamako. Tuaregs are among the tribes living in the area. This indigenous tribe residing throughout the Sahel region, Algeria, Libya, Mali, Niger, and Burkina Faso, repeatedly revolted, particularly in Mali, asking for self-determination. The Tuareg are a native tribe, of which, despite the existing general perception, only a tiny part lives nomadically. In the Tuareg societies, the law of tradition prevailed over Sharia (although Tuaregs are Muslims). Therefore, their matriarchy was maintained, which, together with the Tuareg preference for a secular society, led to conflicts with Islamists. The spirit of the tribe led to clashes with the Mali Government, which offered nothing to improve their living conditions.

Gaddafi, for many years, engaged in a covert war with Algeria to control the Sahara region. Aiming to control the southern border zone of Algeria, he used the Tuareg insurgency in northern Mali and Niger, sparking riots on the one hand and playing the peacemaker's role. However, eventually, he could not achieve his goals (in early 2000) when Algeria could not react because of its war with the Islamists, and Tuaregs turned against the Government in Mali. In 2006, Algeria, using its political and economic leverage in Mali and Niger, succeeded in imposing peace. In July 2006, despite Libya's underground reaction, it made it possible to sign the Algiers Agreement between Bamako (Mali) and Tuaregs. Gaddafi nevertheless continued to stir up the conflict, offering asylum to the "unrepentant" rebels under Ag Bahanga, continuing their funding, and projecting that only Libya could resolve the Tuareg problem. Gaddafi even succeeded in breaking down the Tuaregs of Mali and Niger, taking a section of them under his sway to create a group, along with those he recruited in Chad, to serve his interests.

Terrorism in Algeria and beyond

The events in Algeria in October 1988 are considered a distant harbinger of the Arab Spring. The cause of the uprising then was the demand for reforms, and the economic hardships partly resulted from the low oil prices of 1986. The strikes and demonstrations had led to a mass uprising of the population, led by Islamists, in several Algerian cities. Facing the situation, the Government of the National Liberation Front, FLN, declared a state of emergency and used violence to restore order, resulting in hundreds of deaths and several thousand arrests. In response to the demands, the FLN Government, ruling Algeria since the foundation of the state in 1962, introduced several democratic institutions through a new constitution. The situation created granted Islamists freedom of action, contributing to the rise of Islamism in Algeria. Eventually, it led to the electoral dominance of the Islamists, mainly because of their extraordinary dynamism.

Islamism in Algeria began slowly in the 1980s by claiming that its ideology could ensure the population everything it lacked. The incompetence of politicians and the oil price fall had led the country to poverty. The people were desperate for progress. On the other hand, it is not particularly tricky to promise everything, if not in the present life on earth, at least in the next, in the heavenly. It was not difficult for the "incorruptible" imams to convince the people, disgusted by corrupt politicians. The start was made in universities. The symbols of Islamism were ubiquitous in classrooms. If someone were not a believer, he did not have a place there, or his life would get complicated. Islamism has become the dominant ideology in the country. Eventually, the Islamic Salvation Front (FIS) won the first round of parliamentary elections in December 1991. The National Liberation Front (FLN) forced President Bendjiedid to resign; a republican State Supreme Council took power. It annulled the polls on the grounds that applying democratic principles on this occasion would be the last democratic act in the country.

Persecuted Islamists of the FIS formed several armed groups; the most important was the Armed Islamic Group (GIA), which acted as an urban guerrilla, and the Islamic Armed Movement (MIA), having its bases in mountainous locations. Fighting against ruthless, absolutely deadly, and brutal terrorism, and having the West, if not an opponent, nothing more than a "neutral observer" because of "non-implementing democratic procedures", the interim Government of Algeria finally succeeded after a hard fight to ensure democracy. It led the country to elections in 1999; Abdelaziz Bouteflika was elected President. However, unrepented Islamists set up the terrorist organization GSPC, Salafist Group for (Islamic) Sermon and Battle[176] that continued the terrorist action in the mountainous province of Kabyle.

Democratic Algeria continues to resent the West for its abandonment in the 1990s. The Government has indeed reacted violently, fighting terrorists not always by legal means. The thousands of "disappeared" and the Government's inability to provide relevant data on their fate is indicative. However, the Government claims that there was no other way to fight an illegal army that ambushed and killed citizens in cold blood, entered the villages, murdered all men without exception, and took

---

[176] Groupe Salafiste pour la Prédication et le Combat

women and children as slaves. All foreigners and Christians were undesirable in the country and executed, if possible, almost "on appearance." The deaths of the time victims of Islamist terrorism exceeded one hundred thousand. All these unheard-of barbarities were "justified" from an incredibly harsh religious point of view that has nothing to do with Islam itself since Islam is different from Islamism. Terrorism did not abandon Algeria. Despite the defeat, the GSPC continued its murderous terrorist activity throughout the following period, under the name "Al Qaeda of the Islamic Maghreb" (AQMI-AQIM), becoming the number one enemy of the Algerian state.

Terrorism is not a derivative of a social or political crisis but exploits it. It does not result from radicalizing a social, political, or national claim. Still, it is the extreme culmination of an ideology that has broken its ties with society and the actual world. Salafism, but more generally, any terrorism, when settled in a place, carries out recruitment. To this end, it follows a particular way of analyzing the facts, consequently misleading public opinion by presenting that terrorism is not an ordinary, supposedly political crime. The result is that terrorism remains intimidating, but it is "understandable" and perhaps accepted by many individuals in the context of a supposed ideological struggle. Perpetrators are no longer common killers but "executors."

Therefore, as analysts point out, terrorism is a matter for the security forces alone. Terrorism can represent nothing more than crime since it is just a crime. It also has nothing to do with religion; it could be anti-religious, extreme left, or far right. The fertile ground that feeds terrorism, with terrorists being, in fact, victims, necessitates being analyzed in depth. The distinction between terrorism and the conditions that breed it is essential to avoid creating confusion between the abuser and the victim. The conditions that produce terrorism in many ways are both social and cultural. It often has nothing to do with the economic situation or the social origins of the individual terrorists. In any case, the problem of terrorism is global and, therefore, necessitates a holistic approach. The separate terrorist attacks in Europe, the Middle East, Iraq, Syria, Libya, Mali, and Afghanistan are part of a whole problem, and resolving them will help in the desired direction.

The threat against foreign interests has been more acute in the past. It concerns primarily certain countries such as France, Spain, the United Kingdom, and the USA. In the 1990s and beyond, terrorists avoided hitting oil targets in Algeria until January 2013. The deadly terrorist attack on the gas plant in In Amenas killed many people but exclusively targeted non-Muslims. AQMI has stable structures and organization and an aggressive nature. The choice of international targets by Al Qaida in Algeria is a result of the internationalization of the phenomenon of terrorism in the Maghreb region. It has been chosen as a free territory for its activity and expansion to later hit "targets"' in Europe. As experts point out, the geographical proximity of AQMI's area of action with Europe may have allowed the terrorist activity to jump there through the presence of large communities of peaceful Maghrebins in the continent.[177] However, the Arab Spring and the conflicts among the leaders of the terrorist groups over the undertaking of terrorist operations in Europe prevented the immediate risk of significant outbreaks in the continent. Moreover, the fear of Europeans was

---

[177] Between 5 and 8 million people of Maghrebin origin live in France

transferred to the jihadists with European or American citizenships, fighting against Assad in Syria and probably committing jihadist acts of terrorism elsewhere.

AQMI, which continued its terrorist activity in Algeria, was taken aback by the outbreak of the Arab Spring. After remaining passive for a time, shortly afterward, it started to act by moving its guerrillas to Tunisia to strengthen the Islamic armed movement in the next phase of the Arab Spring and Libya to take up arms against Gaddafi. In addition, its role was central in Mali. Finally, its presence with thousands of other jihadist terrorists from many countries in Syria, organized by various services, became the main military force against the legal Government.

Libya

Libya had a particular state structure with a strong faith in the tribe that held a vital role in the country's political life. The Gaddafi regime, imposed in 1969 on the Libyans, was based on an alliance of the small tribe Kadhafa of the Colonel with the more prominent tribes Warfalla and Magarha. Gaddafi was a brutal dictator; he ruled by torture and corruption and favored only his tribe and allied tribes. His regime, though, in forty years, had taken a Libya with a per capita income of 60 USD and, thanks to oil revenues, had turned it into a country with one of the highest income per capita in the Arab world. Libya's harsh regime, under normal conditions, would not have caused a rebellion against it. Among other things, Gaddafi, inspired by a sense of greatness, was incapable of perceiving his weight in international politics, self-deluded by the compliments of various leaders who coveted Libyan oil and money. Frustrated by the moods of other Arab leaders who did not want to recognize him as the leader of the Arab world, he turned geopolitically toward sub-Saharan Africa, where he found a positive response because of the petrodollars distributed generously.

Gaddafi's policy, always unpredictable, was systematically directed against the neighboring states in the Sahel region. Algeria, distasteful for the expansionist policy and direct involvement of Libya in the internal conflicts of the countries in the area, was always in Gaddafi's sights. The Colonel's repeated attempts to take the Algerian Tuareg on his side impacted their loyalty to the Algerian state. Bandit gangs and terrorists had used the extended border in the desert between Algeria and Libya. By financing mutinies or by using the Tuareg of the Sahel zone through payments, Gaddafi's destabilizing operations in neighboring countries developed in the direction of the creation of the "Great Sahara" in which the leader of Jamahiriya, through his obsession, saw himself as King of Kings (warlords).

THE ARAB SPRING

Developments in the Middle East and North Africa, for decades, depended on the decisions of charismatic leaders able to prevail politically, mobilizing and exercising control over the armed forces of each country. The people were conspicuously absent from political developments other than a formal and usually prescribed vote. The only exception to the introduction of the popular element into political issues, for many years, was the intifada of the Palestinians, which also had no social-economic or political objectives in a narrow sense but the liberation from a foreign power.

The political-social reversals of 2011, called with an over-optimistic approach, "Arab Spring," broke continuity in the political class of the Arab World, which seemed eternal like the Cold War era. History, as is well known, does not have a linear evolution; it proceeds with leaps, the beginning of which cannot be predicted since the building of the necessary conditions is sometimes carried out underground. Therefore, almost always, they are surprising, an element included in the concept of "revolution." However, in the case of the Arab Spring, after the unexpected commencement of events, developments could be foreseen. The mistakes committed by all sides, motivated by prejudices, incomplete reading of data, disregard of historical experiences, and the wrong choice of the criteria, could be eventually avoided.

The recognized term "Arab Spring," although it does not reflect the substance, continues to be used, although it has been criticized because of its results, which are far from spring-related. The observation that the correct terminology would be the expression "Arabic Transition" (attempt towards democracy) is apt if the result of the Arab Spring were positive. The fact is that in 2011, there was a historical discontinuity in the politics of the area. Although these events may not have led to the well-being or amelioration of the economic and security situation of the peoples, they have led to greater involvement of citizens with public issues and the determination of their fate. The citizens have acquired a say in the country's administration, which is undoubtedly progress, a transition to democracy. The Arab World of the Mediterranean basin, after the Arab Spring under any name, will never be the same again.

The term Arab Spring refers to developments in Eastern Europe following the overthrow of the communist regimes resulting from the "collapse of the Berlin Wall'. Although the Arab Spring may have some similarities with the changes in central and Eastern Europe in the early 1990s, it was very different from the outset. The correlations between the two cases, which Western analysts were quick to do, proved unsuccessful. In attitudes, political systems, situations, and times between the Arab countries and Eastern Europe, where the West has used its moral superiority vis-à-vis the Soviet Union, the differences in historical development are too significant for any parallelism.

Moreover, the southern coast of the Mediterranean, except for Israel, belongs to the Arab-Islamic world. Thus, it differs from Eastern Europe's countries, whose accession to the Soviet bloc can only be regarded as a parenthesis since they have always been part of the "Judeo-Christian" cultural sphere. Therefore, any interrelation between the two was incorrect, at least in the view of the Arabs.

The events in Algeria

On Wednesday evening, January 5, 2011, serious riots broke out simultaneously in the central district of Algiers Bab el Oued and on the outskirts of the city, in the center of Algeria's second-largest city, Oran, while the province rose against its marginalization, with riots occurring in many Algerian towns. The following day, on Thursday, January 6, 2011, the situation had calmed down, but in the evening, as soon as it got dark, the events resumed. The police, if it was present, were not visible. The incidents continued Friday with unrelenting intensity in several districts. The episodes spread rapidly and continued in all Algerian cities to end as abruptly as they began, without any particular intervention from the police, on Sunday, January 9, 11. There were reportedly six dead and several hundred police officers and protesters injured. There has been significant damage to banks, shops, particularly cars and luxury goods vendors, and mobile phone agencies. As the vast majority of the protesters were minors, they also burned school records. The targets are indicative of the age and furor of the protesters. Their parents preferred to stay home, leaving the empty streets at the mercy of young protesters, among whom there were numerous criminal elements. Authorities said they imprisoned those arrested but released the minors.

The events ceased when Algerians realized that they were detrimental to their country, as the conflicts began to remind them of the terrorism of the past decade. They feared that the politically imposed Islamic extremism could exploit the situation. The incidents, however, ended when the parents of the demonstrators decided not to participate and did not allow their children to participate further. A direct link to the less violent events in Tunisia was not visible. The Algerian Government has refrained from dramatizing the situation.

The event that triggered the "Arab Spring" and its continuity, mainly with economic demands, started in Tunisia. However, the actions of the practical protest may not have been able to take on the contagious nature they finally received without the simultaneous events in the ever-revolutionary Algeria. Algeria, however, after the first events, did not follow. The reasons for this reluctance were the relatively recent experience of terrorism of the 1990s, the actual freedom of the press that acted as a relief valve, the immediate economic measures taken by the Government as it had very high financial potential, and the wise actions of the police.

Tunisia: The beginning of the Arab Spring

The uprising in Tunisia initially manifested itself as "civil disobedience" caused by the high unemployment rate, food prices, corruption, and lack of freedom of speech. The self-immolation of a Tunisian street vendor, Mohamed Bouazizi, who set himself on fire on December 17, 2010, after the confiscation of his wares, became a catalyst for the Tunisian Revolution and the Arab Spring[178] against autocratic regimes. The ground, however, had already been prepared due to widespread dissatisfaction with the state of the economy, dictatorial governance, and corruption of Ben Ali's regime.

The incidents intensified when Bouazizi succumbed to his burns on January 4; on January 6, the lawyers went on strike, to be followed by teachers. Clashes

---

[178] Grimaldi, Nicole. "Bare & Myriadic Death: Necro-Subjection and the Pandemic Era." 2022, https://core.ac.uk/download/523372702.pdf.

with the police multiplied, and the curfew imposed was not respected. President Ben Ali did not realize on time the extent of the uprising; the situation was out of control after Algeria's events. On Friday, January 14, 2011, Ben Ali declared a state of emergency in the country, dissolved the Government, and promised parliamentary elections within six months. Yet, it was too late. The military and senior figures in Parliament and justice had already decided to take power. While military divisions surrounded the presidential palace, Ben Ali was forced to resign.

At least at the start, the changes in Tunisia were not democratic. It was the balance of power of different factions that should have effectively forced Ben Ali to flee. On the other hand, the regime in Algeria was also the result of a balance. However, the Government in Algeria, compared to that of Ben Ali, was more open and democratic. Many analysts saw similarities in the events in Algeria and Tunisia but rejected the domino effect between them, highlighting the diversity of the two cases.

In another approach, uprisings, as spontaneous collective phenomena, resemble each other, regardless of the direct reason for their incitement. Public authorities generally regard these events as an expression of temporary anger from a marginal group that expresses only a small percentage of the population. However, protest manifestations should be placed each time in the specific context of the social and political system they have broken out. A superficial analysis of this can be dangerous for the political authorities that adopt it if generalized throughout the territory. Besides, the initial assessment of the 1988 uprising in Algeria, which led to the current (2019) relative democratization of the country's political system, was that it came from a "handful of gamins."

Egypt

President Mubarak has been held responsible for the economic poverty of the people and autocratic administration. Mubarak's rule was dictatorial, and in 2005, he was re-elected with only 25 % of the electorate. The regime was facing the Muslim Brotherhood's Islamist threat and had resorted to harsh measures of oppression to confront them. The events started on January 25, 2011, with simultaneous attacks by protesters in Suez and Cairo. The events persisted for 18 days before the army forced President Hosni Mubarak to resign on February 11, 2011. On February 13, the military dissolved the Parliament and suspended the constitution.

The incidents in Egypt were violent from the outset, and, given Ben Ali's previous eviction, they did solely aim at the expulsion of Hosni Mubarak. They included a wide range of events, demonstrations, marches, sit-ins in squares and especially the central Tahrir Square, acts of civil disobedience and resistance, strikes, and uprisings involving many people, which, as it turned out, had different expectations and aspirations. On the "Friday of Wrath" on January 28, 2011, after the traditional prayer, hundreds of thousands of citizens demonstrated against the regime. Prisons were set on fire, and prisoners escaped. There was extensive looting.

In a February 10, 2011 speech, Mubarak said that he was transferring some of his powers to Vice-President Suleiman but underlined that he remained Head of State. However, it was too late. Reactions to the President's speech were fierce. The vice-president announced one day later that Mubarak resigned, and the Supreme Council of the Armed Forces under Mohamed Hussein Tantawi took over the Government.

The ensuing election brought the Islamist Mohamed Morsi of the Muslim Brothers to power, to be overthrown later by massive demonstrations against his Islamist rule.

Libya

The regime of Muammar Gaddafi could, of course, only provoke the desire for freedom and democracy. Still, the Arab Spring "revolution" in Libya cannot be considered either wholly democratic or a spontaneous reaction of a people towards a cruel dictatorship. It was initially an armed uprising of inhabitants of the eastern part of the country as revenge for their neglect for decades and the unfair distribution of oil revenues, together with an armed attempt by the Islamists to seize power. Part of the Tuareg, bought with Gaddafi's money, was among those drafted against the insurgents in Libya. The clashes have been fierce, and the Libyan army prevailed despite the rebels' initial victories.

Western countries could not leave the Libyan people at the mercy of Gaddafi. Security Council took measures to protect the population.[179] Instead, the West allied with the jihadists and other rebels, joining them in combined military operations. NATO countries rejected all attempts of African leaders to find a peaceful solution. NATO's operation exceeded the relevant jurisdiction given by the U.N., participating, in fact, in the war. Its fierce air

---

[179] UN Security Council Resolution 1973 (2011) adopted by a vote of 10 in favor to none against, with 5 abstentions (Brazil, China, Germany, India, Russian Federation), authorized Member-states, acting nationally or through regional organizations or arrangements, to take all necessary measures to protect civilians under threat of attack in the country, including Benghazi.

bombing against any military or administrative target in Libya preceded each time military action of the insurgents on the ground. Eventually, it resulted in the murder of Gaddafi near the latch where he had fled. The Libyan National Transitional Council finally declared Libya "free" on October 23, 2011, and promised a "pluralistic democratic state". However, its foundation was ultimately not achieved, resulting in a failed and fragmented state.

The civil war in Libya began in 2011 with the forming of the National Transitional Council by rebels in Benghazi, which nevertheless disbanded in 2012 after the elections held, and the establishment of the General National Congress (GNC). However, Congress proved to be incapable of limiting the actions of warlords and confronting the Islamic State's emergence. As a result, the new elections on June 24, 2014, were held in chaotic circumstances, with a turnout of 18%, and brought about a complete political deadlock.

The majority of the old Congress (GNC) - which had to dissolve after the elections - did not recognize the new Parliament formed by the polls. The result was the establishment of two governments, one in Tripoli, with the old Congress (GNC), and one in Tobruk, with the elected House of Representatives. Field Marshal Khalifa Belqasim Haftar, the Libya National Army (LNA) commander, allied with the Government of Tobruk. Eventually, all sides signed a Political Agreement on Libya in Skhirat, Morocco, on December 17, 2015. According to the agreement, a Government of National Accord (GNA) under Fayez Mustafa al-Sarraj, head of the Presidential Council of Libya, was established in 2016 in Tripoli.[180]

---

[180] According to article 1.4 of December 17th, 2015 Agreement "The term of the Government of National

The second civil war between Tripoli and Cyrenaic commenced in 2014. Marshal Haftar is engaged with the Prime Minister of the Government of National Accord of Libya Sarraj in a struggle for dominance. Both searched for protectors, sometimes political and sometimes military, depending on geopolitical and international entanglements. Ankara seized the opportunity by supplying arms, ammunition, and jihadist fighters from Syria to the National Accord (GNA) government in Tripoli. The latter supports the "Muslim Brothers" and the Islamist rebels throughout the ongoing second civil war, with Turkey's involvement growing significantly since the end of 2019.

After March 2016, clashes intensified between the two rival parliaments, the House of Representatives (Tobruk) and the General National Congress (GNC) in Tripoli. As a result, the House of Representatives removed the GNA's legitimacy by withdrawing its recognition through a vote in summer 2016. Despite this, the U.N. continued recognizing the General National Congress as legitimate.

The rift between the East and West of Libya deepened following General Haftar's large-scale attack to seize the entire Libyan territory on April 4, 2019, which was unsuccessful. With the military help of Turkey, GNA succeeded in turning away the attackers. The continuing entanglements of various countries, mainly with the supply of war materials and mercenaries, led the U.N. Security Council to take Resolution 2486 (2019)/ September 12, 2019, to impose an arms embargo on Libya.

Accord shall be one year as of the date of granting it a vote of confidence by the House of Representatives. In case the constitution was not finalized during its term, it shall be renewed automatically for one additional year only."

The reversal of P.M. Sarraj's difficult situation was mainly due to Turkish assistance, which broke the U.N.'s embargo, resulting in the GNA's absolute dependence on Ankara. Turkey aspires to control the whole of the eastern Mediterranean. It declared the north-east Mediterranean its Exclusive Economic Zone, disregarding all the rights of the Republic of Cyprus and the Greek islands, including Crete. Considering Libya has opposite coasts from Turkey, it closed the eastern Mediterranean entrance with the combined EEZ of the two countries.

Syria

The events of protest in the context of the Arab Spring in Syria began on March 15, 2011, with political and democratic demands. The claim for removal of Assad was implied, according to the desires of the West. Most Syrians were clearly against a regime change, so the number of demonstrators gradually decreased. The majority, who saw how the situation was evolving in the other Arab countries, especially in Egypt with the prevalence of Islamists, avoided further participation in the demonstrations. The Syrian regime also made some democratic concessions. The Government tried to face the widespread malaise, which came mainly from economic and social reasons rather than political ones, with relatively non-violent policing measures. It made interventions in the financial sector through commodity subsidies and the announcement of political reforms. At the same time, the experience of the turmoil of the past had a catalytic role. What followed after the summer of 2011 had nothing to do with any "Spring." It was a war, through proxies, of the West, allied with Islamists, against the country.

The spread of events

Almost all the Arab countries followed the uprisings in Algeria and Tunisia. In the Kingdoms of Morocco and Jordan, the status quo prevailed with some Islamist shifts, constitutional reforms, and a little help from the Gulf Cooperation Council (GCC). The latter quickly announced that it intended to include them in its structure. There have been various reactions in the other Arab countries, with regimes that have seen the signs of the times promptly and taken appropriate measures, thus avoiding their fall, others toppled, and others being at the edge.

In Morocco, the demonstrations began on February 20, 2011, with demands about economic, political, and social problems haunting Morocco, such as civil liberties and rights, social inequalities, corruption, and free elections. The regime affronted the demonstrations relatively gently; nevertheless, the protests organized by the "Youth Movement of February 20" demanded a new constitution. Finally, on June 17, 2011, King Mohammed VI, in a televised address, promised constitutional reforms accepted at a referendum in July.

In Jordan, the demonstrations in the context of the Arab Spring began on January 14, 2011, with economic demands and calling for the resignation of Prime Minister Samir Rifai. The Muslim Brotherhood followed, organizing a demonstration on January 28, 2011. There was no appeasement despite King Abdullah's efforts, who dismissed the Government on February 1, 2011, formed a new one under Marouf al Bakhit, and met with a delegation of the Muslim Brothers on February 3. The next day, protesters, including the Muslim Brothers, gathered outside the Prime Minister's office demanding reforms and marched to the Egyptian Embassy to support antigovernment protesters in Egypt. Mubarak's fall encouraged the Muslim Brothers, who called on Arabs to learn lessons from Egypt. The demonstrations continued throughout 2011 and 2012, despite occasional promises for reforms to electoral law and the formation of constituencies. At the same time, problems with the Palestinian issue and the presence of Palestinians in the country continued to plague the regime. One of the reasons is that Jordan is bound to discriminate in favor of the natives.

In Yemen, the demonstrations began on January 27, 2011, with a massive protest rally against the rule of Ali Abdullah Saleh. President Saleh's promise six days later not to run for the 2013 elections was followed by the "Days of Rage" on February 3 and 18 and by the "Friday Of No Return» (to the old order of things) on March 11, 2011. The Government reacted violently on March 18, resulting in 52 dead protesters. Since early April, the Gulf Cooperation Council has tried to mediate but faced a series of setbacks by Saleh in the draft agreement he has worked out. Finally, the GCC resigned from its efforts on May 22, 2011, when the Yemeni President refused to sign the deal on the democratic transition for the third time. The next day, a powerful tribal chief, Sadiq al Ahmar, and his armed followers clashed with the army loyal to the Government. The presidential palace was bombed on June 3, 2011, resulting in Saleh's injury. After the President fled to Saudi Arabia for hospitalization, Vice President al-Hadi took over. Saleh declared that he had not resigned despite the crowd's celebrations of his removal. The opposition set up its transitional council. Still, on November 23, Saleh realized that he could only sign the power transition agreement, which had been worked out by the Gulf Cooperation Council, and resign. During the February 21,

328

2012, presidential elections, Al Hadi was elected almost unanimously, this being a characteristic of the Arab approach, even in free elections.

In Bahrain, the Sunni Monarchy was confronted with its numerous Shia citizens. It was rescued only after an armed intervention from its neighbors and the support of the West. The Shiite majority's protests against the Sunni dynasty during the Arab Spring began with the other uprisings in early 2011. The Monarch showed tolerance initially, but a violent confrontation and a raid on the Square of Pearls ensued. A month later, at the Bahraini Government's request, the King declared a three-month state of emergency. At the same time, he invited troops from Saudi Arabia and the Gulf Cooperation Council to secure the regime's status. Clashes with protesters and thousands of arrests followed. Neither Al Jazeera nor the Western media adequately covered the issue. Also, the West did not deal with the violation of human rights and the lack of democracy in this pro-Western country, a member of the Gulf Cooperation Council.

After the U.S. military intervention of 2003, Iraq failed to operate as a normal state. The protests began on February 12, 2011, after a young unemployed man set himself on fire in Mosul, demanding national security, tackling corruption, and reforming public services. They peaked on February 25, 2011, with the organization of the "Day of Rage," in which demonstrators attacked public buildings and prisons, and there were dozens of dead. The protests continued throughout the year, culminating in a rally of Saudi intervention in Bahrain to counter Shiite protesters. On April 9, 2011, the eighth anniversary of the fall of Saddam Hussein, thousands of demonstrators in Baghdad's Tahrir Square protested, among other things, against the American occupation. Muqtada al-Sadr organized a massive demonstration on May 26, 2011, with tens of thousands of protesters. Still, all these protests did not topple the Government. The Iraqi National Movement, representing mostly Iraqi Sunnis, boycotted Parliament for some time, claiming that the Government dominated by Shiites was striving to sideline Sunnis.

Roundup

Depending on its historical background, members' temperament, and cultural level, each society finds a different balance every time. The context in which it operates, the unwritten laws that govern it, and its economic and political characteristics should also be considered. The abroad-imposed "reforms" cannot artificially change this balance.

According to the then Algerian Government, the countries where the uprisings took place were countries with a central political system, without press freedom. They did not take the dimension of regional balance or even the national balance seriously. Instead, they transferred the international environment's pressure on their populations in a challenging economic and social situation. The latter reacted in the opposite direction, rebelling.

The perception of the "Arab Spring," at least in part of the Arab world, does not coincide with that formed in Western public opinion and Western states' governments. According to the former, "no Arab regime has fallen. It is their Presidents who were toppled under the levers of the West. Thousands of citizens called in vain for the departure of their rulers in Bahrain and elsewhere. The reason is that there was no decision from abroad on such an outcome. Many Arabs believe that the Arab Spring was a plan of foreigners to exploit the resources of the

Arab countries and not the will of the majority for reforms. This plan aimed at dealing with the economic crisis that has plagued the West for some years. Only in Tunisia, the events were entirely spontaneous, surprising the West."

"It is false information that has paved the way for military intervention in Libya, which has been the subject of a fierce campaign of disinformation." "History will one day show that the Libyan leader never used his planes to bomb his people." "In Syria, the situation is almost similar. It was a bogus revolution. There were no divisions in the Syrian army, which is based on pan-Arab nationalism and Baathism and remains in solidarity with the Syrian President to this day." "The political transformations that have occurred in Arab states cannot be considered revolutions. The definition of a revolution is far from reflecting what has happened in much of the Arab world. The name Arab Spring is not Arabic, either. It comes from the West, intending to parallel the events of Prague of 1968."[181]

Finally, the Palestinian cause, a central question for the Arabs, did not have a crucial role in these uprisings. Therefore, the theory of the independent nature of each country now appears to be well-founded. However, regime changes occurred only through the army's intervention, either from the country itself or from abroad. In many cases, the Islamists have prevailed. Despite the idealization the West attempts to form, the reality is more straightforward and remains within international power competitions. Islamism, ignited by the Arab Spring, has emerged as a critical factor of development.

---

[181] Views of the researcher Anis Nakache, Algiers, El Moudjahid newspaper, November 2, 2011.

EUROPE

At the turn of the century, there were thoughts within the European Union to establish a "Museum of Europe" to promote Europe's historical and cultural dimension. It was claimed that Europe as a unity began in the 9th century A.D., with the coronation of Charlemagne as Emperor of the Holy Roman Empire in 812. As it was underlined, this was the original starting point of the European edifice. In this way, contemporary Europe would be alienated from its Greek-Roman cultural heritage.

Europe does not have clear geographic boundaries; it is not exactly a continent but part of greater territorial unity, Eurasia. From the beginning of adopting the idea that Europe was a different continent, the differentiating factor was not the geography but the cultural elements of the people living there. However, in 2004, the President of France, Jack Chirac, rejected the reference to a common Christian tradition in the draft European constitution, highlighting the religious neutrality that should govern European states. However, the draft constitution was rejected by a referendum in France in 2005. Thus, Europe was also alienated from its Judo-Christian tradition.

Europe is a concept loosely linked to an area rather than a continent with perfectly defined geographic boundaries. The boundaries of Europe have, therefore, always been mutable. The modern concept of Europe in recent centuries corresponded to Western Europe. It can be seen as generally referring to the European Union and some neighboring individual states. However, from a broader perspective, in the context of the Council of Europe, the concept of Europe could perhaps include areas even of central Asia and countries in the Caucasus. At the same time, Turkey's acceptance, in principle, as a candidate country to the European Union has opened new horizons to the malleable concept of Europe. Europe could be divided geographically and geopolitically into four sections: Western and Northern Europe, the South, Eastern Europe, and the Balkans. These four sections have different characteristics, geographically and socially – politically, and, to some extent, culturally. The European Union's challenge is integrating these four sections into a set of similar characteristics.

Europe's countries are distinguished into land forces and sea forces in another geopolitical approach. Germany is the foremost land power, while Britain used to be the leading sea power. In this approach, Greece, with the largest Greek-acquired merchant fleet, and other countries are significant naval economic powers.[182] Despite its Nazi past, Germany claims a leading role in E.U. because of its size and economy.

The geographic center of Western Europe differs historically and culturally from its periphery, which varies according to the geographic location of each region. The European Union was built based on the social and cultural-political data of the six original members. Nevertheless, it is a system that could not survive after successive enlargements, each time with different textural areas. After an initial "honeymoon" period, the crisis between the center and the periphery upset the illusions of normalcy and equilibrium. E.U.'s redistributive and compensatory policies have not effectively reduced the economic disparities. Governments elected by popular vote could not proceed with concessions affecting their people's finances. Moreover, the ideological differences of

---

[182] G. Prevelakis, EBEA, February 28, 2018.

countries of the periphery, diverging from the liberal model of the core countries, impede the necessary convergence of policies. However, this could lead to a more uniform development of Europe in economic and social terms.

Geographical and climatic conditions are among the reasons for the controversy between Europe's core and periphery. Countries in the Mediterranean exposed to migratory flows, having borders with countries fostering territorial claims or threatening geopolitical backgrounds, cannot be considered to have a similar fate with Western European countries free from such concerns. The project of the common currency of the E.U. could not succeed in ensuring development for all countries, as it was flawed from its conception because Europe lacked a shared fiscal policy.

Formations within and in the vicinity of Europe are created or re-positioned based on geography, creating disputes. The Visegrad Group is a political alliance among the countries of Central Europe, the Czech Republic, Hungary, Poland, and Slovakia, formed before the accession of these countries in the E.U. The name of the group dates to 1335, when the Monarchs of Bohemia (Czech Republic), Poland, and Hungary met in the city of Visegrad. They agreed to create new trade routes to bypass Vienna's then-busy river port and offer more convenient access to European markets. The group sometimes acts as a conventicle within the Union and takes decisions that sometimes oppose the E.U. principles. For example, with the cooperation of Austria, Visegrad countries convened meetings of Southeast European countries, excluding Greece, to cope with the waves of migrants arriving through the Aegean islands.

Within the E.U., in the north and south, around the geopolitical axis formed by the leading E.U. powers of France and Germany, groupings of states whose interests, due to geography or mentality, coincide also created. Especially northern countries form a common front. In the south, the leaders of the countries of the south, France, Spain, Italy, Portugal, Greece, Malta, and Cyprus, meet regularly and discuss regional issues.

The European Neighborhood Policy was conceived in the context of the European Union's cooperation with neighboring countries since 2004. It is a partnership between, on the one hand, the E.U. as a whole and, on the other, each individual neighboring state. The neighborhood concept is different from mere geographical vicinity since it includes community, common fate, and solidarity links. The aim of this policy was, in principle, to avoid creating new dividing lines in Europe following the enlargement of the E.U. to the east with the ten new partners. Still, it was not a process that would lead to E.U. membership.

Two more formations are the Northern Dimension and the Black Sea Cooperation. The Northern Dimension is a partnership among the E.U., Russia, Norway, and Iceland. It is about cross-border and foreign policy issues relating to the geographic area covering northwest Russia, the Baltic, and Arctic Areas, including the Barents Sea. Black Sea Cooperation offers a forum for discussing matters among the coastal countries of that sea. However, the efficiency and geopolitical importance of these schemes are small.

Eastern European countries consider that Russia aims to destabilize them through an aggressive policy.[183] They interpret, and to some extent rightly, that it was not the communist regime that enslaved them but Russia, acting as a nationalist state. The internationalism of the Left was created as a façade of the nationalist-based approaches of the USSR to attract nations to its sphere. The same happened with creating the Pacifist movement in the West when the Soviet Union understood it could not compete with the West in the arms race.

Since the beginning of the century, the E.U. has created the "Western Balkan" group of states in the Balkan Peninsula, where Germany, Austria, and Italy wanted to extend their sway. Slovenia and Croatia became members of the E.U., and Albania, Kosovo, Bosnia, Montenegro, and North Macedonia were supported by the E.U., particularly by Germany and NATO. Serbia was kept on the sidelines. Through the efforts of Turkey and the U.S. Partnership Program (Clinton administration), a geopolitical Islamic arc was created in the Balkans. It includes Muslim countries Turkey, Albania, Kosovo, and Bosnia and Muslim minorities in Greece, Bulgaria, and North Macedonia.

The European Union

The various nation-states within the geographical boundaries of the continent eventually realized that their community of traditions and culture was more important than their historical and economic oppositions. After two bloody wars, they ascertained that peace constituted the most crucial factor for their development. They considered that the safest route in this direction would be their

---

[183] Interview of Polish President Andrzej Duda, November 19, 2017.

economic cooperation, even in the most sensitive sectors at that time, coal and iron (1951, Treaty of Paris). In the second stage, they realized that united, they would achieve more than they could by acting individually (1957, Treaty of Rome). In the next few decades, the practice, combined with security and internal cohesion policies, has shown that the project has been successful. As a result, Europe ensured the highest possible prosperity in its history. However, the errors committed due to the imbalance in the transfer of competencies and collective decisions that favored the big countries caused the alienation of several member-states. The accumulated dissatisfaction could be dealt with only by recognizing the presumption of states' competence in priority.

The Europe of the end of the 20th century, geopolitically facing the Atlantic, envisioned setting up a stable continental space without dividing borders through the Single Market and the Schengen agreement. For their part, the former communist countries sought to join the E.U., believing that by acceding to the Union, they would leave the misery of the past and avoid the Russian danger. After their accession, however, the dominant tendencies of the western-oceanic Europe of their past centuries started encountering land-based continental values, including the safety and hierarchy of the intended purposes. The crux of the European problem lies in the enlargement of the E.U. with countries that have abstained from the historical and geographic being of Europe and its institutional developments after World War II.

Before the construction of the E.U. institutions, Europe was multi-centric and competitive with a particular culture. The "sea values" had previously ensured world domination through colonialism and the two world wars.

The memory remained alive and settled in the people's subconscious. As long as it existed, the Iron Curtain assured its Western orientation. However, after 1990, when the "Europeanisation" under Western Europe's responsibility became a common goal, the balance was overturned.[184]

The untimely enlargement of the E.U. in 2004, with ten states of a different mindset and historical origin, caused malfunctions in the E.U.'s operation. In the Union's interior, economic power inequality and migration and justice variations created problems. In foreign policy, it started discords due to the Eastern European states' pro-Atlantic and extreme anti-Russian policies. The political leaderships of the Visegrad countries attempted to rebuild political and ideological boundaries within Europe. The European Union avoided another mistake by refusing to discuss Turkey's accession further. Instead, it agreed to start accession negotiations with individual countries of the Western Balkans with highly nationalist aspirations. The membership of these countries, with their inherent contradictions, will not contribute to the further integration of Europe. It will only serve the geopolitical ambitions of the German-Italian axis.

In the second decade of the 21st century, instead of a more practical approach, a distancing took place in the E.U. The tendency towards nationalism and the diffusion of Euroscepticism and anti-Europeanism increased, even though it did not represent the majority. The return to the ideology of the state's primary role raises objections. European unification could only be achieved through political and economic integration, and it concerns concessions of national sovereignty. However, several

---

[184] View expressed by G. Prevelakis

European peoples did not accept the haste in this direction and felt wronged by the process.

Unlike its pro-federalist partners, Britain has always had a more "collaborative" approach to the E.U.. It supported the deepening of the trade relationship and the admission of new members to the E.U. despite the problems this would create. Moreover, Britain (and some Eastern European countries) understood the "closer union" trend as leading to nations losing political control. Although the Single Market meant freedom of movement, it also meant losing control over national policies, including migration.[185] This thought dominated the British electorate in the referendum on Brexit in 2016.

The increasing economic divergence among the member-states, combined with the rise of populism, broadened the already existing division. The confidence of the states and their people in the idea of the Union is decreasing. The supranational institution of the European Union is transformed into an intergovernmental organization. There, the influential countries impose their will on the weak. Germany is turning its economic power into a position of leadership. The idea of replacing the 19th-century Balance of Powers system with a regional integration system is no longer valid.[186]

The economic crisis at the end of the first decade of the 21st century has had a considerable impact on European citizens' lives. The financial crisis mainly affected the countries of the south. Greece was affected particularly due to the quirks of its political system and the electorate's behavior. The resulting recession has caused double-digit unemployment rates, especially for the

---

[185] Kate Smith, U.K. Ambassador in Athens.
[186] Loukas Tsoukalis: In defense of Europe, 2016.

young, and drove the social systems to collapse. European Union could not offer solutions to people's social and economic problems due to the stance of some member-states that have not been affected by the crisis.

Moreover, the bureaucratic functioning of Brussels created frustration and discomfort. Besides, the adequacy of the E.U. to respond to international challenges has been called into question. As a result, the E.U could not act as a geopolitical player.

The overall economic problem in Europe stems from internal and external causes. The main problem is the significant economic inequality between member-states in the domestic domain. The lack of flexibility in applying rules of supposedly healthy competitiveness without customs barriers, but with regulations prohibiting the protection of enterprises and services needing assistance, boosts the stronger at the expense of the weaker. In addition, introducing a common currency without the corresponding standard fiscal policies leads to transferring funds from the poorest countries to the richest. There are no compensatory measures, as it would be in a single or genuinely federal state. However, this is Europe, with the European status of the people lagging far behind their national identity. However, the economic crisis has led to the creation of institutions that could, to some extent, meet the demands.

Concerning the external causes, globalization is a central issue, as it contributes to European resources leaking abroad. Of course, the damage is not the same for all European countries; some benefit from globalization and the opening of markets, others lose, and Europe is harmed in its entirety. However, the global economy has benefited from the globalization of trade, and its continuity is in favor of humanity. External causes also include terrorism and the excessive increase of immigrants' numbers with a culture conflicting with the European.

The lack of joint defense and economic policy does not facilitate European integration. Nevertheless, the Treaty of Lisbon established permanent structured cooperation in security and defense. This defense cooperation framework would enable member-states with the will and the ability to develop joint defense capabilities, invest in collaborative projects, and enhance their armed forces' operational readiness and contribution. The Council adopted a decision to institutionalize permanent structured cooperation (PESCO) on December 11, 2017, following the agreement of 25 E.U. member-states to participate. In any case, PESCO does not constitute an alliance to defend European territory. Nevertheless, all this is still a sluggish approach; European states mainly defend their national interests.

However, the withdrawal of Britain from the Union is a positive evolution since its anti-Union policy has always been a suspensory factor. Brexit made France and Germany come even closer and confirm, 56 years after the Elysée Treaty, their close relations with the Treaty of Aachen in January 2019. The Treaty of Aachen strengthened the French-German axis in favor of the values of Europe and contained a mutual defense clause. On the other hand, the conservative axis of Italy–Poland seems to oppose the axis of France – Germany.

Since 2015, mainly with the opening of the borders of Greece – with the urging of Germany – many irregular economic migrants from Asia and Africa passed to Europe through Turkey. The reaction of many European states to the North Corridor of Greece was defensive. However, when their concerns were not answered because of the peculiar mentality of the Greek Government, they closed their borders with Greece. Simultaneously, the link between irregular migration and terrorism or mixing irregular migrants with refugees has intensified the confusion.

The European Union is a singular geopolitical edifice. It lacks the unified structure and the cultural cohesion of a nation-state, as well as the enforcement of sovereignty characterizing federations like the USA or Russia. E.U. is not a united state; it does not behave with the necessary solidarity. After all, every country is left more or less alone to cope with its problems. Moreover, several eastern European states refuse to surrender their sovereignty to a virtually foreign power.

Europe does not have the means to impose the centralism necessary for a self-reliant course. As Europe's bureaucracy attempts to move in this direction, so do the centrifugal forces in the East and West. Britain wanted to return to its imperial dreams; after all, it was never a real E.U. member, and it did not share the objectives of the Union. The Mediterranean countries felt helpless, both in the economic crisis of the second decade of the century and in the question of the continuing immigration crisis. The states of Eastern Europe did not understand, sometimes, the untenable positions of Western Europe and, therefore, were accused (at least) of conservatism.

Germany has opted for budgetary discipline and self-support of its development capacities to meet global competition challenges. It considers that this model is the most appropriate for the rest of the countries of the European Union. However, due to their temper and historically shaped standards, the Mediterranean peoples could not follow the "German rationalism." Economic and developmental tensions between northern and southern

Europeans intersect with differing perceptions between East and West on identity and migration issues.

On the other hand, the dangers of the Cold War era no longer exist. The threat the Soviet Union represented for Europe was not inherited by Russia, despite the efforts of various cycles for a return when the communist danger led to the spreading of an American protective shield over Western Europe. The U.S. Trump felt that they should not be spending money on the defense of a Europe that had become politically and commercially competitive to the States. So the U.S. has taken protectionist measures, including against Europe, moving one step further. Europe, which had taken the support of the United States for granted, was badly surprised.

The new geopolitical environment, a result of the globalization to which Europe has contributed enthusiastically, eventually ousted Europe from the central international stage. On the other hand, the solidarity that Europe wanted to demonstrate has led to many illegal entries of aspiring immigrants, thus creating problems in the economy and social cohesion. Europe no longer has the economic prosperity of the past or the defense protection of America. It is confronted with problems created by itself or issues it did not anticipate their evolution to cope in time with them. Not only governments but European society altogether is responsible for this situation.

Europe could adapt to the new conditions based on political capital accumulated in its happy past. It could then revise its geopolitical model to find a balance between nation-states seeking greater autonomy of movement and the coordination of Brussels.

The European External Action Service
The need for gradual integration of the European states in a supranational international organization such as the E.U. is undeniable. However, it is not sure that the convergence of the E.U. member-states interests has reached the point of granting competence for a common external representation. Therefore, the European External Action Service (EEAS) was established by the Treaty of Lisbon, signed on December 13, 2007, and entered into force on December 1, 2009.[187] This service comprises officials from Council Offices and the European Commission and staff from the national diplomatic services.

As in many other issues, the European Council made too binding decisions for the member-states in haste. However, the E.U. member-states are not coherent; they do not show sincere political and fiscal solidarity, and they do not have common national interests. On the contrary, most of the time, their interests are conflicting. Independent states burdened with dense European history naturally have no understanding of the national interests of others. Eastern European states fear Russia, whereas Western European countries underestimate the risks. Besides, some people within the E.U. are showing pure hostility towards others. Finally, the European Commission, which corresponds to a "government," is not elected by any people and does not give a substantive account to any Parliament. The European Parliament is powerless, and the Council is a formation controlled by the

---

[187] Constitution for the European Union and the Treaty of Lisbon - European Union Legal Materials - Research Guides at Columbia Law School. https://guides.law.columbia.edu/c.php?g=1221803&p=9087251

big and prominent states. The main problem is the different mentalities shaped in Eastern European countries over decades. Still, an organization with many member-states cannot be managed via consensus.

The European External Action Service is governed by its rules and principally serves its interests. Primarily, it supports the aspirations of the Directorate of bigger European states, from which its officials usually come through the mechanisms created. The so-called "E.U. Ambassadors" operate and mostly succeed in substituting the parallel Ambassadors of member-states.

The European Union is a great idea that should not be left to be the victim of hasty decisions, which seem to lead to self-destruction. A review of the issue could perhaps lead to the reintroduction of the previous system. This system responded accurately to reality, while the alternating member-states should carry out the factual Presidency.

The Mediterranean

The Mediterranean is the sea "in the middle of the land." It is in the middle of the three continents, possessing the most significant part of the land worldwide. It is the sea basin where civilization was born and spread and has always been a communication bridge. Navigation in the Mediterranean started early in history for colonization, trade, or piracy purposes. Colonization, with the creation of coastal trade centers, led to the creation of cities and the exploitation of the potential of those regions. Trade generated civilization helped develop culture and contributed to its dissemination. Nevertheless, piracy had been an impediment, sending settlements away from the coasts.

According to geographical–geopolitical analysis, the Mediterranean could be perceived as a separate continent. The core of this "continent" is the cooperation of Europe, mainly with the north-African and other Mediterranean countries in the south.

The south of the Mediterranean region is a zone of instability. Except for the coastal states, it includes disputed Western Sahara, Mali (with the attempt by the Islamists allied with terrorists and criminals to create an entity in the northern part of the country), Chad and Niger, both Sudan and South Sudan (mostly problematic states, terrorism) Somalia (piracy). In the east, the Islamic monarchy of Saudi Arabia, Iran (Islamic Revolution, nuclear), and Afghanistan (Taliban terrorism); in the eastern Mediterranean, the threats of Turkey against almost everybody and its invasions to Cyprus, Iraq, Syria, and Libya dominate. The West alliance considers Turkey a loyal member; in reality, it is the other way around. The Palestinian issue is no longer the protagonist in the play; the Middle East issue stagnates at an impasse with the actual situation.

The Mediterranean is a crossroads connecting the region's countries with all continents. It is linked via Gibraltar to the Atlantic Ocean, via Suez to the Red Sea and the Indian Ocean, and through the Marmara Straits with the Black Sea. Through a river route, it could also be connected to Central Europe.

The importance of the Danube River system – Morava – the Vardar – Axios, ending in the area of Thessaloniki, as a pass for freight transport, is derived from the ability to connect central Europe with the Mediterranean Sea was recognized as early as in the mid-19th century. This route has attracted the interest of China in the context of China's cooperation with Central

European countries "17+1" (CEEC). In 2013, a Chinese company, after study, submitted a plan proposing the revival of the project and determined the way for the next steps. Beijing places this interconnection in the One Belt One Road (OBOR) project. Based on initial estimates, the project's total cost seemed to amount to 5 billion Euros, with the value of the last tranche, Vardar – Axios – Thessaloniki, costing almost 2.4 billion Euros. If implemented, this project will facilitate the transport of products to central and northern European markets, the Caucasus, and the Black Sea. At the same time, the role of maritime traffic through the Black Sea and the Straits would lessen. Thus, the environmentally detrimental project of constructing a canal between the Black Sea and Marmara would be avoided. Respectively, the geopolitical value of all of Central Europe would be increased. The waterway would offer a faster and lower-cost route for shipments. Studies argue that such a path would shorten the journey by four days compared to the existing situation. However, it is not guaranteed that the cost-benefit research eventually would be positive. The melting of the Arctic ice and the development of crossing ships from the North Road may signal a shift in the center of interest. However, it should be considered that these two routes may not be considered competitive but complementary since the Arctic route mainly serves Western Europe. In contrast, the waterway will serve central Europe.

Geopolitically, the Mediterranean could be separated as western and eastern. The western Mediterranean is a sea and coastal zone of peace, stability, and cooperation. The European countries of the north coast have realized the benefits of collaborating with the Maghreb countries. These countries are very responsive because of their historical connections with the former colonial powers. In addition to the multiple bilateral cooperation schemes, the so-called 5+5 initiative, five countries of south-eastern Europe (Italy, Malta, France, Spain, Portugal), and five Maghrebin countries (Morocco, Algeria, Tunisia, Libya, Mauritania) are very active. Although Portugal and Mauritania are not Mediterranean countries, they have been included in the cooperation since they have close ties and interests with others. Efforts of enlargement by adding Greece and Egypt failed; in this case, geography receded to ulterior political motives.

In the framework of the North-South cooperation of the 5+5 initiative, the members discuss issues of geographic interest relating to the Mediterranean environment, such as climate change, desertification, waste management, water resources, biodiversity, coastal protection, and the integrated management of the coastal zone, cleaning of sea and reinforcement of possibilities of action. Energy issues are also being discussed, such as the Mediterranean Solar Energy project, the existing capabilities in this area and their evaluation, the interconnections of the electricity grids, and the perspectives regarding climate protection. Cooperation in the energy sector includes the gas pipelines linking the producer Algeria to European consumers.

Unlike the western part, the eastern Mediterranean is regarded as an area of instability. The Middle East, with the rivalry of Israel–Palestinians, and Syria, and the conflicts among Arab states, between Sunnis and Shiites, but also the underlying dispute over the leadership of the Arab world and the destabilizing behavior of Turkey are creating conditions of concern. Even the situation in Libya, a country participating in the

5+5 initiative, reflects the eastern Mediterranean and not the western part.

One of the Mediterranean's problems is the strong presence of naval forces, resulting from the instability of the eastern part and its strategic importance. The strong naval forces in the Mediterranean of France, Italy, Greece, and Turkey were added to the fleets of the U.S., Russia, and China. As a result, the density of naval forces in the Mediterranean is the largest globally.

Greece, geographically and politically a European, Balkan, and Mediterranean country, is located in the "center of gravity" of the landmass formed by Asia, Europe, and Africa. Together with the Republic of Cyprus, it constitutes bipolar democratic stability in the region. In this light, Turkey not only wants its territorial expansion in Cyprus, but it does not allow the existence of the Republic of Cyprus, which would be a partner of Greece. Greece and Cyprus formed three tripartite cooperation schemes with Egypt and Jordan on the one hand and Israel on the other, on the pattern of the North-South cooperation scheme of the Western Mediterranean (Initiative 5+5), which operated successfully. The United States favors these schemes and includes them in its geopolitical plans.

Ottoman Empire initially occupied the island of Cyprus in 1570 and then rented it to Britain in 1878. However, the West allowed – Britain even urged– Turkey to believe it had rights in Cyprus, although it expressly renounced them by the Treaty of Lausanne of July 23, 1923. Turkey, after a pretext, invaded the island and occupied a large part of the country militarily. The West tolerated Turkey's military occupation of Cyprus for decades. It treats Turkey as a normal country while recognizing it as an equal member of the international community despite violating a basic rule of international law and the statute of the U.N.

Given the situation in Cyprus, Crete has the most considerable geopolitical significance in the eastern Mediterranean for the U.S., with the naval base of Souda. Greece holds geographically and conventionally the most substantial part of the Aegean Sea. Turkey had resigned "from any demands in the Aegean beyond 3 miles -minus Imvros and Tenedos islands in the north" with the Treaty of Lausanne (1923). Despite this resignation, it raises claims (Blue Homeland) on half of the Aegean and the islets not mentioned by name in the Treaty of Paris (1947) with arguments parallel to Germany's Lebensraum. Turkey did not sign the U.N. Convention on the Law of the Sea, does not respect its clauses, and tries to impose its will by military means.

The geopolitics of pipelines and energy

Natural gas is a significant energy source as it is cheaper than oil and less harmful to the environment. The most economical mode of transport is through pipelines. Geopolitically, diversifying sources so that each country does not depend on a single source is raised. Therefore, governments try to diversify the pipelines' routes or use other means, i.e., gas in liquefied form (LNG), transported by ships. According to the UNCLOS, Pipelines could pass through the seabed of the EEZ of any country under some preconditions.

The care to ensure stable conditions in territories from which the oil pipelines pass has been added to the effort of maintaining open transit routes of commerce. This effort has provided additional geopolitical advantages to the countries where the pipelines pass. For example, Turkey argues that it is closely adjacent to 70% of the world's oil and gas reserves and, through its territory, could pass gas from the Caspian to global markets. In this context, it promoted the idea of the Baku-Tbilisi-Ceyhan pipeline for oil and the Transcaucasian pipeline for natural gas.

The Nord Stream pipeline carries 55 billion cubic meters of natural gas from the Vyborg of Russia to Greifswald in Germany. It started its operation in 2012 and fuels parts of Western Europe. The Baltic underwater 1,222 km long conductor is the longest in the world. The construction of two new Nord Stream 2 pipelines is expected to double the capacity. Nevertheless, it faces the objections of the U.S. and some eastern European states that fear an increase in the influence of the Russian Federation due to its energy dependency on it. In any case, the USA focused on avoiding the creation of Russia's energy monopoly in Europe. In this light, they evaluate the pipelines that connect the Caspian to the Mediterranean, bypassing Russia.

The "Turkish Stream" pipeline envisions construction starting from Russia, crossing the Black Sea underwater, and ending at Turkey's pipeline system. Further planning is envisaged with its interconnection with central Europe. However, the European Union opposed the plan because it aimed at disengaging from the Russian gas monopoly.

The Greek-Bulgarian IGB pipeline connects the two countries' natural gas networks.

Through the Mediterranean, the MEDGAZ pipeline (Maghreb – Europe Gas Pipeline) connects the Hassi R'mel field in Algeria with Cordoba in Andalusia via Morocco, supplying natural gas to Spain and Portugal. The TransMed (Trans-Mediterranean Pipeline) -or Enrico Mattei pipeline- connects Algeria with Sicily through Tunisia and Italy. The

GALSI project (Gasdotto Algeria Sardegna Italia) will connect Algeria with Sardinia and northern Italy.

The Eastern Mediterranean EastMed pipeline project concerns the interconnection of the eastern Mediterranean hydrocarbon sources (Egypt, Israel) with Greece through Cyprus and Crete to Italy. This will increase Europe's energy security by diversifying producers and transit routes. The U.S., in favor of Turkey, expressed the view that this pipeline is economically inadvisable. However, in addition to the North Sea fields, European energy sources could be found on the continental shelf of Cyprus and Greece, despite Turkey's harassment regarding searches carried out by Cyprus in its EEZ.

In the context of the Eastern Mediterranean energy cooperation, seven countries of the region held the first ministerial meeting in Cairo in January 2019 to create a gas forum there. The Ministers from Egypt, Israel, Italy, Jordan, Greece, Cyprus, and the Palestinian Authority and representatives of the E.U. and the World Bank attended the meeting. This meeting was "an initiative for dialogue" and adopted a joint declaration having as objectives the creation of a regional gas market, the deepening of cooperation and the strategic dialogue among the countries involved, as well as the exploitation of gas deposits. It created a platform that may take the form of an international organization to create a shared vision and common aspirations among the participating countries. The objective of optimum cooperation on the exploitation of the region's hydrocarbons is to render the eastern Mediterranean competitive in general in the field of energy worldwide.[188]

---

[188] Announcement by G. Lakkotrypis, Cypriot Minister of Energy.

Greece

Greece is left at the end of the book as studying history, geography, politics, geopolitics, and their combination started there, the center of the ancient ecumene; at least geography has not changed much from that time. Greece consists of two peninsulas and many islands, although the second peninsular, Peloponnese, became an island after the opening of a canal in the Isthmus of Corinth — an island connected with the mainland by bridges at the east and west. Mountains, rare fertile valleys, two or three relatively large plains, and the islands define the country's character and its people.

No place in the country is more than a hundred kilometers away from the sea. The sea is dominant everywhere and, since antiquity, has influenced life in the country. Geographical fragmentation formed a people independent and of the most intractable in Europe. Geography and people remain the same, but geopolitics change. The Aegean Sea, which unites the Black Sea countries and the industrial area of Istanbul with the Mediterranean, could control commercial and war navigation through island channels. The Helladic area connects the eastern Mediterranean and Suez with Central Europe. Except for aviation, Greece is connected to Europe through the Balkan motorway, a long and sometimes tricky route, or by sea via Italy. Thus, there is a lack of secure and rapid land connection with Western Europe.

Based on its geographic position and the international political system as it is formed, Greece follows several policies that are, to some extent, independent of each other, although eventually interconnected. In this light, a Balkan, a Mediterranean-

of Canada, an autonomous region belonging to the French offshore complex, the Falkland Islands on the Argentine coast belonging to the United Kingdom, the islands of Guernsey and Jersey, and British possessions near the shores of France. Beyond the peculiarity of Greece's neighbor, inevitably, relations and claims cannot be determined solely by geography.

Greece did not initially understand the problem of immigration. It did not want to stop the migratory flows from the East for altruistic reasons and let them enter Europe. The accumulation of many aspiring immigrants from Asian and African countries in the Greek islands constitutes additional geopolitical trouble. Turkey facilitates this immigration, creating problems for Greece and Europe.

The arc Ukraine – Russia – Turkey – Middle East – Iran primarily falls into the interests of the West. Greece takes a central role as a regional player at the borderline of this arc. The Mediterranean is a scene where threats such as terrorism and irregular migration unfold. The unique position that the West holds for Greece, it seems that sometimes, does not coincide with its interests. The German tendency to project its economic power on the axis-Morava-Danube, which conflicts with the Anglo-Saxon theory of the Perimeter, creates potentially explosive situations. On the other hand, Russia is trying to maintain its sway in North Macedonia and Serbia[190], creating an additional problem for the region.

In the heart of the U.S.'s policies lies its opposition against Russia to the extent that it dominates almost all its geopolitical actions. Concerning local foreign policy in the

---

[190] M. Koppa, Institute of International Relations, April 30, 2018.

eastern Mediterranean, the U.S. is forging two lines of defense to isolate Russia from the East Mediterranean. The first includes Albania, North Macedonia, Bulgaria, and Turkey. It is no coincidence that there are negative feelings for Greece in all these countries. They covet its territorial integrity – but this does not disturb the E.U.

The second line of defense is formed with the tripartite formation of Greece, Cyprus, and Israel, countries with a different temperament from the first line. The second line is precisely what the United States wants to join, with the sole objective of confronting Russia and securing energy. Also, Russia is making its geopolitical calculations, for example, the Russia-Turkey-Iraq-Iran line and its bases in Syria. No wonder Turkey shows up on both sides, as it always has.

Regarding the tripartite with Egypt, the Muslim Brotherhood factor is always decisive. The Islamic and Arab components surpass all others. Therefore, Egypt cannot be a first-rate allied country for the United States. However, the USA accepts the formations with Egypt and Jordan, although it does not want to get involved, perhaps not to risk its privileged relations with Saudi Arabia. If Egypt fell under the Islamists' sovereignty, as was the case with President Morsi, the whole foreign policy of the country would change course. Israel is a more stable country, but its strategic interests can again lead to a closer relationship with Turkey, putting in danger the tripartite cooperation. However, not having a friendly hinterland, it is obliged to shift strategically to the Mediterranean, Cyprus, and Greece.

The Delimitation of the Maritime Zones

The crisis in the Aegean began on November 1, 1973, with the publication of a map in the official gazette of the Turkish Government showing sections of the Northeast Aegean continental shelf offered to the Turkish Oil Company for exploitation.

In claiming that the Aegean islands do not have their continental shelf, Turkey aims to indicate that the Greek islands of the eastern Aegean are within the Anatolian continental shelf (Blue Homeland doctrine). Its ultimate goal is the creation of a special status to occupy the islands militarily. [191]

EPILOGUE

One of the questions raised is whether President Trump's foreign policy represented a tendency of the U.S. in general or it was a peculiarity of a weird person. The world press preferred to underline the second option, but the truth may be found in the first. President Trump seemed to have some central lines around the "America First" axis that resulted in introversion. He was pro-Israeli, forgetting everything about just solutions, but primarily was "against" Palestinians. He tried to resolve the issue of North Korea without much success. In his foreign policy, Trump was obstinate against China (in opposition to Washington's bureaucracy that is adamant against Russia), against Iran (allying the U.S. with Saudi Arabia instead of the E.U.), against the E.U. (considering it as a mere trade competitor), or against its NATO allies (complaining they do not pay enough). He was against Germany because of Russia's Nord Stream 2 pipeline and not spending 2% of its

---

[191] Vassilios Moutsoglou: The Delimitation of the Maritime Zones between Greece and Turkey -. https://professors-phds.com/2020/08/25/28018/

GDP on defense. , and because of the German surplus in the trade balance with the U.S. He was also against all international organizations because they contributed to the diffusion of power. However, international organizations are at the core of integration at the global and regional levels; therefore, their existence is vital for peace and cooperation.

President Trump used to act without consultation deciding and primarily working alone. For example, he had not informed anyone publicly announcing that he would withdraw nearly 10 thousand U.S. troops from Germany, transporting some of them to Poland. He had not revealed it when he was in Berlin; he did not report it to other NATO allies, not even informed beforehand the U.S. Congress.

Trump's America ceased to be the world's dominant power. The lack of visibility showed a broader malaise in American diplomacy. The country's foreign policy lost prestige; the diplomatic service was not consulted or heard. According to Bob Menendez, the senior Democrat on the Senate Foreign Relations Committee, the State Department (under the Trump Presidency) was "at risk of catastrophic failure." Alternatively, according to a foreign Ambassador in Washington: "The U.S. State Department, which used to be important, is destroyed, it does not exist."

Reserve-currency status is often cast as a matter of economic fundamentals.[192] Nevertheless, without a dominant political power defending it, it might not be reckoned as such. The U.S. Dollar's evaluation as a global

---

[192] Dollar dominance is as secure as American global leadership. https://www.economist.com/finance-and-economics/2020/08/06/dollar-dominance-is-as-secure-as-american-global-leadership

currency depends on America's global leadership. The world's economic dominant power may lose its position if the U.S. cannot continue its policy as a moral power in international politics and stops serving the world order to benefit world peace, security, and prosperity. Nevertheless, a few months before the 2020 elections, President Trump succeeded in mediating to conclude economic normalization agreements between Serbia and Kosovo and facilitating Israel's recognition by the United Arab Emirates and Bahrein.

The U.S. urged Europe to join political forces against China. Member-states of the latter are coming out aggressively on the world stage, trying to fill the void left by American introversion. Geopolitical upheavals intensified due to the coronavirus, removing the United States issue from international organizations, alliances, and Europe. The E.U. refuses to be drafted against Beijing, although it does not side up with China.

Despite the U.S.'s opposition to China, E.U.'s relations with Beijing remain strong. German exports to China have risen more than fivefold [193] since 2005, making it its number-one market. The United States stood at number three. For this, most Europeans blamed President Trump's trade policy. They believed that Washington would prefer European disunity and ceased to consider Europeans as the best allies of the U.S. However, Europe tried to limit the erosion in transatlantic relations and ultimately restore European ties with the United States.

---

[193] Op-Ed: Germany's Merkel faces test that will shape EU after coronavirus. https://www.cnbc.com/2020/07/11/op-ed-germanys-merkel-faces-test-that-will-shape-eu-after-coronavirus.html

European and transatlantic aspirations reinforced each other.

European Union, despite its aspirations, could not become a political power. Member-states remain committed to their narrow national interests. Consequently, in issues of great importance, the E.U. does not act as a single political - and military if need be power - except when the individual interests of its member-states coincide.

U.K., France, and Germany aspired to leading roles in global politics. Germany considers that the timing and nature of the U.S.' troop-withdrawal decision were not occasional. Some German officials had cast doubt on whether the possible election of former Vice President Joe Biden in November would alter this trajectory. "Everyone who thinks everything in the trans-Atlantic partnership will be as it once underestimated the structural changes,"[194] said the German Foreign Minister. Considering the stances of Germany regarding issues of siding with NATO Allies, it could not be regarded as a reliable ally in NATO.

In the Middle East, new players emerge. Turkey's membership in NATO is a relic from the past; it does not carry any practical meaning. Together with Germany is not a reliable ally. Fully armed with the most advanced weapons by the U.S., Germany, and Russia, highly militarized Erdogan's Turkey is considered a big and mighty nation, leader of the Islamic World, free from any legal or conventional affiliations. Western countries cannot

---

[194] Op-Ed: Germany's Merkel faces test that will shape EU after coronavirus. https://www.cnbc.com/2020/07/11/op-ed-germanys-merkel-faces-test-that-will-shape-eu-after-coronavirus.html

understand this; they think Turkey is their ally. According to its President, Turkey aspires to be a dominant power in the eastern Mediterranean and a global power, in the same rank as the others.

Russia, under Putin, continues to be an autocratic nation; nevertheless, after the Cold War, its military interventions abroad have been a lot fewer than the West's interventions. Moreover, although it is a nuclear power and a permanent member of the U.N. Security Council, its poor economic performance and NATO's strength deprive Russia of exerting an active global role.

China exerts tight control over the economic cycle; it has an autocratic but more efficient state, whereas the differentiation between state and private firms is unclear. This policy has been performed well, but the results will be seen in the future. China considers its technocratic form of central management sustainable, but this can be true only if globalization continues. On the other hand, as Trump's administration suggested, confrontation could not lead to China's capitulation. The democratization of China is a long-term prospect.

The actual world is in chaos. In many cases, instead of international law, the law of the jungle prevails. Russia annexed Crimea; China attempted to dominate the South China Sea, imposed its rule on Hong Kong, and clashed with India over Kashmir. North Korea continued its nuclear program; migration became a scourge for southern Europe; Myanmar expelled its Muslim citizens; Israel occupied and annexed Arab land. Turkey continued to occupy north Cyprus, bombarded Iraq, and invaded Syria and, through proxies, Libya. The United Nations and the U.S., together with most European Powers, watch as spectators the violation of international law. This indifference allows autocratic imperialist powers such as

Russia, China, and Turkey to implement their expansionist machinations. There is a return to the interwar period (1918-1939) order. However, the next world war will have more than two opponent blocs.

In the early decades of the 21st century, the world is much more interconnected politically, economically, and culturally, more complicated because of the multiple relations between states, organizations, and individuals, and more insecure with various threats of natural or terrorist texture always looming everywhere. Income disparity, protectionism, and rising new powers blur the international scene. On the other hand, democracy in many countries is receding and mutating, and global politics suffer from a lack of leadership. Under President Trump, the U.S. shed its traditional role, and no other country could undertake it. Europe is not an integral power; it has difficulties protecting even its members; it avoids making decisions and lacks a global strategy and military force.

Nevertheless, Europe still needs the U.S. and NATO for its military protection. In addition, the international system is becoming obsolete. The U.N. Security Council expresses virtually only the interests and the will of the five permanent members having veto power.

Recently, there has been a tendency to resolve international conflicts by arms. The continued military occupation of Cyprus, the break-up of Yugoslavia and, in particular, the secession of Kosovo, the American aggression in Iraq, Russia's involvement in Ukraine and the Crimean affair, Syria and Iraq, Libya, the Turkish armed attack on Greece's sovereign rights in the eastern Mediterranean, mark a return to the era of resolving international disputes through the power of arms and the implementation of the jungle law.

In Nagorno Karabakh, there was an unprovoked military attack by the combined forces of Turkey and Azerbaijan. The maps of the Stalinist era cannot be an excuse; wedging war is prohibited under international law.

All these happen under the powerful states' apathetic eyes and the international community that avoids meddling. The U.S., even in the case of its Kurdish allies threatened by Turkey, has refrained from providing support. Neither Russia nor China is the protagonist in resorting to arms; it is Turkey, and it was proved it cannot be prevented by diplomatic means as long as neither NATO nor the E.U. respects their obligations.

International relations are marked by versatility and uncertainty, resulting in the high volatility of modern world relationships, with friendships and rivalries alternating.[195] Security is unstable, and it seems that this situation may not change in the medium term. There is a discrepancy between the theoretical international relations, as reflected in the public discourse, and the reality of the transnational procedures. In the face of political and economic power, determination, and national interest, international organizations are unable to enforce international law or effectively regulate the functioning of transnational relations. Thus, international law continues to recede. The global economy, a significant aspect of the operation of societies, is undergoing the technological-electronic revolution, which is characterized by combining and merging technologies with overlapping boundaries between the physical, digital, and biological domains. The second important aspect, security, is hovering in a context

---

[195] K. Filis, IDIS, April 30, 2018

with vague conditions because of the ambivalence of the societies affected. Irregular migration causes uncontrolled changes in the cultural composition of Europe.

However, given the pros and cons, the world in the early 21st century is the best ever, albeit different, given the absence of linearity in evolution. Life expectancy has increased considerably. Significant progress has been achieved in gender equality and the fight against racism, although there are still steps to be taken. Extreme poverty is reduced. Lower classes have improved their level of life. After 1990, Southeast and East Asian countries developed significantly, surpassing several Western countries. The flow of information, private and public, is global and fast.

Although geography is more or less the same, politics in the 21st century fundamentally differs from the second half of the 20th century.

ANNEX

The U.S.'s re-engage the world.

Speaking to diplomats at the Harry S. Truman Building in Washington on Feb. 4, 2021, President Biden said he intended to "send a clear message to the world: America is back.[196] As he added: "We are going to rebuild our alliances. We are going to re-engage the world."

However, the world America wants to join geopolitically has changed. China and Russia have consolidated their positions as worldwide powers. Besides, several indications regarding the cooperation of those two powers against the West are now apparent. For example, the U.N. Security Council regarding the coup in Myanmar could not adopt a proper condemning Resolution as Britain's proposal was vetoed.

President of China Xi has declared that his country will economically surpass the U.S. soon. Responding, President Biden reiterated that America is second to no one. Geopolitically, China's direct scope might be limited in the China Sea and Taiwan. Still, its geo-economic view extends globally via the Belt and Road initiative.

Russia remains economically weak, but its military might and political will are intact for success worldwide. Biden sent the message that the tolerance period has ended, but President Putin seems to mock the Westerners. Early February's (2021) visit of the High Representative of the European Union, Joseph Borrell, to Russia indicated the current situation in EU-Russia affairs. The opposition

---

[196] Biden Announces End of U.S. Support to Saudi War in Yemen | Wisconsin Muslim Journal. https://wisconsinmuslimjournal.org/biden-announces-end-of-u-s-support-to-saudi-war-in-yemen/

leader, Navalny's issue, drives their relations to their lowest levels. Russia considered it an internal matter and objected to interventions, disregarding that the human rights issues are of international concern. The Foreign Minister of Russia, Lavrov, said that the EU and Russia are opponents on many topics, and aggravation of relations will have unpredictable consequences.

According to Joschka Fischer[197], the European Union stands opposite three "empires": Russia, Turkey, and the United Kingdom. Therefore, a question may arise whether the E.U. could be considered a geopolitical entity. E.U.'s reaction regarding the crises in Syria, Libya, the Eastern Mediterranean, and Nagorno Karabakh is weak. Politically, the E.U.'s death is looming.

Britain's withdrawal from the E.U. relieved the Union of a handicap in its Common Foreign and Security Policy (CFSP) but left Germany as the strong pole in its bipolar (with France's participation) political system.

Despite calls to preserve the West's unity, Germany continues its economic partnership with Beijing. It refuses to freeze the gas pipeline Nord Stream 2 project regarding Russia, ignoring the U.S.'s and France's calls. Moreover, Merkel called Putin to discuss vaccine supply the day Russia jailed Navalny and crushed the democratic protests.

On the other hand, Germany's role as Turkey's geopolitical ally has been crucial in neutralizing the E.U.'s political potential. It overtly impeded the E.U.'s reaction to Turkey's Eastern Mediterranean aspirations and disregarded its military presence in Libya. Germany refused to invite Greece, the closest European neighbor of

---

[197] Former Minister of Foreign Affairs and Vis-Chancellor of Germany

Libya, to the Berlin conference in 2019, lest the Turkish interests were impaired. Merkel's Germany seems to be trying to re-establish its geopolitical alliance system of 1939 with Italy, Spain, Turkey, Bulgaria, and the Soviet Union's successor, Russia. Spain and Italy supported Germany's effort to impede the E.U. from acting against Turkey's aggressive policies. Germany refused to stop the arms provision to Turkey despite war threats against an E.U. and NATO member, Greece.

As President Macron had observed, NATO is also almost dead because of Turkey's hostile stance towards its allies. However, Turkey enjoys the support of NATO's Secretary General Stoltenberg and Germany.

Disregarding any E.U. political unity, Germany is trying to regenerate the old rivalry between Land or Central Powers and sea Powers. The future role of France in the latter is significant. Although not participating in Germany's alliance system, its ties within the bipolar political center of the E.U. remain strong. The severance of these ties might drive an alteration of the political status of the E.U. On the other hand, sea powers like France and Britain focused on the eastern Mediterranean.

The U.S. may be back, but the world is now clearly multipolar. Its foreign policy may be stricter regarding China and Russia, but several variants have changed irrevocably. Moreover, the U.S.'s European allies have lost their confidence in the U.S. due to the Trump administration's aftereffects.

According to Heather A. Conley,[198] the U.S. is aware of the new situation. It realizes that aligning the

---

[198] Senior vice president for Europe, Eurasia, and the Arctic and director of the Europe, Russia, and Eurasia Program at the Center for Strategic and International Studies.

Europeans with their China policy will be challenging. Turkey is another issue of dissent between the U.S. and the E.U. The U.S. certainly will try to reconnect Turkey with the Euro-Atlantic community. Still, it is unknown if Turkey wants to stay within this community as it seems limbo. Moreover, this effort is complicated because the E.U.'s cooperation cannot be assured. After all, Germany and France have different stances on Turkey.

Regarding America's re-engaging the world, it is inevitable that Washington wishes to advance. Nevertheless, it recognizes that the U.S.'s alienation from world affairs is not only a consequence of the Trump administration; it has been happening for the last 10-15 years. Biden administration will have stronger rhetoric than before, but it also has domestic issues to handle. Its main aim will be to restore the U.S.'s reliability and the return to a regime of consultations with its allies.

Biden administration's new Global policy

In its geopolitical approach, the U.S. is trying to apply two policies at once: on the one hand, to pursue the policy of democratization and human rights and, on the other, to promote its commercial interests. Biden follows an approach like that of Trump's America First, though in a different jargon.

The Biden administration seeks to implement a policy of pressure to halt China that risks outmatching the U.S. regarding the National Product by leveraging human rights violations. In this context, it simultaneously imposed sanctions against China by the U.S., the EU, Britain, and Canada on March 22, 2021, concerning Muslim Uighurs' treatment.

The U.S. attitude towards China was indicative during the dialogue in Anchorage in March 2021. On the other hand, the Chinese response was that the U.S. monopolization of international morality was over. Biden's attack on Putin, even before Russia's unjust attack on Ukraine and beyond the confines of diplomacy, also marked the end of a period of relatively peaceful relations. The new U.S. administration seems to assess that Russia has returned to a policy of spheres of influence. As a result, it started to use or threaten the use of force in international issues, such as when it referred to Crimea.

For no substantial reason, the U.S. has created conditions of a quasi-Cold War against Russia and China. It has tried with some success to bring the E.U. together in that. However, the West can hardly form a single position and appear united against its geopolitical opponents. The E.U. cannot identify its policies with Washington against Moscow and Beijing.

Since commercial globalization was chosen as a model of international trade with the abolition of tariffs, it favored less developed but organized economies such as China. China has gradually emerged as the second-largest economy globally, and its growth rates are three times that of America. China, like America, sees the world as a "moral power". It does not impose democracy on regimes around the world. It does not promote any ideology. It simply insists on the economic factor offering prosperity through trade.

China is a country with an authoritarian regime. Still, it is not seeking to extend its influence worldwide beyond its near geographic vicinity until now. China is not seeking a frontal and decisive confrontation with the West but a gradual improvement in its economic position worldwide. However, China does not hesitate to demonstrate its military capabilities in its nearest environment, Taiwan, Hong Kong, and the China Sea.

China's warning to the E.U. not to interfere in its internal affairs, especially those concerning security, was its typical response to sanctions imposed and its rhetoric. However, this time, it went a step further. It set similar retaliation measures against persons in the E.U., including Members of the European Parliament and experts on minority issues in China. In addition, it warned Western companies not to apply their governments' sanctions. Its reaction sends the message that the period of the West blaming China has passed irreversibly and that it will not tolerate such behavior in the future.

Russia, unlike China, is a weak regime. Even if Xi Jinping was incapable of governing, the administration would move on. Russia is not the same, but Putin could remain in power for 15 years more. It is not out of the question that the regime that succeeds him will be more nationalistic and unstable.

West's verbal attacks in a cold war climate fostered by the new U.S. leadership towards Moscow and Beijing, accompanied by sanctions, have led to a rally between Russia and China. On his visit to China a few days ago, Russian Foreign Minister Lavrov spoke of the need to shield the two countries against any new West sanctions, such as turning to off-dollar trade or strengthening technological cooperation. In addition, China signed a 25-year treaty on March 27, 2021, with Iran leading to a dangerous path. Finally, a message of solidarity was sent on behalf of China to North Korea.

The Biden Administration opposed this coalition's alliance with the E.U. and presented the Quad cooperation (the U.S., Australia, India, and Japan) as a shield for controlling Chinese influence in the Pacific.

World politics seem to enter a new face as they always do.

About the author

Vassilios Moutsoglou is Greek Ambassador ad honoris. Studies: Mechanical Engineering (Technical University of Istanbul), Political Science (Pantios University, Athens), Diplomacy (Centre of Diplomatic Studies, Greek MFA).

He has served in Canada, Poland, Saudi Arabia, Belgium (E.U.), and Algeria as a diplomat.

His previous work in the Greek language included published books on:
- The Greek Community in Constantinople -19th century (1998)
- Greek-Turkish Relations- 1955-1999 (2000)
- The Balkans (2002)
- Arab Spring (being an Ambassador in Algiers at the time) (2014)
- The Motives in International Politics (2015)
- The Personality of Turkey (2016)
- The Greek Transition of 1821 (2018
- The Geographical Function of the Geopolitical Puzzle (2019).

From the same author

Decision - Making in Foreign policy

Decision - Making in Foreign policy is a book for those interested in international relations. Its intent is to assist them in understanding the reasons for the decisions made in this domain. Moreover, it might also help them predict the decisions that will be made in the changing circumstances of the international environment. For this, some knowledge of the basic principles of foreign affairs and international law is needed. Therefore, the book is addressed to people who know the fundamentals of geography and recent history.

The Greek Revolution of 1821, Amazon, 2020

The "Greek Revolution of 1821" narrates the process of change of the regime of Greeks from slavery to freedom, culminating in the Greek Revolution of 1821. The book expands upon the stages of the long Revolution that lasted about ten years. The object of this study focuses on the causes and the evolution of the Revolution of 1821. The analysis is done with a contemporary look, mainly by synthesizing the results of previous historical research. In the context of the Greek Revolution, the Ottoman Empire's history is also considered. It was essential to explore the causes of the policy that the Sublime Porte followed.

Printed in Great Britain
by Amazon